Politics and the News Media in Japan

Politics and
the News Media
in Japan

Ofer Feldman

Ann Arbor

THE UNIVERSITY OF MICHIGAN PRESS

Copyright © by the University of Michigan 1993
All rights reserved
Published in the United States of America by
The University of Michigan Press
Manufactured in the United States of America

1996   1995   1994   1993   4   3   2   1

A CIP catalogue record for this book is available from the British Library.

Library of Congress Cataloging-in-Publication Data

Feldman, Ofer, 1954–
    Politics and the news media in Japan / Ofer Feldman.
        p.   cm.
    Includes bibliographical references and index.
    ISBN 0-472-10451-9 (alk. paper)
    1. Government and the press—Japan.   2. Journalism—Political
aspects—Japan.   3. Press—Japan—History—20th century.   4. Press
and politics—Japan.   I. Title.
PN5404.F45   1993
079'.52—dc20   93-31941
                                                           CIP

To Utai and Iri

Acknowledgments

There are a number of people whose advice and encouragement have been of great help in the writing of this book. In particular, I owe a substantial debt to Dr. Tsujimura Akira, Professor Emeritus, University of Tokyo, who read early versions of this book and enriched me with useful comments and criticism, and to Professor Ehud Harari of the Hebrew University of Jerusalem and Professor Ellis S. Krauss of Pittsburgh University for their unfailing assistance and advice in the preparation and development of this study. I have also benefited from intellectual stimulation and criticism from Dr. Alex S. Edelstein, Professor Emeritus, University of Washington; Professor Sone Yasunori and Professor Tsuruki Makoto of Keio University; Dr. Manabe Kazufumi of Kwansei Gakuin University; Professor Iwai Tomoaki of Tokiwa University; and Professor Takeshita Toshio of the University of Tsukuba.

I am deeply grateful to all of the Diet members, their private secretaries, and the many reporters who provided their cooperation for this study. I especially wish to thank Odawara Atsushi of the *Asahi Shimbun,* Saikawa Takasumi of the *Kyôdô News Service,* and Yamazaki Akira and Tase Yasuhiro of the *Nihon Keizai Shimbun,* who devoted so much of their time and energy to simplifying and patiently explaining many of the issues dealt with in this book. Special thanks to Martin Pauly of the Tsukuba College of Technology for reading the manuscript and giving me many useful suggestions and ideas.

Last of all, this book would not have seen the light of day without the sincere work of my wife, Rie, who labored day and night at the keyboard of the word processor, endlessly correcting the various drafts of this book.

Contents

Part 1
Introduction

CHAPTER 1

Topics and Nature of Analysis

This book identifies, describes, and analyzes the various aspects and characteristics of the interrelationships between members of the national Diet[1] and newspeople in Japan. The scope and nature of the news media–politics interrelationship in Japan, the extent to which this interrelationship influences political coverage, and the functions of the press and reporters as information sources to Diet members are discussed. It details the significance of the news media, especially newspapers, in Japanese political life; reporters' accessibility to political news sources; Diet members' access to and exploitation of the news media; the objectives of the interactions between reporters and Diet members; and the perceptions and orientations toward the role of, and the importance attributed to newspeople and the press in Japanese politics. Particular attention is given to reporters from the national dailies: their work patterns, their news-gathering methods, and their daily interactions with their political information sources.

A number of factors led to the writing of this book. Probably the most important was the realization that there is very little information on the contemporary media-politics interrelationship in Japan. Only a handful of studies exist that describe and analyze the role that the news media play in mediating political information between the public and Diet members and that explain Diet members' access to and exploitation of the various channels of mass communication. Particularly, there is little information available in English on the news-gathering processes and methods used by Japanese reporters, their accessibility to information sources and news, and the factors that influence both the contents and scope of the political coverage. This was perhaps a major obstacle to American and European students of communication and politics seeking to compare the nature and scope of the news media–politics interrelationship in their countries with those of a non-Western society such as

---

1. The national Diet is the supreme bicameral legislative body in Japan. It consists of a 512-member House of Representatives (*Shûgiin*), or Lower House, and a 252-member House of Councillors (*Sangiin*), or Upper House. Members of both houses are democratically elected, but each house has a different basis for qualification. Members of the House of Representatives are elected for a four-year term and those of the House of Councillors for a six-year term, with half the members of the House of Councillors elected every three years.

Japan. This book, thus, shall be of interest to students and researchers in the fields of comparative politics, comparative mass communication, and Japanese studies. To facilitate comprehension for readers from different disciplines, the first part of the book serves as an introduction to the Japanese environment, focusing in particular on the structure of media and politics and on several significant recent studies that have examined the nature of political communication in this country.

Basic to the study of the media-politics interrelationship are the mutual relationships between members of the Diet in general, and the information sources in particular, and reporters. This is a key factor for understanding the political continuum that demands contact between the political administration and the press. The latter operates, in fact, within the political systems by conveying information. Seymour-Ure (1968, 266) has elaborated on this concept by suggesting a distinction between horizontal communication between members of the "political public," whose activities the press describes, and vertical communication to the "mass public," for whom the information is provided. Of course, members of the political elite may themselves use the press, as noted by Dunn (1969, 100–107), as a major source of information about the activities of their peers and about other events in the political and social environment. In a study on how British members of Parliament receive information, Barker and Rush (1970, 35–49) revealed the significance of local newspapers and weekly journals as sources of news. Members of Parliament use the press differently than their constituency does, and they have particularly low exposure to television.

To a great extent, the relationship between members of the political elite and reporters determine the scope and the contents of reporting and the means by which information is conveyed to the public. Yet, studies that focus on one group, such as reporters, do not automatically include the other group, the Diet members. What is rational for the former is not necessarily rational for the latter, whose major objectives are to try to gain public attention and support for their political plans, ideas, and political achievements. Conversely, the reporters' primary objectives are to inform and entertain their audience. Obviously, the objectives of the reporters and the Diet members vis-à-vis the public are not necessarily compatible. Nevertheless, neither group can realize its objectives without the cooperation of the other. Diet members require access to the communication channels controlled by the mass media, and reporters must have accessibility to members of the Diet to obtain information, news, and comments. Analysis of the relationship between these groups reveals that not only do they depend on each other to fulfill their individual tasks, but that they often share job-related interests, values, and opinions (for example, Crouse 1974; Nimmo 1964; Sigal 1973). It is a mutually exploitative relationship. Members of both groups recognize the need for mutual trust and know that close contact yields frequent feedback from members of the other group and builds a relationship of understanding. As an outgrowth of such a relationship, many reporters consider themselves, at least in part, to be participants in the legislative process (Blumler and Gurevitch 1981; Dyer and Nayman 1977).

In democracies, it is claimed that reporters play an important role in political communication, for they transmit messages from and information about politicians to the general public. Against a background in which citizens should be informed about their leaders, reporters assume a special role in this context by keeping the public informed: about the quality of their leaders (or candidates for leadership positions), about what the political leaders are doing or intend to do, about political issues and agendas, and about new policies and orientations that might affect the public directly or indirectly. To obtain this information, Japanese reporters often turn to Diet members. The sources of information who have high credibility and reputations for being accurate and astute are those that reporters tend to turn to regularly.

A study of how reporters obtain and transmit political information, and thus fulfill one of the important functions of their role as communicators, presents only one side of the general communication process. The components that determine whether information is worthy of publication are rarely completely controlled by the reporters, therefore it is necessary to examine the "other" side: the government's tendency to provide information and to influence the news media through economic control, news-gathering regulations, censorship, and laws. In the United States, several studies—for example, Carter et al. 1986—have pointed out the activities of the Federal Communications Commission (FCC) in regulating the broadcast media. It is also important to look at Diet members who provide, withhold, or leak information, and to analyze their motives for and attitudes toward providing particular information to specific reporters at a specific time (for example, Chittick 1970; Cohen 1963; Davison 1975).

This book describes the processes and problems involved in gathering political information in Japan from the viewpoint of Diet members and reporters. It points out the fact that since a variety of political parties, party factions, and pressure/interest groups take part in gathering and disseminating political information, the reporter's involvement increases in complexity as he or she attempts to maintain constant contact with all of these groups. Although this book focuses mainly on the processes and methods associated with news gathering, it also explains that contact between Diet members and reporters is not limited to providing and obtaining information. Diet members and reporters meet and interact for other reasons, some of which, as described later, are perhaps no less important than providing and obtaining news. In summary, this book is a study of the reporter–Diet member interaction in

Japan, specifically in *Nagatachô*, Tokyo, the location of the national Diet, the prime minister's official residence, the offices of Diet members, the Diet Press Club, and the headquarters of the major political parties. In a broad sense, the term *Nagatachô* refers to Japanese national politics in general. It is synonymous with the nation's political nerve center, just as 10 Downing Street and 1600 Pennsylvania Avenue are in London and Washington, respectively. This book examines the extent to which the political game that takes place in *Nagatachô*, and that has significant influence on domestic and international affairs, is affected by the distinctive and important role played by Japanese reporters.

Research Design

This is the first work based on surveys of rank-and-file members of the Diet, newspeople, Diet leaders, political party officials, secretaries to Diet members,[2] and others linked to mass media research institutions. The data in this book was obtained over an extended period of time by means of questionnaires distributed to many Diet members; by interviewing many Diet members and reporters from all branches of the news media; and by personal observations while accompanying reporters gathering news. A detailed account on the research method and procedure appears in the Appendix. Briefly, the survey on the relationships between Diet members and reporters in Japan was researched within two time frames. The first, in which extensive data was gathered from Diet members and reporters by a variety of methods, was from July to December 1983. This period covered the last four months of former Prime Minister Nakasone Yasuhiro's first cabinet and the first month of his second cabinet. The second period was from June 1984 to August 1986, during which time meetings were held with selected reporters and Diet members to study their contacts and attitudes toward members of the opposite group over a long period of time.

The information was obtained first through a questionnaire sent or given directly to Diet members from the following parties: Liberal Democratic party (LDP) [*Jiyûminshutô*], the former Japan Socialist party, now renamed the Social Democratic Party of Japan (SDPJ) [*Nihon Shakaitô*],[3] the Clean Gov-

---

2. Each Diet member is entitled to hire two secretaries at state expense, and one of them, most commonly a man, is considered the private secretary. Most of the Diet members actually have more than those two secretaries. Some of them work in the Diet member's Tokyo office and others work in the office maintained in the constituency from which the Diet member is elected. It is noteworthy that secretaries to Diet members are often the "bagmen" for bribes and payoffs, as in the case of the recent Recruit Scandal.

3. The annual Congress of the party held at the end of January 1991 decided to change the English translation of its name from "Japan Socialist party" to "Social Democratic Party of Japan." Its name in Japanese, however, remains *Nihon Shakaitô*.

ernment party (CGP) [*Komeitô*], the Democratic Socialist party (DSP) [*Minshatô*], the New Liberal Club (NLC) [*Shinjiyû Kurabu*][4]—jointly with the United Social Democratic party (USDP) [*Shakaiminshu Rengô* or *Shaminren*] and the *Shinsei Kurabu*. The questionnaire also went to the Diet members of the *Sangiinnokai* group, consisting of independent members of the House of Councillors and members of the Salaried Workers' New party [*Sarariman Shintô*], Second House Club [*Dai Niin Kurabu*], and the Welfare party [*Fukushitô*]. With nine Diet seats vacant at the time of the study, the questionnaire was distributed to 698 Diet members. By November 1983, 402 questionnaires (57.6 percent) had been returned.[5]

The interviews with Diet members and reporters were guided by a set of questions and a list of objectives. Where circumstances permitted, specific questions were asked about the political activities of the Diet member, about contacts between party factions, and about communication among the political parties and between the parties and the bureaucracy. Seventy Diet members, from both Houses of the Diet, were interviewed. In conducting the interviews, special attention was given to the relative size of the political party (and LDP faction) and its strength in the Diet.[6] In selecting the reporters to be interviewed, emphasis was placed on those who report regularly on the activities of the government, political parties, and party factions. As many as 45 reporters representing all branches of the news media were interviewed. In addition, part of the field research was conducted by personal observations, which led to a better understanding of the information obtained in the interviews and through the questionnaire.

Organization of This Book

This book consists of five parts. Chapter 2 provides background information about the Japanese news media and the political environment for the following discussions. Part 2 discusses how accessible political information is to reporters. Chapter 3 focuses on the most important variables that determine the nature and the frequency of the contacts reporters have with Diet members. Chapter 4 identifies the information sources in Japanese politics and reporters' accessibility to these sources. Part 3 outlines the variables associated with the

---

4. After the overwhelming victory of the LDP during the 1986 double elections, the NLC disbanded itself and all of its members joined the LDP.

5. Following the July 1985 Supreme Court ruling regarding the distribution of Lower House seats, the Diet passed a bill early in 1986 that reduced representation in seven rural districts by one seat each and increased it by one seat in each of eight urban districts. As a result, the total number of Lower House members increased by one, to 512. At the time of this study, however, the number of Lower House members was 511.

6. All the data presented below concerning the Diet members have been taken from the *Kokkai Binran* (Handbook of Japanese Diet) 68 (1983).

political news-gathering process. Chapter 5 discusses the competition among various news media channels and examines reporters' tendencies to conform with formal and informal customs. Chapter 6 details how information sources manipulate reporters by leaking or withholding information. Part 4 outlines the important functions reporters play while interacting with Diet members. Chapter 7 details the general importance of information to the Diet members' work and their exposure to information from various sources. Chapter 8 describes how reporters and Diet members perceive the role reporters assume in politics. Part 5 provides an evaluation of the main findings of the study and additional implications and thoughts on the nature of Japanese political communication.

All Japanese names used in the text of this book are given in the Japanese style; that is, family name first. Names are not attributed to the quotations because interviewees were given a written promise of anonymity.

In Japanese vowels can either be short or long. A diacritical mark (e.g., ô) over the vowel indicates that it is a long vowel.

CHAPTER 2

The Media-Government Relationship in Japan

This chapter focuses on the systems and the nature of the news media and politics in Japan. It provides information on the newspaper industry, the status of print media in Japan, and the potential influence the print media has on society. It also details some of the major characteristics of the political environment in Japan and the media's role in it. And by outlining the way the Japanese print media handle political coverage, it serves as a starting point for a study of the nature of the contacts reporters have with Diet members and the political world.

The Japanese Press: Main Characteristics

Several important factors nourish all forms of the news media—newspapers, magazines, television, radio, etc.—on a national scale in Japan. Among them are linguistic homogeneity, Japan's near-perfect literacy rate—one of the highest in the world, at 99.3 percent—and the fact that the Japanese people share basic value orientations, aspects of daily life, and consciousness (Ito 1990). In Japan, strong emphasis is placed on hierarchy and social deference, group orientation, the value of conformity, and dedication to one's group. Group orientation fosters the strength of the institution, distinguishes one group from another, and makes the institutional unit the basis of the Japanese social structure (Doi 1973; Nakane 1972). Individuals are perceived as functioning in various social situations as a result of the interaction of their personalities and their place in the vertical social structure. Awareness of such social situations gives rise to certain needs, particularly the need to acquire information that will help one to know how to act in such social circumstances. Because an individual's social contacts are usually confined to the limits of the circle or place of work where he has daily contacts, in many cases the news media fulfill these information needs. To this end, dependency on the news media may soon become habitual (Arai and Fujiwara 1986; Edelstein et al. 1989, chap. 5). Thus, the cultural aspects of society require that individuals constantly seek new information in order to know how to act. Culture, therefore, can also be regarded as a nourishing factor of the news media in Japan.

9

The Broadcast Media

Japan's news media is among the most highly developed in the world.[1] Japanese broadcasting, for example, is led by NHK (*Nippon Hôsô Kyôkai*), the world's largest public broadcasting system. It is a special government-created nonprofit corporation. Except for a small government subsidy for its overseas broadcasting service, NHK derives its revenue from the fees collected from television viewers throughout the country. It has two television channels (general and educational, consisting of 3,492 general broadcast stations, 3,416 educational stations, and 2,573 stations providing multiplex broadcasting), two AM radio networks (183 stations for general programming and 141 AM stations for educational programming), and one FM radio network (509 stations), all broadcasting nationwide. Currently, NHK is using two channels on the DBS (direct broadcast satellites) to bring its viewers telecasts of major foreign news and sports events.

Virtually equal to NHK in scale, strength, and influence are some 113 privately owned commercial television networks (operating 6,157 stations) and 83 radio networks; the latter consists of 47 AM radio networks (214 stations), one shortwave radio network (two stations), and 35 FM radio networks (142 stations). Commercial stations, which are supported entirely by advertising revenues, were first authorized in 1951 by American Occupation officials. Originally licensed for only local or regional operations, the privately owned stations have grown greatly in number and become linked into informal networks. There are four major commercial television stations in Japan, all with their headquarters in Tokyo: NNN, or NTV (Nippon Television) has 27 local stations in its network; FNN (Fuji Telecasting), 27; JNN, or TBS (Tokyo Broadcasting System), 25; and ABC, or ANN (Asahi National Broadcasting), 20. There is one minor network, Television Tokyo (TV Tô-kyô), with one station each in Tokyo, Nagoya, Osaka, and Okayama. Regional stations depend on the networks for most of their programming, and only around 10 percent of the programming is locally generated. Commercial television programming has become increasingly sophisticated, and there has been a growing trend since the mid-1980s toward broad-ranging news and general information programs. Both NHK and the commercial networks are making a considerable effort to provide the most thorough coverage possible of political, social, and economic news, as well as informative coverage of stories of general and special interest to niche viewers. Nevertheless, the

---

1. All the data concerning the broadcast media is from *Nihon Minkan Hôsô Nenkan-1990* (Japanese Commercial Broadcast Yearbook) (Tokyo: Nihon Minkan Hôsô Rempô, 1991); and *Nihon Hôsô Kyôkai Nenkan-1991* (Japan Broadcasting Corporation Yearbook) (Tokyo: Nihon Hoso Kyokai, 1991).

broadcast media's role is not as significant as that of the print media, especially that of the daily newspapers.

The National Dailies: Circulation and Structure

Newspapers in Japan are either national or local.[2] The national newspapers consist of the "big five," which are all dailies and are probably what many people are referring to when discussing Japanese journalism; namely, the *Yomiuri* (14.5 million circulation), the *Asahi* (12.9 million), the *Mainichi* (6.3 million), the *Nihon Keizai*—referred to also as the *Nikkei*—(4.5 million), and the *Sankei* (3.2 million). Among these newspapers, the share of distribution of the *Yomiuri* countrywide is 36.2 percent and 41.9 percent in the area around Tokyo; *Asahi*'s share is 30.4 and 30.5; *Mainichi*, 14.9 and 10.9; *Nihon Keizai*, 11.1 and 10.7; and *Sankei*, 7.4 and 6.0, respectively.

Until the 1970s there were three major national dailies, the *Asahi*, the *Yomiuri*, and the *Mainichi*, which resembled each other in content. *Asahi* used to lead the nation (and the world) in terms of circulation, followed by the *Yomiuri* and *Mainichi*. Gradually, however, in the late 1970s, the *Asahi* lost this characteristic to its archrival, the *Yomiuri*. At that time, *Yomiuri* had changed its editorial policies, becoming more conservative and progovernment. Also, its livelier makeup, the use of larger pictures, and its devotion of more attention to human interest stories presumably made it more appealing and contributed to the growth in its circulation. *Asahi*, on the other hand, kept its "leftist flavor" on several fundamental issues, such as the imperial system, United States–Japan alliance, and the Self-Defense Forces. It has also kept its image of an "intellectual paper"; serious in tone and somber in makeup, appealing in particular to the nation's intellectuals, and thus regarded as the most influential among the national newspapers. *Mainichi*, once *Asahi*'s closest competitor, has limped behind both its rivals in recent years, unable to recover from the loss of readers after the "oil shock" and burdened by a heavy debt load that required financial reorganization of the company in the late 1970s. Since the late 1970s, conservative newspapers such as the *Nihon Keizai*—the nation's most influential business newspaper, often referred to as Japan's equivalent of the *Wall Street Journal* and viewed as essential reading by most Japanese business executives—and *Sankei* have been steadily increasing their shares.

There are 98 local newspapers, at least one in each of the 47 prefectures. Daily "bloc" or regional newspapers are also published, such as the *Hokkaidô* (1.9 million), the *Tôkyô* (1.3 million), the *Chûnichi* (3 million), and the *Nishi*

---

2. All the data concerning the newspapers is from *Nihon Shimbun Nenkan-1990* (Japanese Newspaper Yearbook) (Tokyo: Nihon Shimbun Kyôkai, 1990).

Nippon (1 million); the circulation of some of these extends into several neighboring prefectures. Among the "bloc" newspapers that compete with the national dailies for readers and influence, the most notable is the *Chûnichi Shimbun*, which covers the densely populated *Chûbu* district of central Japan. This paper heads a group of five dailies that includes the *Tôkyô Shimbun* and two sports papers. The *Hokkaidô* is published on the northern island of Hokkaidô, and the *Nishi Nippon* serves the southern island of Kyûshû.

In all, there are 124 daily newspapers—national, regional and local dailies of general interest, including a dozen sports newspapers, some of which are published at several locations and have wide readership. If the morning and evening editions published under the same name are counted separately, Japan's total daily newspaper circulation is close to 71.5 million, with the big five national newspapers accounting for 41.3 million (57.8 percent) and reaching almost the entire populace of Japan.

Some characteristics of the newspapers are noteworthy. First, the major newspapers all publish a morning and evening edition under the same name as a set.[3] The articles printed in the two editions are edited to maintain continuity from one to the other. Since 93 percent (98 percent for the national dailies) of newspaper circulation represents home-delivery to subscribers (the other 6.5 percent are sold at kiosks in train stations and newsstands on the streets, and 0.6 percent are delivered by mail), the morning and evening editions are usually sold as a set to the subscriber, who thus receives the same paper twice a day. The morning and evening editions of the national newspapers are printed at offices in Tokyo and four regional centers. These newspapers also issue separate editions for various localities—many more editions than newspapers in any other country. *Yomiuri* and *Asahi*, for example, produce 18 major editions in the morning and about 10 in the evening, as well as 100 other editions that vary with the prefecture or area they serve.

The second major characteristic of the press is related to the newspapers' circulation. Japan differs from other countries in that the total newspaper circulation has constantly increased in the last few years: in 1987, the newspaper circulation was 579 per thousand people, the highest in the world. This jumped to 584 in 1989, a figure reflecting that each household in Japan subscribes to an average of 1.3 newspapers per day. Such a wide circulation gives the press the potential for exercising considerable influence on society.

---

3. In 1989 the total circulation of all the Japanese newspapers was 71,457,075 copies. Of them, 49.1 million copies were morning editions and 22.3 million were evening editions. The *Asahi* had 8.1 million copies in the morning and 4.7 million in the evening. The figures (in millions) for the *Yomiuri* were 9.7 and 4.7; the *Mainichi* 4.1 and 2.1; the *Nihon Keizai* 2.8 and 1.6; the *Sankei* 2.0 and 1.1. Of the "bloc" newspapers, *Tôkyô* had 800,285 and 544,145; *Hokkaidô* had 1.1 million and 789,474 copies; *Nishi Nippon* 791,332 and 217,370 and *Chûnichi Shimbun* had 3.0 million and 1.4 million copies in its morning and evening editions, respectively.

Considering that the national newspapers also publish a number of weekly and monthly magazines and assist in the news programming of several network commercial television stations within and outside of Tokyo, it is clear that a relatively large percentage of the population is subject to the direct and indirect potential influence of the national newspapers. Each of the major national dailies has both financial and personal investment in each of the commercial television networks mentioned above: the *Yomiuri,* for example, with NTV; the *Mainichi* with TBS; *Sankei* with Fuji: *Asahi* with ABC; and *Nihon Keizai* with TV Tokyo. This cross-media relationship exists despite regulations that state that newspapers are not allowed to control commercial television stations. Through a variety of means, however, including investments through "sister companies," almost all newspaper enterprises invest more than 50 percent of the station's share in their affiliated television station.

Although communication is its main activity, the press of Japan does not limit itself to this field. The large newspaper companies, in particular, assume a variety of social roles and engage in a range of activities. They list real estate, recording, travel, department stores, and baseball clubs among their activities. (*Yomiuri,* for example, operates Japan's foremost professional baseball team, the *Yomiuri Giants,* founded in 1934 as a circulation gimmick.) They organize cultural and sporting activities; manage clinics, amusement parks (*Yomiuri* operates a 150-acre amusement park called *Yomiuriland*), schools, and publishing companies; finance corporate projects; publish books; and publish magazines: weekly (*Yomiuri,* for example, publishes *Shûkan Yomiuri* and *Yomiuri Shashin Nyûsu*), monthly (*This is Yomiuri, Ozumô,* and *Yomiuri Shimbun Shukusatsuban*), and yearly (*Yomiuri Nenkan, Yomiuri Nyûsu Sôran,* and *Yomiuri Hôdô Shashinshû*) magazines. They also operate radio and television companies. Through Japanese eyes, the newspapers appear as "empires" whose powers extend to almost every sector of the society and whose involvement in society can be assumed to be total.

The Law and Self-Restraint in Coverage

Another important characteristic of the press is its freedom. Freedom of the press, long considered a cornerstone of Japanese journalism, is a feature that the print media has enjoyed without interference since the end of World War II. No laws in Japan specifically regulate the news media. Newspapers are, of course, subject to the criminal and civil codes regarding libel, antimonopoly, and labor laws. But the law specifically recognizes newspapers' right to gather news, to report, and to comment. The Japanese Constitution, adopted by Japan in 1946 under the aegis of the Allied Occupation (1945–52), explicitly guarantees freedom of expression. Article 21 of the constitution guarantees freedom of assembly and association as well as speech, press, and all other forms of expression; it guarantees that no censorship shall be maintained, nor shall the secrecy of any means of communication be violated, but no explicit reference is made to a "right to know" to be exercised by a free press. As noted by Merril (1988), the government in Japan is less inclined to control the press than are other governments. In a 1987 survey of 58 countries, Merril found that Japan is among the 12 countries with the lowest tendency to control the press.

Moreover, the Election Law recognizes the freedom of newspapers (and other news media) to report and comment on elections. Even though Article 148–2 of the Election Law prohibits the publication of news designed to influence an election, and Article 148–3 prohibits the publication of election poll data showing the relative strengths of candidates, these prohibitions are ignored by the national (and some of the bloc) newspapers. All newspapers conduct public opinion polls during election campaign periods and, on the basis of these, they predict the possible outcome of the elections. These forecasts have encouraged voters to vote for other candidates, a phenomenon known as "announcement effect" (*anaunsu kôka*), which will be described later. In recent years, criticism has grown against this practice and the government's inability to enforce the law.

The lack of regulation affecting the activities of the press does not mean, in practical terms, that there is no governmental control of the press. In some cases, as suggested by Kim (1981, 161–63), the government tries to influence the news media through preferential treatment in business management. The newspapers and private television networks are exempted from regular corporate taxes, and the print media enjoys special postal and rail privileges. Some of the major newspaper companies have received allotments of state-owned land at moderate prices on which to build their headquarters, and some cabinet-affiliated agencies financially support the news media. The Japanese government influences the press through provision of facilities for news gathering, access to the briefings of officials, and access to written government materials.

In many cases, the press does not, however, exercise its freedom fully. Its self-restraint in reporting is motivated partly by concern for human lives and partly for what it views as the national interest. One example of self-restraint, or self-imposed limitations, is voluntary censorship in reporting kidnappings. Even when police authorities keep the press fully informed of developments regarding such criminal activity, usually the press will not report any detail that could endanger the life of the victim until after the case is solved. Another example of restraint concerns the attitude the Japanese press shows toward China. In support of the Japanese government's efforts to establish and maintain good relations with the People's Republic of China, the press has tended to avoid any criticism of China since the beginning of the 1970s. Furthermore, motivated by self-restraint, the press has long avoided reporting any news critical of the Clean Government party and its support group, the Sôka Gakkai, a lay organization of the Nichiren Shoshu sect of Japanese Buddhism. Other taboos in the Japanese press concern the imperial family, which is regarded as above criticism.

Because it is not subject to guidance or regulation by government agencies, the newspaper industry differs from most other Japanese industries. Furthermore, unlike the broadcast media, regulated by the Ministry of Posts and Telecommunications through broadcast and telecommunication laws, the newspaper industry has no government body overseeing its activities. On the contrary, some existing laws provide the industry with special benefits and privileges. An example of this is Article 204–1 of the Commercial Code. It stipulates that newspaper companies may restrict stockholders to individuals connected to the newspaper industry, i.e., the employees of the company. Whereas this seems to contradict the general purpose of the stock system, it is an exception enacted in recognition of the newspapers' public-interest status and is intended to prevent any one person from obtaining a controlling interest. It protects newspapers from being subjected to outside pressure. Currently, 14 companies have taken advantage of this code and offer their stock exclusively to their employees. At 23 other newspaper companies, over 50 percent of the stock is held by employees.

Several indicators suggest that the press can maintain its economic independence from public and political organizations. Revenue from sales and advertising data, for example, indicates that since 1980 the profits of newspaper companies have increased yearly, with financial support from outside of the organizations being unnecessary. During fiscal year 1989–90 the newspaper industry enjoyed considerable profit levels carried over from the preceding year. In 1989 alone, newspaper sales, a major source of income for the companies, increased 7.8 percent for the entire industry, the greatest growth since 1982. The major factor contributing to profitability, however, was the growth in advertising revenue. In practical terms, this was reflected by an 18 percent growth in the advertising revenues of the newspaper industry in 1988 over that of the previous year. Nevertheless, because of the dependence of the press on advertising by the leading business, it has frequently been argued that Japanese newspapers, as well as the other news media in Japan, have been "timid" in their coverage of product recalls, product safety reports, cases of massive food poisoning from eating a certain food at a certain establishment, and other forms of unfavorable publicity, because of the pressure from major advertising clients.

Career and Attitudes of Reporters

The fact that newspaper companies are large and profitable organizations allows them to operate autonomously and independently of government or economic overseers; and the fact that the operating and editing of newspapers is accomplished solely by newspaper employees is reflected in a reporter's professional ethics, in the atmosphere of the work place, in the way reporters work and view work. In his comprehensive study based on interviews with 40 reporters, Kim (1981, 44) details aspects related to the nature of reporters' work, the work of editors from different departments, and their recruitment and promotion patterns. Kim noted that, compared with their counterparts in Western societies, reporters in Japan share nearly the same characteristics of newspaper operation and attitude toward colleagues, superiors, and the public. Kim reveals that reporters from the various departments of a newspaper company are competitive, and sometimes even hostile, toward colleagues in other departments. Little respect is demonstrated between reporters specializing in so-called "hard news," such as politics and economics, and colleagues in the "soft news" departments, such as social affairs (Kim 1981, 57–58). The tension exists partly because of rivalry and personality differences, but also because of the peculiar layout of the different pages. Layout editors feel that they must report as much news as possible and rely on eye-catching headlines (Kim 1981, 58).

Studies conducted during the 1970s and 1980s by researchers such as Hayashi (1973), Manabe (1983, 172–209), and Kim (1981, chaps. 3 and 5), have disclosed that Japanese reporters enjoy a rather elevated social status and take pride in their work. Because of a sense of job security and the weight of the seniority system, they are intensely loyal to and have a sense of identification with their company. The work ethic they share may be significantly related to their organization and behavior. Older reporters holding positions higher up in the newspaper hierarchy tend to identify the sense of mission, duty, and service as their work motive, while younger reporters emphasize individuality. Manabe (1983) has noted further that the level of satisfaction with occupation and assignment among reporters increases with age and level of position.

Yamaguchi (1985) studied Japanese reporters' work patterns and focused on their long careers. A career as a reporter is open to a wide stratum of the population on the basis of achievement. Without exception, all reporters entering work at any of the major dailies are recruited through a three-stage process of written and oral competition with rates of success as low as 1 per 150 candidates. Recruits are all new university graduates and come from such prestigious universities as Tokyo, Kyoto, Keio, and Waseda. As part of the working system of a newspaper (or any other member of the news media, such as NHK), a new reporter begins work not at the Tokyo headquarters, but at a local bureau, to gain several years of experience. Usually after five to six years the reporter is then assigned to Tokyo. The work of reporters at the company's headquarters depends on several variables: the preference of a reporter, ability to cover specific types of activities, and the evaluation of the reporter by the head of the local agency where the reporter received initial training. After being carefully evaluated, the reporter becomes a member of a particular department or desk. Each desk of the major news media comprises a large number of reporters. During the 1980s, the political desk of the *Asahi* had 44 reporters, the *Yomiuri* 45, the *Mainichi* 39, the *Nikkei* and the *Sankei*, 30, *Kyôdô News Service* 46, *Tôkyô* 25, NHK 40, and the commercial television stations 22 to 24 each. Upon becoming a member of a desk, a reporter is assigned to cover government agencies in Tokyo for several years until promotion. Promotion ranges from desk work or the deputy head of a department to editorial staff member or the head of a department.

At the major newspapers, desk members direct reporters in the gathering of news, judge the value of news, revise and polish manuscripts, and plan feature stories (Kim 1981, 54–56). Nonetheless, most reporters, not editors, decide what to write, sometimes in consultation with their superiors. The degree of autonomy of reporters increases with experience. But, inversely, it increases with the importance of issues (Kim 1981, 81–82). The importance of the news is usually evaluated by the same reporters according to their training and experience. There is no perceived difference between what the reporters like and what they think the desk prefers. Japanese reporters often believe that they should try to stay within the editorial guidelines of their newspaper, though the policy is rather broad when it comes to imposing restrictions on reporters (Kim 1981, 84–85).

Finally, Kim, (1981, chap. 5) noted that Japanese reporters believe that interpretation or commentary should follow a news report. They do not see their work as being limited to merely reporting, but emphasize the need to provide comments alongside the reports. Additionally, they feel they should act as an opposing element confronting the regime in its work. Like their counterparts in the United States (for example, Dunn 1969; Nimmo 1964), Japanese reporters see their role as one of expressing and shaping public opinion, and informing readers of the variety of opinions. Yet, unlike journalists in the U.S. (Dunn 1969, 11–18; Sigal 1973, 76), they do not see their role as one of participating in government policy making, although some view their activities as indirectly affecting the functioning of government (Kim 1981, chap. 5). This concept is somewhat contradicted by data that I gathered while meeting reporters, as discussed in detail below.

Partisanship and Credibility

The last important characteristic of Japanese newspapers is the code of editorial ethics adopted by newspapers, from the national to the local level. Newspapers are committed to the policy of *fuhen futô, chûritsu kôsei* (impartiality, political neutrality, and fairness). These are the areas of self-restraint and responsibility on which, in the journalist's point of view, freedom of the press depends. The Japanese Canons of Journalism specifically declare that freedom of reporting and editorial writing should be subject to several voluntary restraints. These are lengthy, and state, among other things, that news reporting must convey facts accurately and faithfully; that the personal opinion of the reporter should never color the reporting of the news; that one should always be strictly on guard against the possibility of news being used for the purpose of propaganda; and that partisanship in editorial comments, which knowingly depart from the truth, is harmful to the spirit of journalism.

Public opinion surveys frequently conducted by scholars and the various news media, such as the dailies, have revealed in recent years that an overwhelming majority of readers feel that newspapers should not be partial to any particular political party and should maintain neutrality in reportage (for example, Amamori and Koike 1984). Thus, we find the same trends in Japan as in the advanced Western countries, where readers disfavor politically oriented newspapers. Two reasons are suggested for this tendency. The first is the higher level of education of the citizens. Readers do not want opinions forced on them. There is a significant trend among readers to seek the facts, then form their own opinion. The second reason is rooted in the current Japanese social situation. According to the oft-cited results of the public opinion surveys conducted annually by the prime minister's office, 90 percent of the population believes that it belongs to the middle class, as a result of the elimination of economic class differences. Every year the survey asks a sample of three thousand people, the following questions: "Compared to other people, how do you categorize your own standard of living? Do you think of your own position as lower, lower-middle, middle-middle, upper-middle, or upper?" The percentage of Japanese who view themselves as middle-middle has been continuously increasing to reach the present figure of more than 60 percent. If lower-middle and upper-middle responses are combined together, the figure rises to above 90 percent. Although there has been a controversy as to how to interpret the results, it is increasingly clear that they cannot be dismissed. At any rate, the fact that a large proportion of the population feels it belongs to the same social class is perhaps the reason why readers tend to shun newspapers with an editorial policy that emphasizes political confrontation.

Since the end of World War II, freedom of the Japanese press has been heralded as one of the key safeguards against a resurgence of the militarism that led Japan into the war in the first place. The freedom of the press, its economic independence from any public or political organization, and the editorial pledge to a policy of political neutrality and fairness assure the public that the press cannot be "bought" by any political group. This is regarded as a key factor in the protection of the democratic accomplishments of the postwar era. Two other important effects of the freedom of the press are that the public regards newspapers as reliable and trustworthy, and the relative influence that newspapers have on society. For years, newspaper reportage of social and political issues has been perceived as accurate, reliable, and trustworthy. Academic and public studies frequently report the high credibility that newspapers enjoy. Evaluations by the Japanese of the different news media channels in the 1980s are listed in table 2-1.

According to this table, newspapers, more than television, are regarded as providing information that is detailed, accurate, reliable, and helpful in forming sound judgments and enhancing knowledge. Television is perceived more as a medium of quick information. Books and magazines are not as highly evaluated. Half of the respondents thought books enhanced knowledge and one-fourth thought of them as a source of comparison for judgment and ideas. Magazines were viewed as a source of information about recent trends. About 10 percent regarded radio as an accurate and entertaining medium, but radio generally received a low rating. As recorded in other surveys, the overall evaluation of newspapers was that they are more relevant to society as a whole (with reference to the function of providing the information needed by readers as members of society) than, say, television, which has a greater relevance to daily life. The surveys reveal that people believe that newspapers are better than other news media channels in reflecting readers' opinions, because of their dignity, trustworthiness, and concern for human rights. Similar attitudes appeared in studies exploring and analyzing the public's evaluation of how newspapers cover certain political and social issues or report on the daily routine of political leaders. Feldman and Kawakami (1988), for example, have replicated and extended earlier studies conducted in the United States, in an attempt to study the diverse evaluations of political stories by over one thousand younger Japanese. The study referred in particular to specific dimensions in the categories of competence and trust, community involvement, and personalism and bias and sensationalism. The findings revealed that the political reportage of the print media is highly trusted, that newspapers are perceived as fulfilling their social role, and that the coverage is unbiased and accurately reflects public opinion.

One of the consequences of this is reflected in the reading habits of the Japanese people, who spend a great deal of their time reading newspapers. In the largest survey conducted by the *Nihon Shimbun Kyôkai* (The Japan Newspaper Publishers and Editors Association) in May 1983, involving nine thousand people, the average time spent with various news media each day was 44.1 minutes for newspapers, 144.9 minutes for television, 48.6 minutes for radio, 17 minutes for magazines, and 25 minutes for books—for a total of 4 hours and 39 minutes a day (Amamori and Koike 1984). As figure 2-1 shows,

TABLE 2-1. Evaluation by the Japanese of Different News Media According to Several Criteria (in percentages)

Criteria for Evaluation	Order					Do Not Know	No Answer
	1st	2nd	3rd	4th	5th		
Accurate information	Television (59.8)	Newspapers (50.5)	Radio (11.9)	Books (2.9)	Magazines (1.0)	14.5	5.0
Provides detailed information	Newspapers (60.0)	Television (46.0)	Magazines (9.4)	Books (7.8)	Radio (7.4)	6.5	4.2
Useful for one's work	Newspapers (45.2)	Television (23.8)	Books (19.6)	Magazines (11.2)	Radio (8.0)	17.2	10.3
Useful for daily activities	Television (65.3)	Newspapers (59.1)	Radio (8.7)	Books (4.1)	Magazines (2.3)	6.5	5.5
Provides large amount of information	Newspapers (56.0)	Television (47.8)	Magazines (12.1)	Radio (8.7)	Books (4.3)	6.3	5.4
Verifies information from various aspects	Newspapers (49.5)	Television (35.9)	Magazines (16.5)	Books (10.7)	Radio (5.2)	13.4	6.8
Contributes to enhancing the level of knowledge and general education	Books (50.4)	Newspapers (46.5)	Television (22.6)	Magazines (11.2)	Radio (4.8)	7.3	5.0
Provides information on trends	Television (63.7)	Magazines (48.7)	Newspapers (12.9)	Radio (3.8)	Books (3.3)	6.9	5.8
Provides useful shopping information	Newspapers (37.2)	Television (34.3)	Magazines (31.9)	Radio (2.9)	Books (2.6)	16.9	8.9
Amusement	Television (78.2)	Magazines (26.9)	Radio (12.3)	Books (11.0)	Newspapers (10.7)	3.7	4.8
Comparable to one's judgments or ideas	Newspapers (47.3)	Television (26.4)	Books (24.4)	Magazines (9.8)	Radio (4.6)	17.2	8.5
Reliable	Newspapers (47.1)	Television (33.3)	Books (10.7)	Radio (5.1)	Magazines (1.4)	25.7	9.8

Source: Nihon Shimbun Kyōkai Kenkyūjo, *Gendai no shimbun dokusha to masukomi sesshoku no jittai: Zenkoku shimbun shinraido sōgō chōsa 1983-nen* (Contemporary Newspapers' Readers and Exposure to the News Media: The 1983 National Survey on the Reliability of Newspapers) Tokyo: Nihon Shimbun Kyōkai Kenkyūjo, 23.

Note: Figures enclosed in parentheses indicate the percentage of respondents who evaluated each news medium separately, according to specific criteria.

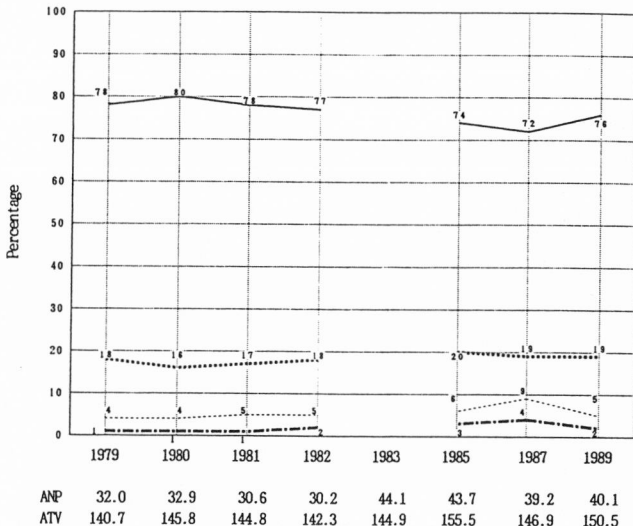

	1979	1980	1981	1982	1983	1985	1987	1989
ANP	32.0	32.9	30.6	30.2	44.1	43.7	39.2	40.1
ATV	140.7	145.8	144.8	142.3	144.9	155.5	146.9	150.5

ANP—Average time spent reading newspapers (in minutes)
ATV—Average time spent watching television (in minutes)

—— Proportion of those who read newspapers daily
•—•• Proportion of those who read newspapers occasionally
······ Proportion of those who rarely read newspapers
—— Proportion of those who rarely watch television

Fig. 2-1. Frequency of contact with newspapers and television. The figure indicates the results of the eight surveys conducted from 1979 to 1989 by the *Nihon Shimbun Kyôkai*. There were no data available for 1983. (*Source: Nihon Shimbun Kyôkai Kenkyûjo, Dai hachikai zenkoku shimbun shinraido chôsa* [The Eighth National Survey on the Reliability of Newspapers], *Shimbun Kenkyû,* no. 458, September 1989, 52.)

the average daily time that people spent reading newspapers in 1989 was 40.1 minutes, 1 minute longer than the figure obtained in the previous survey.

The decline in the time spent in reading newspapers continued for some years, then stopped in 1989. The 1989 survey's figures showed that 76 percent of the public "read newspapers daily" and 19 percent "read newspapers occasionally," for a total of 95 percent of the public reading newspapers. The number of people who "read newspapers daily" increased by 4 percent from that of the previous year. Many said they "always" read the television and radio schedules. Other "always"-read items were city and local news, followed by sports stories and home and women's columns. In short, the "light reading" articles were the ones read the most. Even so, political stories, which belong to the "serious" category of reading materials, usually fare well, ranking fifth among the 15 different types of news items that were "always" read. Conversely, economic news, foreign news, commentaries, and editorials, also in the "serious" reading category, usually do not fare well.

Influence of the Print Media

Yet another implication is present in the tendency of the public to evaluate highly the neutrality and the role of newspapers in Japanese society: the influence the print media have on society. Given the fact that the Japanese are avid readers and tend to revere the printed word, spending a great deal of time reading newspapers and accepting the content as being accurate and trustworthy, newspapers have been able to consolidate their exceptional influence. Items reported in the national newspapers, for instance, are very often taken at face value. The interpretation that newspapers place on facts is likely to become the generally accepted interpretation. At times the press is able to assert a dominant influence in the shaping of public sentiment and opinion, on both domestic and international issues (Kawakami and Feldman 1988). Newspapers were responsible for encouraging citizens' movements and countermeasures to governmental policies regarding such environmental problems as industrial pollution and destruction of land. By revealing the wrongdoings and corruption of political leaders and officials to the public, newspapers directly influence the attitudes of the public toward the political world. (Most notably, the coverage of the Recruit Scandal and the womanizing affair of former Prime Minister Uno Sosuke affected the voting behavior during the 1989 general elections.) In particular, the press is perceived as the driving force behind the negative images that the Japanese have of Diet members, most notably the prime minister, who is regarded as distant, disagreeable, and impersonal (Feldman and Kawakami 1989).

The impact of the press, when observed from a broader perspective, sheds light on the important role the media play over Japanese society as a whole. Tsuruki (1982), for example, noted that more than 30 percent of the Japanese people are under direct and indirect influence of the same major dailies, which gives the dailies an extraordinary power. Because of this fact, Tsuruki views the media, particularly the newspapers, as one of the most important factors that have contributed to the standardization of information and knowledge in Japanese society; to the rapid standardization of culture, to the extent that there are no longer differences in ways of talking, dressing, and living between rural areas and the large cities; to the increasing homogeneity of lifestyle and attitude; and to the disintegration of the class structure, to the degree that 90 percent of the population regards itself, as discussed, as belonging to the middle class. A similar view regarding the role of the media was emphasized by Arai (1989). Arai noted that because there are a small number of national newspapers with wide circulation that are read by a large segment of the public, and because people use a limited number of television channels that are collaborating in their news and entertainment programing, people are exposed to almost the same information. This results in closing the cultural gap between different segments of the public and between different aspects such as gender, age, socioeconomic status, and place of residence. Moreover, the result of this media exposure is reflected in the process of dramatic change that Japanese society now experiences, and is expressed in an overall sense of satisfaction with life and the resultant support of conservative movements, a sense of helplessness in politics and society, a growing lack of interest in communicating with other people, and a belief in materialism.

The capability of the press to influence the behavior of voters at election time has been the focus of numerous studies. Special attention has been paid to the potential influence of the print media through surveys it conducts during election campaigns, a phenomenon mentioned earlier as "announcement effect." The major newspapers in Japan conduct public opinion polls during election campaigns. Based on these polls, they predict which of the candidates in each of Japan's 130 constituencies is likely to be elected and which candidates have only a slight chance of winning. These predictions directly and indirectly influence the activities of the candidates and, no less important, the electorate, to the extent that in recent years the election predictions have been quite different from the actual results. Candidates predicted as being behind others or facing a struggle are motivated to try harder to mobilize more supporters and to convince voters of their ability. The candidates who are predicted as being in a safe position, or as leading by one step, may feel that they are safe and lose the tension, and feel such relief that they may not continue to work hard in the last few days of the campaign. This, in turn, may influence potential voters, especially late in the campaign, a critically important time during which candidates make an all-out effort to win the support of voters who are undecided.

Under Japan's medium electorate system, candidates of the same political party run against each other in the same electoral district in many cases. As a result, voters may find it difficult to distinguish the platforms of the different candidates and may easily change their choice of candidates on the basis of election predictions. Some may even refrain from voting for a candidate who has a high probability of winning in the election and support the candidate with the least chance of winning (Tsujimura, 1976a 87–91). Kabashima (1988) has illustrated more clearly the nature of the effect of newspaper announcements during the 1986 double-election campaign. Aimed at exploring the question of whether the news media influence the outcome of elections, Kabashima polled over two thousand people across the country. He found that as much as 16 percent of the people were influenced by newspaper announcements. This points out the relative significance of the percentage of voters who tend to either change their vote from one candidate to another or refrain from voting as a result of newspaper election predictions. Demographically, Kabashima noted, the group of those who tend to change their vote from one candidate to another consists of men, mostly high school graduates living in urban areas and working in the service industry. The group which, after following the announcements in the newspapers, tends to refrain from voting is comprised of mostly young men and women in their twenties; students, female office workers, and urban dwellers. The findings suggest that voters who have a keen interest in politics tend to switch candidates, and those who have a low political interest tend to refrain from voting.

About a dozen empirical studies have focused on the ability of the Japanese press to place various political, social, and economic issues on the public agenda and to determine what people think about, especially during election campaigns. In other words, these studies have tried to examine the agenda-setting effects of Japanese media and the extent to which the news media play an important role in constructing social reality, particularly on the local-community politics level (for example, Iwabuchi 1989; Kobayashi 1990). Takeshita (1983, 1988) conducted a somewhat distinctive and comprehensive study on the agenda-setting role of the Japanese press. Focusing on one city, Wakayama city in Wakayama prefecture, he did content analysis on television news and the national dailies, in addition to interviews with local community voters. Takeshita's most significant finding was that the strength of agenda-setting influence is positively correlated with the extent to which someone has an interest in politics and exposes himself or herself to the news. An increase in the level of interest in political affairs and events and in the extent of exposure to news is related to a stronger agenda-setting effect and predicts a greater association between the media's emphasis and the voter's salience. Furthermore, exposure to newspapers' news coverage appears to result in a stronger and more significant agenda-setting effect on voters than does exposure to television.

The most recent studies conducted during and outside election campaigns clearly revealed the ability of newspapers to influence political cognition and behavior. Feldman and Kawakami (1991), for example, showed that newspapers do exert more influence on the public than television. Exposure to newspapers strongly correlated with political awareness, including concern with and discussion of politics with family and friends; with participation in political meetings and campaign activities; and with the intention to vote in coming elections. High interest in and knowledge of politics is correlated to paying more attention to political coverage in the print media. The situation differs with television. Generally, exposure to television is associated with low—if not negative—political cognition and behavior and with less of an ability to evaluate political leaders.

Notably, several studies revealed the considerable influence the press exerts on, and its ability to affect, decision makers and government bureaucrats. Kabashima (1990) and Kim (1981, 101–2) among others, noted that the press serves as an important source of information for members of both groups, who have a high degree of sensitivity to reportage and depend on it to gauge public opinion, attitudes, and the evolving policies of various ministries on a given issue. Nevertheless, the data that I gathered while interviewing Diet members, which is presented below, reveal different, even contradicting results, suggesting that not all Diet members heavily depend on the media to obtain specific types of information.

The Nature of Japanese Politics and Newspapers' Political Coverage

Two Political Camps

As is true in any other country, Japanese politics has its own traditions, history, institutions, and culture. Perhaps the most pertinent dimension to the present discussion is the fact that Japanese politics is characterized above all by the political and ideological bipolarity of two groups, or camps, in a predominant party system: the conservative camp (*hoshu jin'ei*) and the "progressive" (i.e., left-of-center) camp (*kakushin jin'ei*). From 1955 until the mid-1970s, the Liberal Democratic Party (LDP), considered to be a "catch-all" party, was the only conservative party. Throughout this period, key support for the party came from big business and agriculture. In 1976, a small group of LDP Diet members broke away from the LDP in protest against "money-power politics" and established a second conservative party, the New Liberal Club (NLC). Following the LDP's landslide victory in the 1986 double elections, the NLC disbanded, and all of its members rejoined the LDP. One of the distinctive features of the LDP is that it is an alliance of factions based on personal loyalty to one another rather than on ideological differences. Most party business is conducted by all of the factions. An example of this is the maneuvering for the highest political positions in Japan—the prime minister (who concurrently serves as party president), the 20 cabinet ministerial portfolios, and the 3 top party posts—by all LDP factions. In principle, cabinet posts are appointed in accordance with the size of each faction—the larger factions receiving the most posts.

To secure cabinet posts and influence, faction leaders frequently engage in rounds of power play in a closed circle. Usually, the faction with the most members plays the role of kingmaker. It holds the key to the presidential election and can easily control the activity of the prime minister. Additionally, it usually obtains the most desirable posts, such as the secretary general of the party and cabinet portfolio of finance, construction, and international trade and industry. Maneuvering over policy-making, however, is conducted within the framework established by, and is therefore a result of, the outcome of leadership maneuvering. Factional competition is thus centered around the party's presidential election. The continued rivalry and intrigues among the leaders of the various factions, which have brought frequent change to government, occupy a central spot in Japanese politics and, as a result, in Japanese political communication. The significant role LDP factions and faction leaders play in how reporters gather news is disscussed and examined in detail below.

The progressive camp in Japanese politics includes the Japan Communist party (JCP) and the Social Democratic Party of Japan (SDPJ). After a dispute over the SDPJ's strong socialistic leanings, a group of SDPJ Diet members broke away from the SDPJ in 1960 and established the Democratic Socialist party (DSP). The Clean Government party (CGP), which at times counts itself along with the DSP as a middle-of-the-road party, was formed in 1956. The CGP, considered the political arm of the *Sôka Gakkai* Buddhist religious organization, claims a family-total membership of around 10 million people. Although the CGP and Sôka Gakkai had officially severed ties in 1970, they are the same in terms of overlapping leadership. The base support for the CGP is in the lower-middle-class to middle-class urban vote. The party does well in most low-income and low-education areas. Support for the other parties of the progressive camp comes predominantly from organized labor, intellectuals, and urban dwellers (Curtis 1988). After implementation of the Proportional Representation System in the Upper House election in 1983, several small parties emerged—the United Social Democratic party (USDP), Salaried Workers' New party, Second House Club, and the Tax party. Because they were formed by a very small number of Diet members having little political influence, several of these miniparties faced crisis situations. Some, including the Welfare party and the Tax party, disbanded during the 1980s and early 1990, and their Diet members joined the LDP.

The LDP has monopolized political leadership for more than three decades. Part of the ruling party's success in staying in power for so long has been its ability to provide, as a "catch-all party," at least minimal satisfaction for all the sectors supporting it. The party enjoys a dominant position in the Diet and over cabinet and government offices. Major policy decisions inevitably revolve around the LDP and its internal political processes because of its long monopoly of leadership. This enables the party to continuously influence the Diet, ministries, and other government organs, with its own members assuming a growing role in maintaining close personal contact with bureaucrats and interest groups (Sone 1986). To the average Japanese, the LDP is the party responsible for Japan's prosperity in recent years. In fact, all of the dramatic change since the end of World War II is a tribute to the stability and efficiency the government has provided under the leadership of the LDP. Japan has become overwhelmingly urban, the people are more prosperous, better-educated, and better-fed than during any time in the past; and the people have the world's longest life expectancy. The LDP is also considered the party responsible for the successful diplomatic and security policies achieved in the last 35 or 40 years.

In contrast, the opposition parties appear to be weak and to lack competence. To many Japanese, the opposition, headed by the SDPJ, does not offer a viable alternative to LDP policies. As a result, the party does not appeal to a growing number of voters or to the general public as whole. Because some of the opposition parties—particularly the SDPJ—have remained deeply wedded to their traditional ideologies and basic support groups, and are therefore resistant to change, they appear less efficient and fated to permanently remain opposition parties without even the slightest interest in assuming power. And, as will be discussed later, this fact has a significant impact on the news-gathering process of reporters, and in a broader sense, on the nature of political communication in Japan. A major problem for the opposition has been the difficulty in bridging the different stances of the various parties, especially with regard to the Japan-U.S. Security Pact and the Self-Defense Forces, and in forming a coalition of parties that could snatch political leadership away from the LDP. During the 1980s, the policies of the CGP and DSP regarding the Japan-U.S. Security Pact and the Self-Defense Forces have become increasingly pragmatic, while the SDPJ has remained firmly opposed to both, insisting (despite the fact that the majority of Japanese people support the existence of the Self-Defense Forces), that the Self-Defense Forces are unconstitutional. During the 1980s, as a result of its failure to offer any convincing policy proposals, the SDPJ suffered setbacks in elections for both houses of the Diet, and failed to take the power away from the LDP. Voters snubbed the SDPJ's persistent stance of political negativism and the ambiguity of the party platform.

Things began to look up for the SDPJ when Doi Takako, law-professor-turned-politician, became the first ever woman leader of a Japanese party. Ms. Doi led the SDPJ to "victory" in the elections of both houses of the Diet in 1989 and 1990. With the SDPJ making a tremendous leap forward, it helped the opposition snatch a majority in the House of Councillors from an LDP weakened by popular anger over the following scandals: the involvement of the ruling party's leaders in the Recruit-insider trading scandal, centering on the sale of shares of a Recruit subsidiary before their public listing, enabling the purchasers to make huge profits; the extramarital affairs of Prime Minister Uno; the government's introduction of the 3 percent consumer tax; and the LDP's agricultural reform policy, which aimed at preserving farmland but favored large-scale, highly productive farms that could compete in an open market. However, after the LDP's major defeat in the House of Councillors election, the SDPJ and the other opposition parties could not resolve their political differences to achieve a policy consensus and form a united front against the LDP. In Japan's general election of February 1990 for the House of Representatives, the LDP, led by former Education Minister Kaifu Toshiki, won 275 seats, a stable majority of the total of 512 seats. On the other hand, the middle-of-the-road CGP and the DSP suffered losses apparently because potential DSP votes flowed to the SDPJ. The JCP fared poorly, probably due to the political changes taking place in the Soviet Union and eastern Europe. As a result of the two elections, the LDP and SDPJ now account for over 70 percent of the 252-seat Upper House and over 80 percent of the 512-seat Lower House.

Uniformity against the LDP

A growing interest by communication researchers concerning the way Japanese newspapers handle daily coverage has instigated criticism in recent years regarding the tendencies and political stances of various newspapers. The common thread running through this criticism is that newspapers are almost identical in their reportage, selection of news, and even in their headlines, makeup, and format; and further, that there is a great deal of uniformity in the degree of emphasis attributed to a particular news item in all of the newspapers, with items selected for major treatment being remarkably similar. Some will go so far as to say that the distinctive character of Japanese newspapers is that they have no distinctive character. Some critics have pointed out that during the postwar period the more than 120 Japanese daily newspapers have never engaged in controversy among themselves on any issue (Kase 1978). More significant is the prevalent view that the press as a whole comprises a united front against the LDP and its leaders. Newspapers are regarded by almost all researchers of Japanese journalism as having a progressive attitude, left-wing orientation, and antigovernment stance, and as being critical of the LDP and tolerant of the opposition parties (Kim 1981, 1). During the 1970s and the 1980s, some researchers have been more consistent than others in claiming that newspapers differ in their degree of criticism of the LDP. Based on content analysis of the way social and political events were usually handled by daily newspapers, Tsujimura (1976a, 199–208) has suggested a scale on which the most prestigious paper, the *Asahi,* is the most critical of all vis-à-vis the government, followed by the *Mainichi,* the

Yomiuri, the *Nihon Keizai*, and the *Sankei*. Brown and Lee (1977) noted that the latter two newspapers are usually regarded as having a progovernment attitude.

By examining a number of case studies, Tsujimura (1976b, 1981) revealed the anti-LDP government stance the press has, and how much of a discrepancy there was between public opinion and newspaper editorials vis-à-vis the government or government policies. Antigovernment editorials in the major newspapers, according to Tsujimura, did not represent or reflect public opinion. Tsujimura noted that all major newspapers were against the government drafts for the San Francisco Peace Treaty in 1952 and Japan-Korea Normalization Treaty in 1964. This was the stance of the newspapers, although public opinion polls clearly showed that the public supported the government in both these instances. Additionally, newspapers have persistently campaigned against the Self-Defense Forces and were sympathetic to workers' strikes, whereas the public tended to show support in the first case and took a negative stance in the latter. Ito (1990) elucidated that during the 1960s and up to mid-1970s, the major newspapers were favorable to the Socialist bloc and socialism, idealizing China and North Korea, and unfavorable to the Japanese and United States governments and their policies. They also criticized South Korea and the Self-Defense Forces and were cynical about the Japanese imperial system.

In a bid to explain this tendency of the press, some have assumed that the more Japanese newspapers attempt to increase their circulations, the more progressive they become in pursuing the course of left-wing commercialism (Tsujimura, 1976a, 198). This assumption is related perhaps to the view that a newspaper's progressive attitude will be of more interest and attract more readers. Others, such as Kyogoku (1987, 196–204), have documented the traditional "spirit" of the newspapers, since the onset of modern Japan some 130 years ago, as always opposing the incumbent government as a type of effective, long-lasting opposition. The general concept is that in contrast to the European and American counterparts, newspapers in Japan underwent a constant change in a relatively short period of time. However, since the 1870s—about a decade after the Meiji Restoration, when newspapers became a widespread medium of communication for the first time—newspapers have carried some "anti-government coloration." (This would not include the period in the thirties and forties when racist and ultranationalist forces came to the fore.) In particular, after the end of World War II, newspapers, as a reaction against their own role before the war, started to adopt a strong tendency against authority, against government, and against the establishment. Furthermore, they even started to take a strong critical stance toward traditions of Japanese culture. Tsujimura (1981), for example, analyzed the year-end and new-year editorials from 1946 to 1980; he noted that the criticism against the conservative party (the LDP) and the government, the Japanese, and Japanese culture, appeared in 43.5 percent of the editorials.

Several important aspects are related to the study of the media and politics in Japan. On one hand, there is the strength of the print media, derived from its enormous circulation, reliability, and importance in Japanese society. Although the press pledges itself to policies of neutrality and fairness, it is perceived as constantly criticizing the LDP and the government, assuming the role of public watchdog over the political leadership. On the other hand, the political environment is characterized by a strong party that has dominated for over 30 years and is opposed by several parties, led by the SDPJ, which are unable to consolidate their strength and pursue political leadership.

Two questions are relevant here. One concerns the way in which the strength of the press affects the interaction between Diet members and the members of the press, the tendency of the Diet members to take advantage of the huge circulation of newspapers to suit their publicity needs, and the tendency of Diet members to depend on the print media as a source of information. The other question is related to the political environment and the way in which the existence of the two political groups, one more established and dominant than the other, affects the functions of reporters gathering news and the nature and content of the political coverage by the press as a whole.

These two related questions are discussed in the chapters to follow.

Part 2
Gathering Political Information in Nagatachô

CHAPTER 3

Accessibility to Political Communicators:
The Views of Reporters

Meetings with Diet Members

Perhaps the most conspicuous phenomenon visible to an occasional visitor to *Nagatachô* is the sight of many reporters everywhere. This phenomenon is even more salient to those visiting the Diet Building: many reporters moving from one side to the other of this huge complex, coming and going from one floor to another, entering and leaving the various committee rooms and the plenary chamber. They are even seen in the restaurant. Dozens of reporters frequently cluster in the corridors, leaning on each other's shoulders, forming a circle around a Diet member or any other politician talking to them. Reporters are also seen everywhere in the three huge seven-story buildings across the road behind the Diet Building—two of which house the offices of members of the House of Representatives and the other containing those of the House of Councillors.

From morning until late afternoon and, in many cases, even after most government and political party offices surrounding *Nagatachô* are dark and deserted, reporters are seen entering and leaving Diet members' private offices. The frequency of such comings and goings is such that many Diet members see it as an integral part of their routine office work. Commenting during the late evening on their hectic schedule, Diet members may refer to a meeting of their political party, party faction, or committee in the Diet. They might mention that they met representatives of a certain interest group or with other groups of bureaucrats, but they never fail to disclose that they also met at least one reporter.

Frequency of Meetings

Generally speaking, reporters have very easy accessibility to all Diet members. News-gathering methods adopted by the press (discussed later) facilitate meetings between reporters and Diet members. In fact, reporters can easily approach cabinet members and even the prime minister. Reporters assigned to the political desk—such as on-the-spot reporters, desk members, and political editors—have a special badge on their lapel and a special card with their photograph, which permits them to move freely in all facilities concerned with the political affairs of the country. This includes the Diet Building, the headquarters of the political parties, the Diet members' private office buildings, the prime minister's official residence, and all of the government agencies, most of which are within walking distance of *Nagatachô* in the *Kasumigaseki* district, or a few minutes' ride on the train in the *Ôtemachi* district. Reporters need only to make a telephone call to any Diet member's office and inform the secretary of their intention to drop by. Many reporters do not even bother to make a telephone call; they simply knock on the door and ask to see the Diet member.

Easy accessibility to Diet members is not limited to reporters from the political desk. It is also a legacy of reporters from other sections, such as the economic and social desks. Some of them may find it useful to meet with a particular Diet member to complete a certain story or to obtain a comment about information collected earlier by their desk. These reporters can usually receive a special one-time entrance card to meet the Diet member in the private office or in the Diet Building. Nevertheless, meetings between political desk reporters and Diet members are much more significant and more prevalent than are meetings with reporters from other sections.

Diet members, for their part, rarely refuse to meet with any reporter who wishes to see them for any reason. A Diet member's perspective was succinctly expressed by one SDPJ Diet member who claimed: "When a reporter wants to pay a call, I consider it an urgent matter and give it top priority. Reporters are always welcome visitors and my door is open to them whenever they want to meet me. Sometimes I even postpone other appointments to meet reporters."

Meetings between Diet members and reporters do not always take place in the Diet member's office or the Diet Building. In fact, reporters meet Diet members almost anywhere: in the Diet Building or one of its committee rooms, at the headquarters of political parties, at one of the government bureaus, and even in the prime minister's official residence. Moreover, meetings extend beyond the workplace and Diet members often meet reporters in their private residence, at restaurants, and even on golf courses. The latter is where, in recent years, especially top echelon Diet members, such as LDP faction leaders, prefer to practice so-called "golf-politics"; i.e., between drives they chat, seek to achieve mutual understanding on a certain problem in Japanese politics, and show their friendship to the reporters. When I asked a reporter to explain the significance of getting up early in the morning on a day off, such as Sunday, leaving the children wishing to go to the beach on a hot day, and instead driving five hours outside of Tokyo only to watch several leaders smile, joke, and play golf together in front of several television cameras and other reporters, the reporter answered:

> On such an occasion, far away from their gray offices in the closed cubicle of *Nagatachô,* in the open field, loosened from their ties and suits and formality, I can not always get, in fact I cannot get at all, any details on decision-making process in the government, nor what Japan intends to do in the recent international crisis, or what the ruling party is working on right now. But, the information that I can get is not less valuable; that is, on the atmosphere that exists between those political figures who play golf in front of me. The way they joke with each other; the way they greet each other; the way they praise the other for a good drive; even the way they look at each other, tells me a lot about their interpersonal relations, the extent that they like or dislike their colleague, the degree that one tends to agree with the other, and on the interpersonal power structure that exists between them. This is not less important than getting their verbal opinion on a specific policy matter. To be a political reporter means, in the first place, to understand the real mood that exists behind the words and ideas of political leaders.

Moreover, Diet members also meet reporters in special study groups, in the form of a seminar, organized in a rental conference room in one of the hotels in the *Nagatachô* area behind the Diet members' office building. Ordinarily, once a week, a group of reporters, often joined by editorial writers and members of the political desk from several news media, meet with a certain Diet member, usually an outspoken figure, to hear the Diet member's opinion about a certain pending issue on the political agenda. Here again, however, the orientation is to get more hints on the atmosphere and the general mood that exists in the particular political cycle that the speaker belongs to, such as an LDP faction or the LDP headquarters, than to get details on a specific policy matter.

There are several other forms of meetings between Diet members and reporters, but for the present discussion the important factors are that reporters have constant contact with Diet members, inside and outside *Nagatachô,* and that the nature of each meeting differs along several criteria discussed below. In order to get the overall picture of the nature of this contact, Diet members were asked first to indicate the typical frequency of meetings they have with reporters. Their answers are outlined in table 3-1.[1]

---

1. The question was: "Does the Diet member meet any reporter (from newspapers, radio, or television)? If yes, how many times in the course of a week? (1) He/she does not meet them at all; (2) once a week; (3) twice a week; (4) three or more times a week; (5) he does meet them but the number of times is unknown."

TABLE 3-1.   Frequency of Weekly Meetings between Diet Members and Reporters

Political Party			Weekly Meetings			
		Once a Week	Twice a Week	Three or More Times	Diet Members Meet Reporters, but Number is Unknown	No Meetings
Sangiinnokai	(N = 9)	1	2	6	0	0
NLC	(N = 12)	1	1	8	2	0
DSP	(N = 32)	5	3	9	15	0
CGP	(N = 50)	8	4	8	30	0
SDPJ	(N = 79)	11	11	27	30	0
LDP	(N = 213)	22	22	99	70	0
Total	(N = 395)	48	43	157	147	0

Note: In seven cases the answer was not clear.

Several significant points are reflected in the Diet members' answers. As table 3-1 reveals, not one Diet member noted that they do not meet with any reporter in the course of a week. They all meet with reporters at least once a week. The tendency to meet with reporters once or twice a week is reflected in 11.9 and 10.6 percent of the cases, respectively. Significantly, however, reporters tend to meet with close to 40 percent of the Diet members three or more times a week. Nearly this same percentage of Diet members meet with reporters on a regular basis, but noted that the frequency of meetings is not a constant factor and depends on the political climate at a given time; for example, during times of cabinet reshuffling or before an election. These may be only a few of the factors that create an environment for frequent meetings between reporters and Diet members, as will be discussed in chapter 5.

Another significant point related to meetings between Diet members and reporters is that nearly 40 percent of the ruling LDP members meet with reporters three or more times a week. In the case of the number 1 and number 2 opposition parties, the SDPJ and CGP, nearly 34 and 16 percent of the Diet members of these parties meet with reporters three or more times a week, respectively. Furthermore, a large number of Diet members from small political parties, such as *Sangiinnokai* and the NLC,[2] also frequently meet reporters. On the whole, the fact that Diet members from different political parties meet reporters about three or more times a week is remarkable, and reflects a tendency for reporters—or both sides—to meet as often as possible.

---

2. These parties are defined as "small" on the basis of the number of members and political influence. In the case of the NLC, at the time of this research it had not yet entered a coalition with the ruling LDP.

This tendency, potentially, can facilitate the flow of varied, and even conflict-ing, information, interpretations, and views, held by large and small political parties from both ends of the political spectrum, to the public.

Political Experience and Meetings with Reporters

The tendency of reporters to meet as often as three or more times a week with a large number of Diet members raises the question of whether these Diet members with whom the reporters meet most often have special characteris-tics that attract reporters to them and that distinguish them from any other group of Diet members.

One characteristic that may be important is the experience a Diet member has in Diet activities. It is suggested that there is some correlation between the number of times elected to the Diet and the frequency of meeting reporters. The more experience Diet members have, the more they tend to participate in diversified political activities and to be involved in more policy-making roles on different levels (such as their political party and the Diet). For instance, in the case of the ruling LDP, those elected more than three or four times become vice ministers or vice chairpeople of committees in the Diet or in the party, and those elected five to seven times receive minister posts or chairs of committees in the Diet, or serve as vice-secretary general of the party. More-over, those elected more times will have more contacts with people from other political groups, which, in turn, will further broaden their own knowledge. A more experienced Diet member will have more first-hand knowledge concern-ing the various activities they directly participate in. Also, a more veteran Diet member will have significantly more access to other kinds of informa-tion, such as about other groups participating in politics, which will be pro-vided to them by personal communication with colleagues, either Diet mem-bers or other persons with whom they have cultivated contact during their long tenure in the Diet. In their pursuit of reliable information and analysis, re-porters may tend then to meet especially with experienced Diet members. The latter will draw the attention of reporters as a potential and useful news source and, based on their experience, a source of opinions and views about various political activities and developments.

To analyze the above characteristics, attention is focused here on those Diet members who tend to meet with reporters most often, that is, three or more times a week. This is because previous examination did not reveal any significant points for those who meet reporters less frequently, that is, once or twice a week. Figure 3-1 shows schematically the relationships between the number of times a Diet member was elected to the Diet and the tendency to meet with reporters three or more times a week. In view of the different significant aspects that characterize the role and the composition of the two

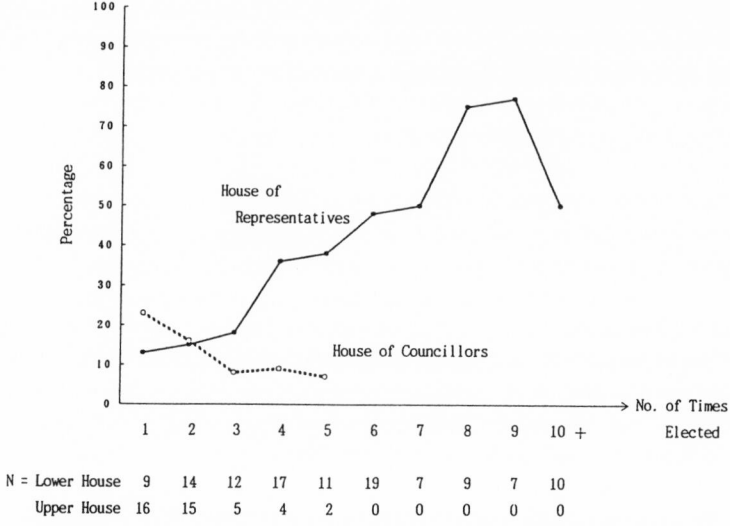

N = Lower House   9   14   12   17   11   19   7   9   7   10
    Upper House   16   15   5   4   2   0   0   0   0   0

Fig. 3-1. Relationship between number of times elected of members of the House of Representatives and House of Councillors and meetings with reporters three or more times a week. The graph indicates the relative percentage of Diet members who meet reporters three or more times a week, per number of times elected.

chambers of the Diet,[3] the figure gives the variables divided by the two chambers.

Study of the meeting habits of members of the House of Councillors as expressed in this figure shows an initial decline, followed by a stabilization in the cases of those elected three or four times, then falls off again for those elected more times. On the other hand, regarding members of the Lower House, the figure indicates a somewhat exponential increase until eight or nine elections, when it suddenly levels off, then decreases sharply. Interestingly, a comparison of the two graphs shows a correlation between the given variables; schematically, however, one is almost a mirror image of the other.

Regarding the House of Representatives, four distinct levels can be seen:

3. Each chamber of the Diet has a different basis for qualification. The membership of the House of Representatives is 512 and the term of office is four years. Historically, however, general elections have been held on average every two or three years. The corresponding figures for the House of Councillors are 252 members and six-year terms. Half of the members of this chamber are elected every three years. Of the two chambers, the Lower House is the more important. It has constitutional priority over the budget and can override a decision by the House

the first level relates to those elected up to three times, of whom about 12 to 18 percent meet with reporters three or more times a week. The second level relates to those elected four to seven times, of whom about 36 to 50 percent meet with reporters three or more times a week. The third level relates to those elected eight or nine times, of whom 75 to 77 percent meet with reporters three or more times a week; and the fourth level relates to those elected ten or more times, of whom some 50 percent meet with reporters three or more times a week. These four distinct levels suggest an interpretation of the tendency of reporters to meet with certain Diet members.

The first level consists mainly of members elected only a few times, thus having less political experience. Consequently, the potential interest of reporters in meeting with them to obtain information is lower. The second level consists of middle-echelon members—holding positions such as, in the case of the LDP, vice ministers, vice chairpeople of committees, or even chairpeople of committees within the party—who possess a slightly higher interest potential to reporters. The level having the highest interest potential to reporters, as shown in figure 3-1, consists of members elected eight or nine times. Most of these Diet members have climbed the political ladder through such posts as—in the case of the LDP—ministers (some even served twice in this post), chairpeople of committees in the Diet, vice secretaries general of the party, and so forth; or they are chairperson, spokesperson, or head of committees of the opposition political parties. Worth noting is the gap between those elected seven and those elected eight times. Table A-2 in the Appendix indicates the gap at the point where members have been elected seven times. This gap derives from the fact that only about 44 percent of the Diet members elected seven times participated in the present study, whereas 57 percent of those elected eight times participated. This gap might have been reduced had the number of those elected seven times been higher.

Of greatest interest is the fourth level. Two explanations may be offered to account for the sudden drop in Diet member–reporter interaction. First, a Diet member elected more than 10 times has become too entrenched within the framework of the Diet to provide interesting information to reporters. In the words of one reporter:

> Such Diet members can offer stories from today until next week. One cannot, of course, ignore their experience; some of these veteran Diet

---

of Councillors regarding a bill or the selection of a prime minister. Politically, most cabinet ministers come from the House of Representatives, and because members of the Lower House are elected from smaller districts, they are closer to the voters' concerns and attention. Nevertheless, one cannot ignore the role played by the Upper House. Potentially, an opposition majority in the Upper House can greatly slow the passage of legislation and force the ruling party into greater compromises than it would otherwise contemplate.

members could teach in any prestigious university a great deal about Japanese politics and its dynamics, decision-making process, and internal structure. One can study a lot from them on the relations between one group of Diet members and another, and on how Japanese politics might function better. Some of their stories are very interesting. But during the time that I have been covering *Nagatachô* I have found that in most cases their stories are of little relevance to the political news that I have to write. So, on a regular basis, I do not meet any of these veteran Diet members at all.

Except the very few Diet members who serve as leaders of the opposition political parties or of LDP factions, former prime ministers, or other top-echelon members, such as the speaker of the House, most Diet members elected more than 10 times have moved beyond the range of such activities as policy-making or running party affairs and now constitute something akin to "elders of the tribe." Due to their advanced age (some of these Diet members are in their late seventies, others in their eighties) and the fact that usually they are not involved in a large number of activities of the Diet or their parties or factions, they have a lot of free time to meet any reporters interested in meeting them, but offer, as noted, "only stories."

The same explanation can be applied for those from the Upper House, who were elected five or more times, which means more than 30 years in the Diet. Those elected three or four times to the House of Councillors may also fall into the category applied to levels two and three of the Lower House; for example, some of them are, or were, ministers, while others serve, or had served, posts such as chairperson of committees in the Diet and in their political parties, and they are thus of potential interest to reporters.

Although explanations can be suggested as to why reporters tend to meet Diet members elected more times, there are questions regarding those elected one or two times in the Upper House and one to three times in the Lower House. The high tendency of these younger Diet members to meet reporters does not make sense if one considers the assumption that reporters tend to meet more experienced Diet members to obtain information. Moreover, it is hard to believe that Diet members from the small and less powerful political parties (for example, *Sangiinnokai*) meet reporters as often as three or more times a week.

The frequency of meetings with both the members of the small political parties and the least experienced Diet members may be related to two factors. First, reporters meet Diet members, but not necessarily, as was assumed, for obtaining information. This brings up the question of why reporters meet Diet members—which accounts for such frequent meetings. The second factor is that reporters indeed meet less experienced Diet members and those from the small political parties, but because of the great number of news agencies in Japan, not all of these reporters are from, say, the leading national newspapers. In other words, if, as Diet members indicated in their responses, they meet reporters so often (and presumably give them information), not all of the information obtained from Diet members has the potential to reach all of the people throughout the country. Further study is needed to identify the specific reporters who meet Diet members and the news channels that they represent. Taken from a broad perspective, these two questions—identifying the reporters who meet Diet members and the reasons for their meetings—are interrelated. It is suggested here that by identifying these reporters one can deduce the reasons for the meetings. Hereafter the discussion will focus on these specific reporters.

Meetings with Reporters

Most Frequent Meetings

Because there are so many reporters representing various news media within *Nagatachô,* many Diet members are motivated to meet and tell them about themselves and about their activities. To a great extent, because of the huge circulations of the national newspapers, each reporter represents a channel to the Diet member for approaching millions of people all over the country. On a regular basis, each Diet member may, of course, have general preferences concerning meetings with reporters from the national or local newspapers or television stations. Some Diet members may prefer to meet most often, for example, with local newspaper reporters before an election to remind their electorate that they intend to run again. Because Japan's electoral system is mostly locally oriented, the local newspaper (the one that is published in the prefecture the Diet member represents) serves at election time as the most useful vehicle to send messages and appeals to supporters. At other times, these Diet members may prefer to meet reporters from national newspapers, to gain publicity on a national level. To be sure, Diet members, as will be discussed later, do not play a passive role in their relation with reporters; instead, they constantly try to attract reporters and to initiate meetings with as many as possible, hoping to realize various objectives through them. Which reporters do Diet members meet with most? Table 3-2 outlines the most frequent meetings with reporters from a particular newspaper, television station, or radio station.[4]

---

4. The question was: "From what field of the news media does the Diet member meet reporters most often? Indicate one of the following channels: The *Yomiuri,* the *Asahi,* the *Mainichi,* the *Nihon Keizai,* the *Sankei;* local newspapers; NHK (including the educational channel); commercial television; radio; *Jiji Press; Kyôdô News Service;* other _____; unknown."

TABLE 3-2. Most Frequent Meetings with News Media Reporters

Political Party	Daily Newspapers						Television		Radio	Wire Services		Others*
	Yomiuri	Asahi	Mainichi	Nikkei	Sankei	Local	NHK	Commercial		Jiji	Kyōdō	
Sangiinnokai (N = 9)	1	5	1	0	0	0	0	0	0	0	1	1
NLC (N = 12)	1	6	1	0	0	2	1	0	0	0	1	0
DSP (N = 32)	1	4	1	1	4	7	4	3	1	4	1	1
CGP (N = 51)	1	15	2	1	0	17	9	0	0	2	2	2
SDPJ (N = 81)	4	8	5	1	0	26	13	6	0	3	12	3
LDP (N = 217)	15	37	7	8	6	58	42	5	0	9	22	8
Total (N = 402)	23	75	17	11	10	110	69	14	1	18	39	15

*All of those who answered in this column referred to bloc newspapers.

Clearly, Diet members meet reporters from various news agencies. Most Diet members, about 66 percent, tend to meet reporters from the national, local, and bloc newspapers. Some 27 percent of them meet reporters of local newspapers. The *others* column in table 3-2 refers to other newspapers. All Diet members noted that they referred to bloc newspapers in this column, however. Because the bloc newspapers are distributed in a specific and limited area, such as Tokyo and the island of Hokkaido, and because their content and makeup are oriented to specific readers who live in these areas, these newspapers can be considered more as local newspapers than national dailies. In this case, the frequency of meetings with local newspapers automatically increases (to 31.1 percent). Of the national newspapers, the *Asahi* is dominant regarding its reporters' meetings with Diet members; nearly 19 percent of the Diet members have frequent meetings with the *Asahi* reporters, followed by the *Yomiuri* reporters, with which nearly 6 percent of Diet members meet. From this viewpoint, the *Yomiuri,* which has the largest circulation in Japan, is not regarded with the same importance, giving the *Asahi* greater political significance. On the other hand, representatives of all the television channels, NHK, and the commercial stations, have frequent meetings with only 21 percent of the Diet members, and radio stations have insignificant contact with Diet members.

Another notable point is the large number of Diet members who meet with reporters from the wire services; more than 14 percent of them meet reporters from *Kyôdô News Service* and *Jiji Press.* Surprisingly, this figure is higher than the number of meetings with some of the national newspapers, such as *Mainichi, Nihon Keizai,* and *Sankei.* The tendency for meeting with the wire-service reporters is interesting in itself, since the wire services provide news, feature stories, and editorials mainly to local newspapers; this finding suggests that Diet members have, potentially, another channel for transmitting updated information to local newspapers, and thus to voters from their constituencies. Taken together, table 3-2 indicates that 125 Diet members (31.1 percent) meet with reporters from local (and bloc) newspapers, 57 (14.2 percent) meet most often with reporters from the wire services, 83 (20.6 percent) with television reporters, and 136 (33.8 percent) with reporters from national newspapers. With regard to the question of which reporters Diet members meet with most, only one-third of the Diet members' information potentially passes directly through national newspapers' reporters to the national dailies.

Political Experience and Meetings with Reporters

As previously discussed, one of the crucial factors governing meetings between Diet members and reporters is the experience a Diet member has in Diet activities. This factor will be examined further in this section. It is assumed that a Diet member elected many times will have the experience, knowledge, and involvement in political activities that, in the reporter's view, make the Diet member someone whose experience can meet the reporter's needs for information. Table 3-3 correlates the number of times a Diet member has been elected to the Diet to their meetings with reporters from a particular news medium.

From the table, it is hard to find any obvious correlations between the two variables in the case of commercial television, radio, and each of the national newspapers. A correlation can be observed in four instances, however. The first one is related to the *Jiji* and *Kyôdô* wire services; the more experience one has in political activities, the smaller the tendency to meet reporters from these agencies. These wire services provide news mainly to local newspapers, and the tendency of Diet members to meet with reporters from these agencies is very obvious for those members elected one to three times (the less experienced Diet members), for reasons suggested above. The second point is related to the *others* label. As previously stated, Diet members referred to the bloc newspapers here, which are also local newspapers. Again, the less political experience one has, the greater the tendency to meet bloc newspaper reporters. Moreover, a correlation can also be observed in the other two cases, of local newspapers and NHK television. Figure 3-2 shows these correlations schematically. In addition, this figure presents a closer study of the tendency for Diet members to meet with reporters of all the national newspapers. As previously mentioned, no obvious correlation can be found concerning meeting with any particular national newspaper. Thus, to find a general tendency, the five big newspapers were combined to form one category.

In the case of local newspapers, it can be seen that a large percentage of Diet members having less experience meet reporters quite often but, graphically, this tendency decreases exponentially as experience increases. For example, a relatively large number of Diet members elected 1 to 3 times meet reporters of local newspapers, whereas those elected 9 or 10 times do not meet them at all. This phenomenon is in direct contrast to that of NHK. In other words, many of those elected 9 or more times tend to meet NHK reporters more frequently, whereas only a few of those elected once or twice meet them at all.

As the figure shows, three distinct levels concerning local newspapers are identified. The first is related to Diet members elected up to three times, of whom about 25 to 40 percent meet with reporters of local newspapers. There is a sudden shift in the frequency of contact for those elected four times, and a similar decreasing trend appears in those elected up to seven times, or 14 to 34 percent. The third level occurs when a Diet member has been elected eight

TABLE 3-3. Ratio of Number of Times Elected to the Diet to Meetings with Particular News Media Reporters (in percentages)

Number of Times Elected	Daily Newspapers						Television		Radio	Wire Services		
	Yomiuri	Asahi	Mainichi	Nikkei	Sankei	Local	NHK	Commercial		Jiji	Kyôdô	Others*
1 (N = 70)	7.1	12.9	1.4	0.0	0.0	40.0	2.9	0.0	0.0	5.7	17.1	12.9
2 (N = 94)	3.2	12.8	2.1	0.0	1.1	37.2	4.3	5.3	0.0	5.3	23.4	5.3
3 (N = 67)	10.4	16.4	6.0	1.4	1.4	25.3	12.0	9.0	0.0	13.4	3.0	1.4
4 (N = 47)	0.0	34.0	2.1	2.1	4.2	34.0	19.1	2.1	0.0	0.0	2.1	0.0
5 (N = 29)	0.0	17.2	10.3	10.3	6.9	20.7	24.1	3.4	3.4	0.0	3.4	0.0
6 (N = 40)	2.5	35.0	0.0	7.5	7.5	12.5	32.5	5.0	0.0	0.0	0.0	0.0
7 (N = 14)	14.3	14.3	14.3	7.1	0.0	14.3	35.7	0.0	0.0	0.0	0.0	0.0
8 (N = 12)	8.3	16.6	8.3	0.0	8.3	8.3	41.7	0.0	0.0	0.0	8.3	0.0
9 (N = 9)	22.2	0.0	22.2	11.1	0.0	0.0	44.4	0.0	0.0	0.0	0.0	0.0
10 (N = 20)	10.0	20.0	5.0	5.0	0.0	0.0	60.0	0.0	0.0	0.0	0.0	0.0
Total (N = 402)	5.7	18.7	4.2	2.7	2.5	27.4	17.2	3.5	0.2	4.5	9.7	3.7

*All of those who answered in this column referred to bloc newspapers.

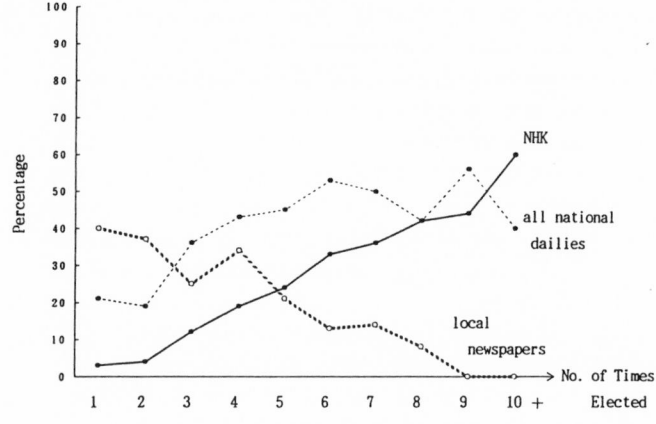

N = National dailies 15   18   24   20   13   21   7   5   5   8
    Local newspapers 28   35   17   16   6   5   2   1   0   0
    NHK   2   4   8   9   7   13   5   5   4   12

Fig. 3-2. Correlation between meetings with NHK, the national and local newspapers' reporters, and number of times elected. The graph indicates the relative percentage of Diet members who meet NHK, the national and local newspapers' reporters, relative to the number of times elected to the Diet.

times: 8.3 percent meet with local newspaper reporters, and this figure decreases with more elections. The first level obviously consists of Diet members elected fewer times, with less political experience, influence, and reputation. Consequently, on one hand (as was explained with reference to figure 3-1), the potential interest of reporters from national newspapers to meet these Diet members is lower. On the other hand, to establish their own reputation and to pass on information about their activities to their districts, these politicians need to meet reporters representing their own constituencies. The second level reflected in figure 3-2 consists of middle-echelon Diet members having a slightly higher interest potential to reporters from national newspapers. Those elected four to seven times have already established their reputations in their constituencies and their positions in their political parties. There is a shift at this level toward a higher degree of contact with national media reporters rather than with local newspaper reporters.

An interesting point shown in figure 3-2 is that those elected four times meet with reporters from local newspapers more often than those elected three times. The explanation is that at the time of this survey, about 16 of the latter were among the 25 vice ministers, who, because of their relatively important political posts, tend to be in contact more with the national newspaper reporters covering their agencies, and tend to neglect meetings with local newspapers. (This will be discussed broadly in the next chapter.) These Diet members represent 16 of the 67 elected three times (see Appendix), about 24 percent, accounting for the deviation in the group. Those elected four times simply maintain the same tendency as those elected one or two times. From this viewpoint, those elected three times are the exception. The opposite tendency—in the case of the national newspapers—is reflected in the sudden jump of those elected three times as shown in Figure 3-2 since they, as vice ministers, have close contact with the mass media on a national level.

The third level reflected in the case of the local newspapers in figure 3-2 consists of Diet members who have already established their reputations and contacts with supporters. Most of their activities are covered by the national newspapers or television newscasts. They have already developed tools for providing information to their constituents besides local newspapers during their tenure in the Diet. More elections corresponds with the shift from meetings with local newspaper reporters and an increased tendency for meetings with national newspaper reporters. In other words, less experience in the Diet leads to a greater reliance on meetings with local newspaper reporters, whereas greater experience leads to increased meetings with national newspaper reporters, thus revealing two directly reflective tendencies.

Four levels can also be seen regarding the meetings with national dailies' reporters as reflected in figure 3-2. The first concerns younger Diet members elected 1 or 2 times, 19 to 21 percent of whom meet with reporters from national newspapers. The second level shows that, for those elected 3 to 7 times, the figure rises to 35 to 52 percent. Two more shifts follow, involving those elected 8 or 9 times and again for those elected 10 or more times. A somewhat similar trend is reflected in the case of NHK. It is clear that the more times a Diet member is elected, the greater the tendency to meet with NHK reporters. It is interesting to note that about 60 percent of those elected 10 or more times meet with NHK reporters; in comparison, there is a drastic drop between national newspapers' reporters–Diet member interaction, after the latter are elected 10 or more times. This factor can reveal—in a broader sense—the sources of news for NHK. Most Diet members elected 10 times or more are heads of political parties or faction leaders within the LDP, but this group also includes former prime ministers, former ministers, and former heads of committees. A few of them continue to participate in the policy-making processes in their parties or on the national level, but the majority do not assume any such role. From this viewpoint, NHK reporters tend to pay less attention to whether one actively participates in policy-making, and relying more on the experience Diet members have gained in their work, a factor which is perhaps significantly more important to NHK than to newspaper reporters.

All in all, the data presented until now indicates several significant points. First, 246 Diet members, 61.2 percent, meet with newspaper reporters (136 Diet members meet with reporters from all the national newspapers and 110 Diet members meet with reporters of local dailies), compared to meeting with television reporters (NHK or commercial, 69 and 14, respectively) or radio reporters. This may reveal the patterns of exposure of the Diet members to reporters of the print media, in view, perhaps, of their huge circulations and potential influence; or as will be discussed later, it may be a consequence of the newspaper reporters' work pattern, which obliges them to be in constant contact with Diet members, which is not true for broadcast media reporters. Second, table 3-3 and figure 3-2 suggest that 50 percent or more in each group of Diet members elected a certain number of times meets with reporters from newspapers, with the exception of one group—those elected 10 or more times, most of whom meet with reporters from NHK. These tables and figures also indicate that, comparatively, most information from Diet members elected 1 or 2 times has the potential of going to local newspapers, and information from those elected 3 or more times has the potential of being passed on to the national level. In the case of those elected 10 or more times, since most of them meet with NHK reporters, this channel has the potential of most clearly reflecting their thoughts and opinions.

Objectives of Reporter–Diet Member Interaction

Motivations for Meetings

The notion emphasized thus far is that the primary objective of meetings between Diet member and reporters is to provide (or obtain) political information. The reporters must obtain news from Diet members and, based on the information thus obtained, write stories; this is, after all, the essence of their work. In fact, unlike work done by reporters in other sections, the nature of a political reporter's work requires constant meetings with Diet members in order to observe any change or any shift of activity occurring in political dynamics. When asked during interviews to reveal the nature of their work, political reporters in particular often compare it to and distinguish it from that of reporters who work at other sections. In answering a related question, one political reporter noted:

> A reporter from the social news section, for example, can sit in one place waiting for an event to occur and can then collect information and write their story. But I, as a reporter from the political section, have to know,

from moment to moment, exactly what is going on, and to supply my newspaper with information, not only about what has just happened, but also information concerning contemporary trends and even some assumptions of what may occur in the near future. And because in many instances in Japanese politics the "near future" can take place within a few hours, I must be "in the swim" constantly, close to the Diet members.

And as an editorial writer noted:

The wider the range of Diet members a reporter has contact with, the better his ability to observe the dynamics of the political world, mainly by hearing opinions and viewpoints held by various, even conflicting, Diet members and by observing their daily routine work.

Moreover, political reporters must not only supply their desk regularly with political information for routine daily coverage, but also need to contribute, from time to time, special feature stories. The latter demands that they understand any existing or emerging trend in politics, and this may stimulate even more direct contact with Diet members. On the other hand, as previously indicated, Diet members do not play a passive role in their interaction with reporters, and they take full part in their meetings. They also initiate some of the meetings, likewise trying to meet as many reporters as they can. And, as has been elucidated, meetings between reporters and Diet members encourage a versatile and complex network of mutual relations and interrelations.

Why do Diet members meet reporters of the media? Is their sole objective to provide information or do they have other objectives in mind? At the preliminary meetings preceding this study, I met with Diet members' secretaries and asked their views on these questions. There was no clear answer. Secretaries, sometimes consulting with the other secretaries working in the same office, were not sure if there was really only one answer. In their view, a Diet member tends to meet with reporters, not for one particular reason, but perhaps for several reasons, some of which are interrelated. Initially, secretaries felt that Diet members meet with reporters to inform them about their activities, but may have other motives as well. For example, a Diet member may meet with a reporter because they are friends and they like to chat about various issues in a relaxed atmosphere. This chat, as one secretary said, "is not necessarily about politics, but about, say, their common interest in golf."

In this social or friendly atmosphere, which serves as the basis for their meeting, the Diet member and the reporter also exchange opinions and views, and their relationship continues beyond working hours and the workplace. They may play golf and drink together during the weekend. Or, Diet members

TABLE 3-4. Purposes for Meeting with Mass Media Reporters (N = 402)

Purpose	Providing Information	Obtaining Information	Social or Friendship Basis	Maintaining Good Relations	Others	Unknown
Number of Diet Members	206	228	115	170	35	9

may meet with reporters because they want—more than anything else—to maintain good relations with the press. Such Diet members may simply wish, for instance, that reporters not forget that they exist. Thus, the reasons that the secretaries of Diet members referred to most often were identified and included in the questionnaire presented to the Diet members. Table 3-4 indicates the purposes for which Diet members meet reporters.[5]

Since 402 Diet members participated in the study, the figure shows that most Diet members answered affirmatively about meeting reporters for more than one purpose. In other words, meetings between Diet members and reporters go beyond the sole purpose of Diet members providing information to reporters. The general purpose seems to be a two-way transmission of information. The purpose of obtaining information from reporters is remarkably higher than any other stated purpose, however. Twenty-five Diet members answered that the only reason they meet reporters is to provide information, and 13 others claimed that the sole purpose was obtaining information. A social or friendship basis was claimed as the sole purpose by 9 Diet members. Finally, as the sole purpose, maintaining good relations was stated by 27 Diet members, noting that meeting with reporters has nothing to do with exchanging information but is rather intended just to maintain and nurture the personal side of these relationships. It illustrates, as will be disscussed later, that rapport precedes cooperation; greater attention has to be given to maintaining the affective, rather than the instrumental, side of relationships.

Meetings with Specific Reporters

Figure 3-3 shows a closer view of the objectives of Diet members in meeting with reporters of a specific medium—national newspapers (N = 136), local newspapers (N = 110), and NHK (N = 69). The figure refers to 315 (78.4 percent) of the 402 Diet members who took part in this study.

---

5. The question was: "For what purpose does the Diet member meet reporters from the news media? (1) providing information; (2) obtaining information; (3) social or friendship basis; (4) maintaining good relations; (5) other _____; (6) unknown." Other questions were: "Do you meet reporters regularly?"; "From which newspaper(s)?"; "Do you prefer to meet specific reporters? Why? What is the purpose of these meetings?"

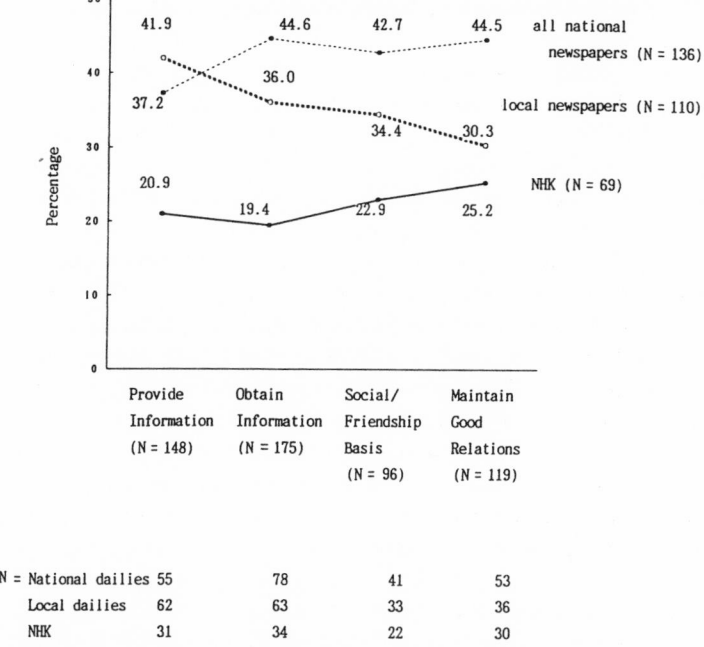

Fig. 3-3. Purposes of meeting specific media reporters. The graph indicates the relative percentages of Diet members who meet reporters of a specific news media for a specific purpose.

In general, 148 Diet members meet with reporters from national newspapers, local newspapers, or NHK to provide information; 175 meet with them to obtain information; and 96 and 119, respectively, meet with them on a social basis or to maintain good relations with the press. This pattern suggests that of the 206 Diet members who meet with reporters to provide information (as reflected in table 3-4), 148 (or 71.8 percent) provide it to the national and local newspapers and NHK, and the other 58 Diet members (28.8 percent), provide information presumably to the wire services, bloc newspapers, or commercial television and radio broadcast stations. Similarly, of the 228 who meet reporters to obtain information (table 3-4), 175 (76.8 percent) obtain it from national or local newspaper or NHK reporters, whereas the other 53 (23.2 percent) receive information from reporters of other news channels. Figure 3-3 illustrates that the largest group of Diet members (most of them with perhaps less political experience) provides information to local newspaper reporters and the smallest group provides it to NHK reporters. This is because, in comparison with newspaper reporters, the contact between NHK reporters and Diet members is not as close. Also, NHK reporters meet with fewer Diet members; have smaller staffs of reporters on a routine basis in *Nagatachô;* and, for news gathering, concentrate on the more experienced Diet members, such as LDP faction leaders and political party leaders, as is outlined in table 3-3. In practical terms, the tendencies regarding local newspaper and NHK reporters suggest that most information provided by middle-experienced Diet members (those elected four to nine times), who now serve in key positions such as ministers, vice ministers, heads of committees, and so forth, is provided to national newspaper reporters.

The figure clearly indicates that whereas a greater percentage of Diet members provide information than obtain it from reporters of the local newspapers and NHK, the opposite trend exists in the case of the national newspapers. Significantly, the number of Diet members who meet reporters from the national dailies for the purpose of obtaining information rates the highest. This tendency has several explanations and important implications. While the following chapters explain the meaning of this tendency, it is noteworthy here that such an attitude is related to the fact that national newspaper reporters meet with more Diet members and, as was shown, most of these Diet members have long experience in the Diet; some of them hold top posts in their political parties and the government. Since national newspaper reporters have more extensive resources than, say, local newspaper or NHK reporters, Diet members have a propensity to obtain more and varied information from them. Details on the nature of the information that reporters give to Diet members and on the extent to which such information is used follows. Finally, figure 3-3 suggests that only about 55 Diet members (about half of the 136 Diet members who regularly meet national newspaper reporters) serve as potential sources of information to the national press. Furthermore, in each of the other categories listed in figure 3-3 ("obtain information," "social/friendship basis," and "maintain good relations"), the largest number of Diet members appears to interact with reporters of the national dailies. Thus, the major reasons for meeting with reporters of the national dailies appear to be twofold: to exchange information and to maintain good relations.

Political Information and Quasi Sources of News

Several factors have been pointed out in the preceding discussion. The most important are that reporters frequently meet with members of the Diet and that the purposes, or objectives, of these meetings vary with both parties. Moreover, both parties have more than one reason for meeting. In general, the purposes of their meetings are to exchange information and, at the same time, to maintain their relations. In this kind of long-lasting interaction, 206 Diet members described their part as providers of information to the print and broadcast media on the local and national levels. The Diet member's function in this regard vis-à-vis local newspapers is easily understood. Reporters from these newspapers look for information that is the most relevant and of direct interest to their prefectures, including the activities of Diet members from neighboring districts. Diet members, especially the younger ones, who meet with local newspaper reporters, are in a position to provide information for voters and potential supporters, to let as many people as possible know their names, activities, and involvement in matters for promoting and improving local or prefectural issues. In this type of relationship both parties obviously benefit since the Diet members help to fulfill the needs of the local press. There is, however, a question regarding the large number of Diet members (86, or 21.4 percent of the 402 who participated in the present study) who reported that they provide political information to national newspapers and television reporters. Do all of them really provide information to these channels? If yes, what type of information do they provide?

Because both the national newspapers and television stations work on the national level, their coverage, in comparison with local newspapers, is intended to address the broad interests and concerns of the general reader (or viewer) from all parts of the country. Local newspapers tend to concentrate on the activities of one, two, or three individual Diet members, especially in their feature stories on the activities or opinions of their "prefectural" Diet members. However, the national news media must, a priori, deal with the activities of political parties, party factions, or the bureaucracy; and significantly, as appears to be the case, their frequent focus of attention is on political figures who lead the nation in posts such as prime minister. Within the limited space (or time) the various print and broadcast media have, they must deal with broad issues of concern to the general public and respond to the different tastes of their audiences. Thus, whereas local newspaper reporters might have a tendency to obtain all the information that the Diet members from their respective prefectures are willing to provide, the national news media reporters may have a preference for selected information, and seek to obtain it from certain and specific Diet members.

The nature of such information, or news sources, may depend on the flow of events or on the political or social situation at a specific time. Naturally, preference for certain information means paying less attention to or attaching less importance to other types of news. With many political activities and events to cover, in addition to informing the public about the positions held by the competing groups on various issues, the media tends to play up some topics, to emphasize certain positions more than others, and to allocate more coverage to specific political groups and less to others (Feldman and Diskin 1988). In view of the above assumption, the question is, if indeed the national news media reporters have a tendency to select particular news items, what kind of information do they want and prefer to obtain? And, among the many Diet members they have contact with, are there preferred individuals, aside from the more experienced Diet members, which reporters evaluate higher than others as sources of information?

Selectivity of Political Information

As the primary step in answering the above question, political reporters were asked to indicate the kind of information they most prefer to obtain from Diet members. In particular, reporters were asked to specify the sort of data they are most interested in professionally, and which they consider the most important and essential to them while writing political stories.[6] One factor considered in asking this question was that the type of information reporters want to obtain depends on the political climate at a given time. That is to say, the coverage of political activities during, for instance, a cabinet reshuffle or the period preceding an election, tends to focus on topics related to these particular events, while coverage of regular and daily political events is "neglected" or "postponed." For this reason, reporters were asked to refer solely to a situation of regular and routine political activity, characterized by no special events. The reporters' views were rich and varied. Nevertheless, a certain perspective was common to all of their answers. Almost all of the reporters tended to distinguish between three levels or spheres of information they are most interested in obtaining. The first sphere concerns the general activities of the Diet as a whole and the activities of the various political parties. The Diet is the focus of attention particularly when it is in session, and information regarding the various committees of the Diet are of special interest. Reporters from the national newspapers are most interested in obtaining information about the activities within and among the many political parties and the ruling party's factions as well as the activities of the prime minister, the cabinet, and the ministers.

The second sphere of information reporters are concerned about is related to the functioning of the bureaucracy. When asked to refer to the specific information they prefer to obtain, without exception reporters mentioned the daily routine work of public officials in various ministries; and particularly on the way government agencies communicate with one another or with other political organs, such as political parties and interest groups, while drafting or changing a certain bill before implementation. The activities of certain minis-

---

6. The questions were: "Is there a particular kind of information that you have a professional interest in obtaining while meeting Diet members in general or your sources of information in particular? If yes, what kind of information is it?" And, "What kind of information do you consider the most important and essential to you while writing political stories?"

tries, such as the Ministry of Finance, is of special concern to reporters before and during deliberations on the budget in the Diet. The work of other bureaucrats, such as those in the Foreign Ministry, is of interest while major international events occur. Last, reporters want to obtain information on a broader scope with regard to the way a certain political activity is derived from and related to existing demands within the public; or, to what extent a specific political or social measure will answer the public demands or affect either the general public or certain segments of it, such as interest and pressure groups, labor unions, etc. Taken from a broad perspective, these three levels are closely related and interdependent. In fact, activity on one level is very often affected by or affects the other levels.

Graphically, these levels can be conceptualized as three concentric circles, each larger than the previous one. The first circle, which can be regarded as the inner one, refers to activities centered on and involving political groups in *Nagatachô*. *Nagatachô* is a major site of information about the political process and decision making, much as in the United States the largest national news producer is Washington, D.C. It is estimated that about 50 percent of all the news generated in a day comes out of Washington (Hess 1980, 95), and although related empirical data for *Nagatachô* is unavailable, it can be estimated that such a study would reveal a close figure. This is because most decisions of government and the ruling and opposition parties are announced in *Nagatachô*. It is the prime forum in which party influences over issues of the day can be ventilated. Daily opportunities to elicit reactions of government, as well as the political parties and factions, to breaking news stories and unfolding events are presented in questions to political leaders (and Diet members) who work in *Nagatachô*.

In this regard, and from the viewpoint of reporters, *Nagatachô* includes three significant political institutions that make *Nagatachô* the most important and rich source of information about politics in Japan: the Diet (about reporters seeking information detailing its regular functioning as the highest organ of state power, its plenary sessions, and the work of its committees); the cabinet (the activities of the government, the prime minister, and the ministers); and the political parties (the LDP and leading opposition parties, such as SDPJ and CGP, whose headquarters are, in most cases, within walking distance of *Nagatachô*). By gathering information in *Nagatachô*, reporters can find answers to questions such as: what the issues of the day are; how these issues are debated (or negotiated) by the main political parties, factions, and their leaders; what kind of policies government intends to adopt for coping with current problems; and how policies are perceived by other political players.

The second circle, larger than the previous one, includes more and larger organs with a broad range of other activities. Specifically, it includes the activities of the various government agencies, most of which are located in the *Kasumigaseki* area in Tokyo, not far from *Nagatachô*. To a political reporter, some of the activities of several agencies are of greater interest than others. For example, the activity of the Ministry of Foreign Affairs and the Ministry of Finance are routinely of more interest than, for example, the Ministry of Labor or the Ministry of Health and Welfare. This is because the activities of the former have much more relevance to the function and philosophy of various political parties and interest groups. *Kasumigaseki* is the arena in which fluctuating power relationships (between the ruling party, the government, and the bureaucracy) are mirrored and played out, and the demands and viewpoints of key subgroups of the society that are confronted with the bureaucracy are resolved. Information such as what measures a particular ministry intends to adopt; how another ministry will react to a new bill proposed by the government; what kind of pressure a certain group of Diet members will put on certain bureaucrats, can be collected by reporters in the *Kasumigaseki* circle.

The largest circle, which surrounds the previous one, is the public circle. Political reporters are interested in the way Diet members react to public opinion, about how the cabinet intends to meet the desires of the people concerning a certain issue, and on the extent to which a new policy issue will affect the public.

A prominent factor common to these three circles is the great importance reporters attach to information related to the ruling party. In the first circle, the "*Nagatachô* circle," the activities of the LDP factions are the focus of the reporters' interest. An editorial in one of the national dailies remarked:

> It is quite natural for anybody who writes about Japanese politics to see the activities of these factions as the core and the most significant in Japanese politics. Consequently, in all the dailies, related information is highly evaluated as important for the composition of the political page.

Of particular interest in this regard are the daily activities of, and the relations between, the faction leaders; the nature of the contacts the various factions have among themselves; the type of information that the factions exchange with one another; and the strategies and tactics each faction intends to adopt to pave the way for its leader to become the party leader, which means the prime minister. Such information is regarded as the most important, followed by information about the prime minister's activities and the activities of the LDP as a whole, in particular, the functioning of the party's two major committees: the Policy Affairs Research Council and the Executive

Council. Information about contacts between the ruling party and opposition leaders, and news about opposition party activities are next in importance. Last, reporters seek information about the activities of the Diet. This structure illustrates the notion that reporters have a preference for a certain type of information even in the "*Nagatachô* circle," and that they evaluate the activities of the ruling party as more significant than those of the national Diet.

Even in the second circle, the "*Kasumigaseki* circle," reporters show more interest in information related to the activities of the ruling party. Information concerning the LDP and its contacts with bureaucrats is of greater importance to reporters than information related to the latter's regular work. A view held by one member of the political desk was:

> Writing a story about a draft or implementation of a certain bill while ignoring the role of or opinions held within the ruling party toward that bill, could not disclose all sides of the issue or will carry no significance.

Another reporter noted:

> From my viewpoint, to cover the activities of the bureaucracy and the work of public officials means to refer mainly to what the LDP members think or intend to do regarding a certain policy.

The activities of the members of the LDP's committees that are parallel to each government agency and a certain minister or the parliamentarian vice-minister are in this connection also of interest to reporters. And although reporters are also interested in the relationships between each bureaucracy and interest groups, and the bureaucracy and labor unions or the opposition, on a daily coverage level they are not evaluated as highly as information about LDP's role vis-à-vis the bureaucracy.

The "public circle" is the final one. Reporters believe that information regarding the opinions held by Diet members about the general public should often be mentioned in political stories; likewise, information about voters and supporters and about the expectations from and reactions of the public to certain political activities should be mentioned. Some of the aspects reporters see as being of interest to the general reader (or viewer) who wants to know about the dynamics of Japanese politics are contacts between labor unions and the ruling or opposition parties and meetings between a group of supporters and leaders of parties or factions. More than all of these, however, reporters, again, evaluate as most important the activities of the LDP vis-à-vis the general public; contacts between the LDP members and pressure groups; and information about the activities of the *zoku giin* ("tribe Diet members"), those powerful, experienced LDP members who have acquired special influence with certain ministries, agencies, and industries during their Diet service, and who work for the interests of certain interest groups.[7]

The clear preference of reporters' interest in the LDP is hardly surprising. The reporters and editors I spoke to often stressed the idea that Japanese politics is viewed by them as "one party." The LDP's activities affect every day-to-day aspect of the Japanese people and the country as a whole in the domestic and international arenas; thus, it is important to devote much attention to the party's movements. As much as possible, reporters avoid trying to obtain information from members of the opposition parties and concentrate on members of the ruling party. To reporters, the LDP suggests a diversity of information about what one editorial writer called "real politics." In contrast, members of the opposition can offer only theoretical information which has no special significance in day-to-day politics.

In other words, one of the consequences of the LDP being in the dominant position in Japanese politics is that it also dominates the daily political coverage of the press. The implication of such a phenomenon is reflected most obviously at such important times as during an election campaign. Newspapers tend to pay much heed to the ruling LDP; compared to other parties, LDP-related stories are larger, have more photos, and are more often allocated space on the front page. A potential voter thus has the opportunity to gain knowledge about the ruling party and its leaders, the contents of their speeches, and their opinions and ideas on policy and campaign issues, but less

---

7. In the traditional pattern set in the immediate postwar years, each industry came to be associated with a particular LDP faction, and pressure groups' channels of influence were organized along factional lines. Each industry thus contributed political funds to one specific LDP faction leader to manage and strengthen their factions, and with the power of their factions behind them they would pressure the government bureaucracy and the ruling party executives to adopt the desired policy. During the 1980s, however, a growing number of interest groups started to channel their demands through the LDP's headquarters, especially through the party's influential Policy Affairs Research Council (PARC), the *Seichôkai* (Hirose 1984). This council consists of 17 divisions that cover roughly the same administrative issues as the ministries. The Diet members who work at these divisions gain wide personal connections and accessibility to bureaucrats in the relevant ministries. Through these personal connections they monitor developments and influence them through support for legislative proposals by government bureaucrats. Diet members—particularly LDP members who have worked in one of the PARC divisions a long time, and who share an interest in a particular area of public policy related to this division—become *zoku giin*. Through years of continuing contact with a relevant ministry or agency and the relevant interest groups, these Diet members become powerful by gaining wide-ranging information and in-depth knowledge in a certain policy area, such as construction, transportation, or agriculture. This know-how enables them to exert pressure on government bureaucrats, or to intervene or exert influence regarding any important matter handled by the bureaucracy that is of interest to a specific pressure group.

about each of the competing parties or candidates (Konoe 1987). This bias in coverage might work for the benefit of the party that wants to appeal to and mobilize more support from the public and voters. Knowledge about the party stances on various issues and acquaintance with its leaders' activities and speeches, more than about the activities of the other parties' leaders, are all to the advantage of the LDP in its campaign activities (Feldman and Diskin 1988).

Obtaining Political Information

The focus of the above analysis is on the kind of information reporters are most interested in. Hereafter the discussion turns to the second question introduced above: Are there certain Diet members, among the many that reporters meet with daily, from whom the reporters prefer to obtain information? The fact that most of the information that reporters are interested in is related to the ruling party suggests that it can be obtained directly and most easily through contact with members and officials of that party. This is indeed the case. In other words, most of the information reporters would like to obtain for political coverage can be obtained from sources within the LDP. Before identifying these sources, however, the question of sources of information to reporters deserves special attention in view of the wide contacts reporters have with many Diet members.

Generally speaking, from the viewpoint of a political reporter, all political information regarding the aforementioned three circles can be obtained by contacts with two different groups or levels of sources. Reporters distinguished these groups according to three criteria: by the number of their members; the positions these figures hold in the Japanese political world; and, of course, the nature and scope of the information they possess and can provide to the reporters. Members of the first group, or level, consist of a relatively large number of potential sources. Their main characteristic is that, from a reporter's viewpoint, they have a limited knowledge about political activities and events; in fact, as one reporter noted, "they can provide information only about the activities which they directly participate in."

Moreover, these sources attract the attention of reporters following specific—planned or incidental—circumstances or events; they do not draw the attention of reporters for a long period of time. These sources can be divided into two subgroups. The first includes figures who are not elected officeholders; some do not even have direct and daily connection to the political world. This subgroup includes, for example, doctors, who attract reporters especially when one of the leading Diet members requires medical treatment. This was the case concerning former prime ministers Yoshida Shigeru, Ohira

Masayoshi, and Tanaka Kakuei; or when Miyazawa Kiichi was stabbed.[8] Other members of this subgroup include scholars, especially those from the prestigious University of Tokyo, who serve as the prime minister's or opposition party leaders' advisers; representatives of pressure groups and labor unions, who support opposition parties such as the SDPJ and DSP; leaders of citizen's campaigns; and bureaucrats at the levels of section chief (*buchô*), bureau chief (*kyokuchô*), and, the highest post for a professional bureaucrat at a certain ministry, administrative vice-minister (*jimujikan*). All these routinely deal with politicians, especially LDP members, in matters concerning decision making. This group of sources also includes the secretaries of Diet members. These secretaries, in the words of one reporter,

> know everything about the Diet members, down to their bed partner the night before, are extremely talkative, and, like their bosses, want to maintain good relations with reporters. For these reasons they often tend to disclose very useful information. Most of the time, their bosses don't know about their meetings with me.

A secretary, for example, can tell a reporter about a Diet member's efforts to get political donations and his recent achievements in these endeavors; or may show the reporter their boss's schedule, indicating the Diet member's meetings and contacts with other politicians, bureaucrats, and supporters. Depending on the political climate, such information is of great significance to a political reporter. A secretary can also give a reporter leaks on what strategy the boss intends to use as a gimmick in a coming election; or, not less interesting, on the strategy the Diet member intends to use to attract press and reporters' attention. Last, the sponsors, the people behind the scenes (*kuromakuteki jimbutsu*), those who provide support to Diet members, especially financial, can also serve at times as sources of information about the activities of a certain Diet member.

The first level of sources also consists of another subgroup—politicians, some of whom hold top positions in the government or the Diet. The speaker or the president of both chambers of the Diet, for example, though they hold top positions in Japanese politics, are regarded by reporters as possessing information limited to the administrative procedures of the Diet. Reporters meet with them only a few times while in office, notably at the opening and closing of a plenary session of the Diet. In these instances reporters have an opportunity to hear their opinions or ideas about the session, the bills that

---

8. That doctors appeared in front of the news media and reported daily on the condition of their patients drew public criticism regarding their professional ethics about disclosing private matters.

should be taken care of, and about other events on the political agenda. Similarly, heads or members of committees in the Diet may inform reporters about specific issues their committee is working on and perhaps certain questions they intend to ask in the coming meeting. A reporter I talked to emphasized that contacts with these figures, however, depends on the way a certain committee works; if some interesting (or provocative) topic is placed on the agenda, reporters may have frequent contact with its members. At other times, heads or members of committees do not have constant meetings with reporters. This subgroup of sources also includes some members of the opposition parties, who can provide some ideas about how their groups perceive certain political issues. But perhaps the most conspicuous figures in this group of news sources are ministers and vice ministers. Although they can potentially provide information about a wide variety of issues and their ideas—as will be explained later—reporters view them as being able to provide only information related to their specific work at a certain ministry.

The general opinion held by reporters is that meetings with members of this group can provide them with what one editor termed "nothing more than 'crumbs' of information," closely related to these members' own activities. In the view of an editorial writer, this group should be regarded more as "quasi sources" rather than sources. This reporter agreed that data obtained from members of this group may sometimes serve as a starting point for digging up more details. Most of these figures, however, tend to have "low-quality information." They can provide some insights about the political momentum or specific political events or mood, from their own viewpoint, but can rarely provide broad observations and information about the political parties, factions, and bureaucracy because their own information is actually limited. Information that the members of this group have and can provide to reporters does not deal with matters which have, in most cases, an immediate or dramatic impact on the political world. They are not the figures who decide the political agenda of parties and the Diet, and they do not affect the course of the policy-making of the country. And in most cases, information from these figures will not appear in the regular daily political coverage. Essentially, reporters prefer to obtain regular political information from a certain, limited group of Diet members. This group comprises the reporters' "sources of information" and a broad discussion about this group and the way news is obtained from its members is given in the next chapter.

CHAPTER 4

Reporting on the Diet: The View from a Press Club

Sources of Information

What are the criteria that make a person a source of information to Japanese reporters, that is, what distinguishes them from other people? My meetings and interviews with a large number of reporters reveal that to a great extent such a query represents a paradox in Japanese journalism. Members of the political desk and reporters agree that political information should be gathered from as many sources as possible. One member of the desk said: "Reporters should endeavor to obtain information from many people who represent various groups actively participating in the political world."

Reporters agreed with this concept, noting an awareness that they must maximize their news-gathering and information capabilities to obtain all information concerning a given political activity or trend and, as one reporter said,

> To cover it from all possible angles by obtaining as much information, ideas, and comments from as many sources as possible, journalists must gather information from reliable, trusted people and seek *hosoku shuzai* (supplementary sources) to obtain a broader picture of a given political or social event.

Gathering information from a variety of sources enables reporters to approach any phenomenon with a wide viewpoint of references while writing stories for their desk. Nevertheless, reporters and desk members agree that everybody cannot be a source of information. Because of limited time for gathering news, and limited space to publish the stories, reporters must select their sources and focus on certain people who they see as having specific characteristics that make them sources of information for the press.

Characteristics of Information Sources

The characteristics that reporters refer to narrow the circle of those who can serve as sources of information to only a handful of people, thus contradicting the belief that many people are needed to obtain the information. In particular, reporters refer to several, distinct criteria when discussing these sources. To reporters, a source of information must have, first, knowledge—not superficial or general ideas about what is going on—but knowledge that is acquired through direct, personal involvement in various political activities. Thus, a source must be a person involved in political activities; not an observer or someone who has heard something, but someone who takes a direct and active part. Based on personal involvement, a source should know everything about the activities of various political groups, but more importantly, about the activities of and viewpoints held by leaders of political parties and their factions and bureaucrats—"yesterday, now, and in the future," in the words of one editorial writer.

Not all those who have knowledge of or involvement in political activities can be regarded as information sources to the press. A real source of information is a person who can give reporters an idea of what is happening in a political party and, at the same time, how such a given event will affect the work of the bureaucracy and the public. Thus, a real information source is a person who can supply a broad range of information that will include the three circles—the *Nagatachô, Kasumigaseki,* and the *public*—those circles that reporters have so much interest in. An information source should be able to tell reporters about the activities in each of these circles and, more significantly, about the extent to which trends in one circle may affect the others and how the activities in the three circles interact and interrelate with each other. Such a person is viewed as not only thoroughly knowledgeable, but as one who can help reporters form a framework in which to analyze or interpret any particular political activity and to put it into the broad context of the nation's political life.

Information about the above three circles can be gathered through contact with, for example, high-ranking bureaucrats. The political reporter, however, shows a clear preference for obtaining related information from elected politicians. In some exceptional cases, reporters may view a bureaucrat or party official as an "additional source"; but as a rule, an information source must be a Diet member. There are several reasons for this attitude. One is that, in the view of reporters, bureaucrats or party officials tend to see things from a rather narrow perspective, related basically to their workplace; in most of the cases they even tend to release information to benefit themselves. Diet members, on the other hand, are not only considered more newsworthy (as news actors) but also as more reliable observers. Most important is the reporters' belief that it is easier to approach—and thus establish a trustworthy and close relationship with—a Diet member than a bureaucrat. This close relationship enables a reporter to get a wide range of information from the inside on various issues, including the work of the bureaucracy as a whole.

All Diet members cannot be information sources, however. The choice of information sources reflects how Japanese reporters see the "political world"; these sources are chosen because of their position, role, and responsibility in relation to the perceived political environment. To be regarded by reporters as a reliable information source, one must be appointed by a political party (or party faction) to fulfill a specific post that includes exerting influence over issues of public concern and the political agenda. This influence should not be limited to one, two, or three issues, but a series of activities, such as Diet deliberations and consultations between political groups, all of which affect the functions of the cabinet, political parties, party factions, or other elite or public groups. That a Diet member is appointed to a certain ranking position suggests exactly what a reporter expects from sources of information; that thay have the right connections, experience, knowledge of Diet activities, and knowledge of the activities of their political party or party faction. When such a Diet member provides information they can also, based on their experience, compare current issues to past situations or insightfully analyze any emerging political trend. Thus, an information source is one who has knowledge about activities of political parties and the functions of the bureaucracy; is familiar with how a given political activity will affect the public; and can exert continuous influence on political activities because of status in a political party.

How many Diet members have such characteristics? In the views of most reporters, editorial writers, and political desk members who were interviewed for this study, the number of Diet members having these characteristics is quite low. In fact, according to these newspeople, fewer than 25 Diet members qualify as information sources, making it worthwhile to meet with them, obtain the real information, and write about it. Interestingly, all reporters from the various newspapers and wire services mentioned the same names and positions of their information sources.[1] Among these were the chief cabinet secretary; the LDP faction leaders; the new leaders (or the neo-new leaders[2]); the three leading officials of the ruling LDP (*san'yaku*);[3] and the leaders of the SDPJ, CGP, DSP, and JCP.

---

1. The question they were asked was: "Who are your sources of information? What are their names and positions?"

2. The term *neo-new leaders* refers to Diet members who hope to take the prime minister position in the coming years to lead Japan into the twenty-first century. Among them is Watanabe Michio, who heads former Prime Minister Nakasone's faction, and Ozawa Ichiro and Hashimoto Ryutaro, leading figures in the Takeshita faction.

3. The three leading officials (*san'yaku*) consist of the secretary-general of the LDP (*kanji-chô*), the chairperson of the Executive Council (*sômukaichô*) and the chairperson of the Party Affairs Research Council (*seimuchôsakaichô*). The secretary-general is considered to be the second most important post in the party, following that of the party president (*sôsai*), who is also

Few Reliable Information Sources

Two explanations were offered by the reporters for their tendency to rely on these particular Diet members as information sources, the majority of whom are LDP members. The first was summed up by one editorial writer who said:

> Although a relatively large number of people may participate in the decision-making process, at the national or political party levels, the number of those in the forefront and who are privy to the whole decision-making process—from the drafting stage to the enactment of new policies or more controversial matters—and who have access to details is actually small. They do not exceed the leaders of LDP factions, oppositions party leaders, the leading officials of the LDP and their aids.

Second, reliance on these political leaders might prevent contradiction in information obtained. A reporter explained:

> Covering a certain event by obtaining information from two Diet members, each having basically different views, experiences, and ways of thinking, may result in different information and interpretation of the same phenomenon. To prevent such a complication, and avoid having to later verify the correct version from third, fourth, and fifth persons, a reporter prefers to meet the highest-ranking Diet member who participated in a given political event—this means a political party or party faction leader, or a chairman of an LDP's committee—and write a story based on their viewpoint.

Professionally, there is a significant factor to such a tendency. Information obtained from such a person, reporters believe, will convince the desk members of the reliability and validity of the information. Thus, reporters may have many connections in the political parties or the party factions they are covering, but only four or five Diet members serve them as real information sources, depending on the issue. In the words of one reporter:

> I have met about 70 members of the faction that I have been covering for the last 5 years and I have good connections with 10 of them. Usually, to obtain information, I meet with 3 or 4 members who really know all the details.

---

the prime minister. The secretary-general is in charge of the daily administration of the party as well as candidate selection and fund-raising. The chairperson of the Executive Council is in charge of the party's basic policies, and the responsibility of the chairperson of the Party Affairs Research Council is to review all matters related to policy affairs that are formulated by the bureaucracy.

Schematically, two distinct levels of information sources from whom reporters can obtain information can be identified among the Japanese political elite. The first level consists of information sources at the national level, such as the nation's political leader and the chief cabinet secretary. The second level is at the political parties level, represented first by the LDP divided into its faction leaders, the new leaders (or the neo-new leaders), and the three leading officials of the LDP. In the case of the opposition parties, the information sources are those who hold similar positions to those in the LDP. Table 4-1 outlines the major information sources in Japanese politics.

Focusing on Diet members holding higher positions has both its merits and weak points. An information source's high position makes the information provided to reporters very valuable. It is in this context that the quality of a story's source affects its news value. In many cases a piece of information that such a Diet member provides a reporter is trivial and has no significance to daily politics. But, because it was obtained from this particular Diet member, reporters tend to attach great importance to it, and it appears as an item in the political coverage. And, in Japan, the more elite the source of information, the more newsworthy the story. Thus, the personage of the information source frequently gives meaning and significance to a certain information item; and the emphasis is on the fact that the information source revealed something, rather than on the weight of the information itself. Since reporters consider these information sources as those who know the fine details, they often lean on them with "closed eyes." This is, of course, an open door to many Diet members to use the press for their needs by leaking information. Some reflections on this concept follow in chapter 6.

That the number of information sources is limited has two implications; and, if graphically represented, would resemble a circle. First, almost all information sources function in the same capacity for all channels of the mass media, and almost all reporters from the variety of newspapers and wire services have contact with the same individuals. Consequently, most of the information they obtain is, more or less, of the same nature. Second, dealing with the same information sources limits the scope of information possible to obtain and transfer to the public and to the decision makers who are therefore unable to obtain a wide variety of information through the mass media agencies. This creates a situation in which officials must often seek alternative sources for information they need for their work (discussed in chapter 7).

Reporters' Clubs

Organization and Structure of Clubs

How do reporters approach information sources and obtain information from them? In Japan, contacts between information sources and the press take place in the framework of the so-called *kisha kurabu* (reporters' clubs or press

TABLE 4-1. Main Political Information Sources in Japan

Prime Minister's Official Residence
    Prime minister
    Chief cabinet secretary
    Deputy chief cabinet secretary
    Prime minister's private secretary

Political Parties

LDP

    LDP factions
        Faction leader, faction boss, and former prime ministers (4 or 5 Diet members)
        "New Leaders" (or "Neo-New Leaders") (2–3 Diet members)
        Diet members close to each faction's leaders (9 or 10 Diet members)

    LDP Organs
        Three key officials
            Secretary general
            Chairperson, Executive Council
            Chairperson, Policy Affairs Research Council
        Chairperson, Diet Policy Committee

Opposition Parties (SDPJ, CGP, DSP, and JCP)
    Chairperson
    General secretary
    Chairperson, Diet Administration (or policy) Committee
    Chairperson, Policy Board

Note: The number of information sources is actually fewer since some Diet members hold more than one of the posts listed in this table. For example, the prime minister is usually also a faction leader; he can be, in addition, one of the "New Leaders." Similarly, some of the "New Leaders" and some Diet members "close to the leaders" hold posts in the LDP organs.

clubs). The press clubs are the ultimate factor to be considered in any attempt to understand how newspeople gather daily information; in particular, what sort of information they obtain and from which information sources, and how the information is provided to reporters. In a broad sense, the press clubs shape much of the nature of the relationships between information sources and reporters, affect the contents of the information provided to reporters, and even affect the role and orientations of reporters.

A press club is a formal association of reporters assigned to one beat. Each of the perhaps one thousand different agencies of the government, law courts, police headquarters, political party centers, and major economic organizations in Japan allocate a large room for use by reporters responsible for covering that agency for their news organizations. This room serves as the "club," the base and operation room for the reporters to gather, confirm, organize, and write all the news that emanates from a certain location; to receive briefings, handouts, press releases. and other communications; and to interact with their information sources. Located on the second or third floor of each government-agency building or party headquarters, near the office of the head of the particular agency (such as the minister or secretary-general), each club has anywhere from a dozen to three hundred or more reporters, depending on the nature of the agency and its importance.

Press clubs also exist in other countries, e.g., the National Press Club in the United States. A similarity can be found also between the press club and the Lobby, a formal association of newspaper and broadcast journalists who work out of the Palace of Westminster in England, considered to be the key mechanism through which a considerable amount of political information from government finds its way into the public domain (Tunstall 1970; Cockerell et al. 1984; Seymour-Ure 1968; Williams 1972). But the Japanese club is said to differ from them in structure and functional characteristics. *Kisha kurabu* is not simply a mechanism for gathering information. It is a social setting to which reporters belong. Within this setting, reporters make friends, pass along gossip, and share customs and secrets. In fact, the original objectives of the press club were, among other things, to cultivate mutual friendship between reporters; to form a type of pressure group to deal with information sources; and to enable reporters to mutually adjust their activities while gathering information (Hirose 1986). The press club has become so established in Japanese journalism and politics that it is regarded as a system, i.e., the *kisha kurabu seido* (press club system). This system is the most effective way to distribute information to the public, and once a person joins a club there is no way, at least on the surface, to prevent the information he or she obtains from being published.

To assure smooth functioning of the clubs, one (in some cases two) of the reporters serves as secretary (*kanji*) for about a month or two, taking responsibility for all the administrative issues in the club. This includes mediation and coordination between the reporters and the Diet members or bureaucrats they are covering and organizational matters related to the reporters' work. Differing from press clubs in other countries—which are organized and sponsored by the establishment, or the information sources—a Japanese press club is organized and managed by news media associations such as *Nihon Shimbun Kyôkai* (Japan Newspaper Publishers and Editors Association) and *Nihon Minkan Hôsô Renmei* (The National Association of Commercial Broadcasters in Japan). Membership in a press club is limited to the representatives of 114 companies that belong to these associations of the Japanese media. Each company pays about six hundred yen per reporter as a monthly membership fee (*kurabu kaihi*), which entitles its representatives to participate in the club's activities. Reporters who work for political parties, religious organizations, unions, periodicals, and the foreign press are barred from entering the clubs. Because it is difficult, almost impossible, to gather genuine news from any important organization in Japan without going through the press club, there has frequently been criticism in recent years from foreign reporters and foreign news organizations about the exclusive nature of the press club system. Following this, a few press clubs were opened to foreign correspondents so they could attend conferences. There are over 40 press clubs in Tokyo alone. Table 4-2 lists the major press clubs in Tokyo.

The largest and most important press club, for example, is the *Nagata kurabu,* or the *Kantei* ([Prime Minister's] Official Residence) as it is known

TABLE 4-2. Major Press Clubs in Tokyo

Name of Club	Location/Coverage Charge
Governmental and Municipal Offices	
Naikaku kishakai (Nagata kurabu)	Prime minister's official residence
Shûgiin kisha kurabu	House of Representatives
Sangiin kisha kurabu	House of Councillors
Hôsô kisha kurabu	Ministry of Justice
Gaimushô kisha kurabu (Kasumi kurabu)	Ministry of Foreign Affairs
Zaisei kenkyûkai & Zaisei kurabu	Ministry of Finance
Mombu kishakai & Nankyoku kishakai	Ministry of Education, Culture and Science
Kôsei kishakai & Kôsei Hibiya kurabu	Ministry of Health and Welfare
Nôsei kurabu & Nôrin kishakai	Ministry of Agriculture, Forestry and Fisheries
Tsûsanshô kishakai (Toranomon kurabu)	Ministry of International Trade and Industry
Kôtsû seisaku kenkyûkai, Un'yushô kisha kurabu & Kôtsû kishakai	Ministry of Transport

(*continued*)

TABLE 4-2.—*Continued*

Name of Club	Location/Coverage Charge
	Governmental and Municipal Offices
Yûsei kisha kurabu, Yûsei terekomu, Iikura kurabu & Mimpô renrakushitsu	Ministry of Posts and Telecommunications
Rôdôshô kisha kurabu	Ministry of Labor
Kensetsu kurabu	Ministry of Construction
Naisei kisha kurabu	Ministry of Home Affairs
Bôei kisha kurabu	Defense Agency
Keizai kenkyûkai	Economic Planning Agency
Kagaku gijutsu kisha kurabu & Kagaku kishakai	Science and Technology Agency
Kankyô mondai kenkyûkai	Environment Agency
Kokudo kisha kurabu & Kokudochô senmonshi kishakai	National Land Agency
Kaihatsu kurabu	Hokkaido Development Agency
Sorifu kisha kurabu Okinawa kaihatsuchô tantô yokakai	Okinawa Development Agency
Jinjiin kurabu	National Personnel Authority
Kaijô hoanchô kisha kurabu & Muroto kisha kurabu	Maritime Safety Agencies
Keishichô kisha kurabu & Nanashakai	National Police Agency
Naisei kurabu & Shakai kurabu	National Fire Defense Board
Kishôchô kisha kurabu	Meterological Agency
Kunai kishakai	Imperial Household Agency
Kokuzeichô kisha kurabu	National Tax Administration Agency
Yûraku kurabu & Kajibashi kurabu	Metropolis of Tokyo
Keisatsuchô kisha kurabu	Metropolitan Police
Shôbô kisha kurabu	Metropolitan Fire Defense Board
Shihô kisha kurabu	Courthouse
Tôkyô kôkû kishakai	Haneda and Narita airports
	Political Parties
Hirakawa kurabu	Liberal Democratic Party
Shakaitô kisha kurabu & Yatô kurabu	Socialist Democratic Party of Japan
Kômeitô kisha kurabu	Clean Government Party
Minshatô kisha kurabu	Democratic Socialist Party
Kyôsantô kisha kurabu	Japan Communist Party
	Private Organizations
Keizai dantai kishakai	Keidanren (The Federation of Economic Organizations)
Kinyû kisha kurabu	Bank of Japan
Kabuto kurabu	Stock Exchange Market

by journalists. Located in the prime minister's official residence, close to the Diet Building in *Nagatachô*, this club has 370 members, representing 70 branches of the news media. Their domain of responsibility is to cover virtually any aspect of the activities of the cabinet and the prime minister. This is the number-one spot in coverage and corresponding visibility for the reporters. It is therefore a prime journalistic assignment. Second to the *Nagata kurabu* in importance is the *Hirakawa kurabu*, which has almost 150 reporters. The *Hirakawa kurabu* is in the ruling Liberal Democratic party headquarters, at *Hirakawachô*, facing the Diet Building, and is responsible for covering events dealing with party affairs and leading party members. Within press club circles, the *Hirakawa kurabu* is considered to be unique in that it "moves" between two locations. When the Diet is in session, the club members shift to the press club in the Diet Building, which consists of two clubs: one covering the House of Representatives and the other the House of Councillors. At other times, it is in the LDP headquarters.

Other important and noteworthy press clubs are those in the Ministry of Foreign Affairs (*Kasumi kurabu,* in the *Kasumigaseki* district), which has 180 reporters; the Ministry of International Trade and Industry (*Toranomon kurabu,* in the *Toranomon* district), and the Ministry of Finance (*Zaisei kenkyûkai*), each of which has 130 reporters. About the same number of reporters belong to the opposition parties' club (*Yatô kurabu*). This club is located in the headquarters of the SDPJ, and each of the main news agencies assigns up to four reporters to cover the activities of all the opposition parties. Each reporter thus covers the activities of one party, either the SDPJ, CGP, JCP, or DSP. In addition, there are up to 80 reporters in each of the clubs close to the Ministry of Education, Culture, and Science, and the Bank of Japan.

Although each club accommodates reporters from various news media, representatives of the 15 major Japanese news media companies dominate the clubs by their work style, organization, and well-equipped facilities. These are the *jôchûjûgosha* (literally, the 15 companies permanently located in the clubs), whose reporters are in almost every major press club. The *jôchûjûgosha* consists of representatives of eight newspapers (the "big five," i.e., *Yomiuri, Asahi, Mainichi, Nihon Keizai,* and *Sankei;* and three bloc newspapers, the *Chûnichi* [or *Tôkyô*], *Nishi Nippon,* and *Hokkaidô*), five television networks (NHK and four commercial broadcasting companies licensed on a prefectural basis: NTV [or NNN]; TBS [or JNN]; Fuji TV; and ABC [or ANN], and two news agencies (*Kyôdô News Service* and *Jiji Press*). Conspicuous by its absence from the group is a fifth commercial television broadcasting channel: *TV Tôkyô.* Because of lack of enough manpower and financial difficulties, *TV Tôkyô* must rely mainly on the news agencies, such as *Kyôdô,* for regular daily information. On rare occasions *TV Tôkyô* temporarily assigns a reporter to a certain club to cover an event deemed too important to be ignored.

Each of the 15 permanent companies (especially those of the print media) usually sends a large staff of reporters to each of the main clubs in Tokyo. For example, major newspapers such as *Asahi* and *Yomiuri* assign up to nine reporters to *Nagata kurabu,* and other newspapers send at least five reporters to cover the activities of the cabinet or the prime minister through this club. To have the implications of a given event that breaks during the course of the day immediately analyzed by a specialist in the relevant area, the various news media assign reporters who, in many cases, are from different sections— political, economic, foreign affairs, or social—to the same club. Each of these reporters can provide—based on their own field of specialization—a different viewpoint and interpretation of the same event, contributing to more in-depth coverage of the political world's activities. For sending reporters to a specific club, each of the news media use different criteria and take different measures. The number of reporters assigned to a certain club and the reporters' areas of specialization depend on several variables, such as the political climate and political agenda, and mainly on the nature of the newspaper and the kind of stories it emphasizes. A newspaper such as *Asahi,* for example, which allocates much importance and space to political stories, sends more reporters to the press club that covers the opposition parties, than, say, *Nihon Keizai,* which emphasizes economic news, and which assigns more reporters to cover the activities of the Ministry of Finance.

A reporter is usually assigned to a press club from one to three years, then shifted to another club. On the one hand, news in a certain agency or a political group generally is continuing and interrelated; yesterday's comment is related to last week's debate, and action in February is related to action in November. Thus, it is useful to have the same reporter working in a certain press club over a period of time, and to have him observe the agency within the context of past actions and future options. On the other hand, the system in which a reporter is assigned to a club for only a short time is based on newspeople's beliefs that reporters can benefit from an assignment change, acquiring experience in different fields and thereby broadening their knowledge about various activities, and that their stories benefit from this broader knowledge and experience. A second explanation for this shifting is the assumption that if reporters work at a specific club for a long time, they become too friendly with the Diet member or the bureaucrat they cover and might bias their reporting in that person's favor. Reporters who spend too much time in a press club may even develop a tendency to see the world as their source does and absorb the source's values and perspectives, until source and reporter become "virtual allies" (Sigal 1973, 144). As Gans (1980, 144) noted, the

Watergate scandal story in the United States was discovered by outsiders, general reporters, who were not compromised by the close relationships that had been established between political reporters and their sources of information. Japanese editors therefore avoid assigning a reporter to one club for very long.

Teamwork in the Club

Reporters from the same news media company assigned to the same press club constitute a team (*chimu*). One of the reporters, usually with long experience covering various activities in two or three different clubs for an average of 10 years, will serve as captain (*kyappu*), and stories will be written and sent by telephone, facsimile machine, or messenger to the headquarters of their news agency under his or her supervision and responsibility. Each team of reporters works autonomously. Most of them go directly to their assignment posts in the morning and keep in contact with their headquarters by telephone. Removed from the direct supervision of the desk most of the day, the team is largely responsible for deciding what to cover and how to cover it. They are expected to generate news on their own initiative, although at times they are assigned stories from the desk.

Several characteristics related to the almost identical activities of reporters from different news agencies in the clubs are worth noting. Each of the major news agencies has its own niche, consisting of one or two desks and a few chairs in the press club. This serves as the news agency's headquarters at this particular location and the center of the reporters' work. Writing stories, leaving or receiving messages, telephoning to or from the headquarters of the news agency, receiving various announcements or cancellations of urgent press conferences, are some of the things taking place at this desk. Most notably, the daily meeting of each team is held at this desk. As a routine, the reporters enter the club each workday (and frequently on Sundays and national holidays) in the late morning, usually around 10:00 A.M. At about that time each news media company holds a daily team meeting. Such meetings are held in each club to discuss the latest political, economic, international, and miscellaneous events that may have a direct or indirect influence on the regular, routine work of the political world in general and on the agency that the reporters cover in particular. This is done in an effort to foresee the implications that might result from the news, to assess what kind of developments they must pay special attention to, and who (in their working domain) can possibly provide them with certain types of information regarding such developments.

These meetings also serve as an opportunity for reporters to be informed about the latest needs of the desks in the headquarters for certain information, on the need for more details or background data about a given issue for a specific edition (either the afternoon or the following morning edition) or for a special feature, or cover story. Thus, team meetings help to set the day's framework and schedule for each team and to focus the activity of reporters in accordance with the needs of their headquarter's desk or the climate in the agency they cover. At the same time that each club holds its team meeting, reporters from the major news agencies assigned to the clubs in the *Nagatachô* district, close to the Diet (such as the *Kantei, Hirakawa,* and *Yatô kurabu*), frequently meet in the rooms of their company at the *Kokkai Kisha Kaikan* (Diet Press Assembly Hall) Building. In this building, located on a corner, one side facing the prime minister's official residence and the other the Diet Building, each of the major news agencies has its own room, which serves as something akin to a "frontlines-headquarters" close to the center of which the major political events occur. Equipped with several tables and chairs, telephones, television sets, facsimile machines, and a huge board hanging on a wall listing the telephone numbers of all the press clubs in which the agency has reporters, these rooms can also accommodate meetings with up to 30 reporters from three or four important clubs close to the Diet. Such meetings are often held in the presence of messengers, desk members, and at times even the political editor and the vice-editor. Their objective is to coordinate the activities of the various teams covering the political world in different clubs for the same news agency, in a bid to achieve coverage that is as broad as possible.

The regular workday of reporters begins after the team meeting and continues until evening. There are occasions, such as at the time of cabinet reshuffles, when reporters stay at the club until late at night or early hours of the following day. Likewise, there are times when reporters need to gather information at locations other than the club. On a regular day, when there is no urgent need for certain types of information or a feature story, reporters spend the morning covering press conferences or listening to briefings given by various persons in the agency they cover, such as a minister, department director, or section chief. At noon they have lunch, and then, remaining in the club until around 2:00 P.M., write stories for the evening edition of their newspaper, watch television, read magazines, play mah-jongg, take naps, or write articles for periodicals as a part-time job. As will be discussed later, these periodicals are a frequently used channel for information that, for various reasons, cannot be published in daily newspapers. From 2:00 to 4:00 P.M., reporters make rounds to meet and chat with officials at the agency in search of information; and the hours after 4:00 P.M. are spent in receiving handouts, listening to lectures by representatives of the agency, or in writing stories for the next morning's edition of their newspaper.

After 2:00 P.M. only one reporter from each newspaper or news agency remains in the club, fulfilling the role of "person on duty," handling phone calls from their newspaper or attending urgent press conferences. In some cases, this is a junior reporter who has not yet accumulated much work experience; in other cases reporters take turns at this post, changing every two or three hours. Until a few years ago that system caused many headaches for the desk, especially when there was a need for the entire team to meet quickly to cover a sudden development. Recently, however, each reporter assigned to a club carries a beeper and can be reached anywhere during the day to receive a message about any urgent development.

Coverage of Diet Committees

The major goal of reporters at a particular press club is to know everything that's happening in the agency to which this club belongs. This requires regular and constant surveillance. The reporters call at each important office daily, talk to any of the same people, read the routine reports provided to them by the agency they cover, and attend regular meetings of the leading figures in this agency. Reporters, however, do not spent all day at the building of the agency they cover. Their work obliges them to know and to cover the overall activities of the agency, which means that they must also write stories about issues related to the agency's work that occurs outside the building. One such implication is that reporters must cover the various Diet committees that examine law bills, budgets, treaties, and petitions, or conduct investigations related to their agency. To understand this sort of assignment it is significant that, on a regular basis, the national Diet is covered by several groups of reporters simultaneously. Such groups include those that cover the activities of the ruling party's members and those that cover the opposition parties. All of these cover the routine work of the Diet and, in particular, the regular meetings of both the House of Representatives and the House of Councillors. Since the former has 18 standing committees (*jônin iinkai*) and the latter 16, however, it is almost impossible for the few reporters who cover the activities of Diet members from various parties to gather information about every committee's activities, decisions, personal administration, and agenda.

Nevertheless, in its determination to keep a close eye on the work of the Diet committees, the press has adopted an original approach to achieve this objective. This approach is derived from the fact that—except for committees on budget, house management, audit, and discipline—the committees roughly overlap the various government ministries and agencies. For example, the Foreign Affairs Committee has jurisdiction over activities covered by the Ministry of Foreign Affairs, and the Education Committee covers the Ministry of Education. In their will to assure appropriate coverage of each committee, the news companies expect reporters who work at a press club near a certain government agency to also cover the activities of the committee corresponding to that agency. Thus, reporters who work at the Ministry of Foreign Affairs cover the activities of the Foreign Affairs Committee, and the meetings of the Education Committee are covered by reporters from the Ministry of Education, Culture, and Science. In principle, committee meetings are closed to all except Diet members. Regularly, however, representatives of the news media enjoy the special privilege of attending the meetings of all the committees (similar to the Lobby correspondents in Britain; see Tunstall 1970), except the Discipline Committee. This committee, which seldom meets, is responsible for maintenance of internal discipline and punishment of members for disorderly conduct. Some of the debates in committees such as the Budget Committee and the Foreign Affairs Committee are even televised live, which is perhaps an important reason why they attract great interest by the general public.

Because reporters must also write stories about the work of the committees, they must spend time in the Diet to attend the committee meetings to hear discussions, observe negotiations between the parties involved, and be present during debates and testimonies. Because reporters cover the regular work of a certain agency and, in addition, cover the activities of the committee related to that agency, they become—to a great degree—experts on the general work and on many of the issues related to that agency. Reporters are so familiar with the work of the agency they cover that many Diet members try to take advantage of this for their own benefit. They frequently consult with reporters and receive advice about the functions of the agency and about the types of questions they should ask in a particular committee meeting. Some of the important dimensions of this side of reporters–Diet members contact will be discussed in chapter 6.

Generally speaking, each committee is covered by representatives of the team that works at the affiliated agency. There is, however, one exception. This is the Budget Committee, considered to be the most important of the Diet committees. In recent years, discussions about the budget have become more and more important. This is because decisions regarding the budget have not only a tremendous impact on domestic affairs, but they also influence Japan's attitudes toward other countries in the West and in Asia, including international organizations such as the United Nations. Members of many different groups, from the ruling and opposition parties, bureaucrats from government agencies, and interest groups from various segments of the public, have great concern about the nation's budget and the way the Diet and its related committee work on it. Because the Budget Committee covers many different topics of interest to various groups of the general public and should be analyzed and explained from an expert viewpoint, the news agencies, especially the major newspapers, have adopted a unique approach in a bid to provide their consumers with the most comprehensive information possible about this committee. While each press club team consists of a number of reporters, each of whom is expert in a different area, the major newspapers and other news media assign reporters, not from different sections of the same news agency, but from different press clubs, to work together and to cover the Budget Committee. The logic behind this approach is the assumption that each reporter in such a group has detailed knowledge about the daily work of "his" or "her" agency: thus, the reporter can explain how a given measure discussed by the Budget Committee would affect that agency or ministry, or a specific group of the public, from the viewpoint of the agency with which they are affiliated.

In the last few years, since some of the most frequent hot topics of interest to the public in the Budget Committee are defense and the growing role Japan assumes in the international community, reporters from the Ministry of Foreign Affairs and the Defense Agency have often t een mobilized into a team to cover the work of the Budget Committee. The tex.m of reporters that covers the Budget Committee's work comprises a task force. Each of the national dailies calls this team by a different name (in the case of *Asahi* it is called *Yosan Iinkai Tantô,* or Budget Team) and employs different criteria for constructing this task force. Regularly, it consists of five reporters: a captain, usually someone whose familiarity with the Budget Committee's work was gained while at the Ministry of Finance press club; a reporter from the Defense Agency press club; one from the Ministry of Finance press club; and one from the Ministry of Foreign Affairs press club. The fifth reporter serves as an assistant to the others and may belong to any of the other clubs. This task force is organized to cover a very limited event on a temporary basis for about two to three months. It is usually organized when the budget is formally presented to the Diet by the cabinet in the latter part of January of each year and is dissolved when both the Upper and Lower Houses Budget Committees finish their work at the beginning of April. Of particular interest to reporters on the task force is the work of 50 members of the House of Representatives Budget Committee (where the proposed budget is first sent for deliberations), who examine all possible aspects of the budget.

The work of such a task force is especially intensive during the short period in which the main (or general) interpellations (*sôkatsu shitsugi*) take place. During this period, all cabinet ministers and the prime minister must attend the meetings of the Budget Committee, which last several days, from morning until evening, and answer questions, mainly from opposition party members regarding various political issues. In fact, the Budget Committee has become an arena for debate on every possible issue and the questions raised during the main interpellation period are not limited to the budget itself; defense issues, foreign policy, education reforms, and wrongdoing and corruption of Diet members—such as the Recruit scandal—are some of the topics frequently discussed. During the general interpellation, meetings of the Budget Committee are covered daily and broadcast live on television and radio, thus attracting much public attention. At this time, many members of the committee try to bring up many controversial issues and make provocative statements to gain publicity. Not less important, however, is the fact that the live television coverage enables each member of this committee an opportunity to appear on the screens of millions of viewers all over the country. How can one resist such coverage? Understandably, thus, this affects the behavior of many Diet members on the committee. First, whereas a Diet member may be absent from any other of the committees he belongs to, only a few will not be present in the Budget Committee; in fact, the meetings of this committee are always overcrowded. Many of the Diet members who participate in the meetings of the committee use several tricks in a bid to catch the camera. e.g., they move nervously in their chairs, nod their heads quickly, laugh loudly, etc.

Because the meetings of the Budget Committee are broadcast live on television, reporters can thus monitor the televison in their press club and write full reports on the meetings. However, the reporters who cover the work of this committee are not particularly interested in the nature of the questions and answers during the meetings, but are keenly interested in the general mood of the meetings. Because reporters must also write some feature stories, in addition to daily stories, they look for interesting behind-the-scenes stories and anecdotes of the committee and for emotional reactions of Diet members; this type of information they can obtain only by attending the meetings.

News Gathering at *Nagatachô*

Press Conferences

What is the role played by the press club in the process of gathering political information in Tokyo? Generally speaking, the club system facilitates the gathering of information from information sources by two major methods. The first is press conferences. While meeting with representatives of the news media, a Diet member or a high-ranking bureaucrat in an agency addresses the reporters, then answers questions to clarify their ideas. The most important press conferences for political reporters are those held at *Nagata kurabu* in the prime minister's official residence. Press conferences are held every two or three months by the prime minister in this club. Because of their significance, these conferences are broadcast live on television and radio. The prime minister also meets the press when the need arises to address several issues about the political, economic, social, or international agenda and to answer reporters' questions. Special press conferences are held with Japan's top leaders before or after elections, following dissolution of the Diet, after inauguration of a new cabinet, before the prime minister leaves for an important international meeting, and before or after meeting with one of the world's leaders. In addition to the prime minister, reporters at *Nagata kurabu* have constant contact with the prime minister's private secretary; the deputy chief-cabinet secretary; and, most important, with the chief cabinet secretary (*kanbô-chôkan*), who serves as top spokesman for the cabinet.

The chief-cabinet secretary meets reporters regularly, at least twice a day—around eleven o'clock in the morning and around four o'clock in the afternoon. Ordinarily, except on rare occasions when the need to meet the press arises, such as at the time of cabinet reshuffles or emerging international problems, the press conferences last about 15 to 20 minutes each, although sometimes the meetings do not exceed 3 or 4 minutes. In each of the meetings with the press, the chief cabinet secretary first briefs reporters, then answers any questions ranging from domestic politics and the agenda of the cabinet to foreign policy and social issues. The chief cabinet secretary is considered to be the most well versed in Diet affairs, and one of his roles is to coordinate policies among cabinet members (to the extent that many of them were termed "top cabinet managers" or "cabinet signboards"). Because of this, and the fact that this Diet member holds multifaceted daily press conferences, the chief cabinet secretary is considered to be the best information source about government issues.

Besides the chief cabinet secretary, all cabinet ministers hold press conferences for the reporters who work in the press club closest to their office at least once a week. Usually at these conferences, the ministers describe the latest (or coming) cabinet meeting from their own viewpoint; examine to what extent a new program adopted by the cabinet benefits or is detrimental to their ministry; and give the press their opinions concerning the latest trends in domestic or international politics and their views on issues related to their ministry, e.g., a new bill. In some cases, the parliamentary-vice minister (*seimujikan*) and the administrative vice-minister (*jimujikan*) also meet the press, especially when their ministry intends to issue a new policy, or when they intend to introduce a new bill in the Diet or to discuss a related matter in one of the affiliated comittees.

Other important press conferences are those held for reporters in the *Hirakawa kurabu* by the secretary-general of the LDP, from whom reporters also receive regular briefings and political information. Leaders of the main opposition parties—the SDPJ, CGP, DSP, and JCP—also appear every two or three months before the members of the press clubs who cover the opposition parties and give their opinions concerning various political issues. When the Diet is in session, the *Yatô kurabu,* the press club that covers the opposition parties, is one of the busiest clubs. During this season, each of the opposition parties holds a meeting of its Diet Administration (or Policy) Committee every morning around nine o'clock. Following this meeting, each chairperson of the committee from the different parties conducts separate press conferences to brief the press on the content of the meeting. In addition, the meetings of the policy-making central executive members (*chûô shikkô iinkai*) and the executive board (*kanbu*) of each of the opposition parties, which take place once a week, are also followed by press conferences. While observing the regular activities of the *Yato kurabu*, I was impressed by the fact that the leaders of each opposition party use every opportunity to conduct meetings with the press. In addition to daily conferences with the news agencies, these parties organize press conferences at times when they are trying to initiate a reaction to the ruling party's activities, when they intend to take a certain countermeasure or to suggest a specific matter to the government or the ruling party. In many cases, the opposition parties attract the attention of reporters and there are many press conferences with opposition party representatives. Nevertheless, little related information appears in the media. Although about 40 percent of the voters support various opposition parties, the political coverage of these parties is far below this proportion (Feldman 1989).

Press conferences, as held by the different government agencies and political parties, are viewed by reporters as only one channel for receiving information from officials. Reporters see the press conferences as a useful channel for acquiring the most official, most formal, stances held by the official who represents a certain governmental agency. One editorial writer admmitted:

> Meetings with officials in press conferences serve as a good ground for obtaining the dry facts, a general statement, or description of the state of affairs or the *tatemae,* the formal truth, rather than the core of things, the most important information."

Most reporters believe that the main speaker, whether a Diet member or a bureaucrat, is unable to talk freely while meeting a large number of reporters in a huge hall. A speaker such as the chief cabinet secretary or the secretary-general of a political party must carefully weigh each word while speaking to tens or hundreds of reporters and will never divulge all the facts. When asked to elaborate on this notion, a captain at *Nagata kurabu* explained:

> They might be tempted to tell more anecdotes in an attempt to satisfy us, the reporters, by showing that they are trying to perform their duty or are complying with the requirements of their job, but rarely reveal the full detailed truth.

This, reporters believe, can be obtained outside the press-conference hall.[4] Equipped with considerable background knowledge, provided in the conference, reporters look for detailed information to complete their stories. This they can obtain by practicing another, and perhaps the most important, method of gathering information in Japan, through the *ban*.

Beat Reporters

The *ban kisha* (beat or watch reporters) refers to a group of 5 to 15 reporters, each representing one of the news agencies that is permanently at the press club. In other words, the *ban* consists of reporters from the major news agencies in Japan—national and bloc newspapers, the wire services, and the national and commercial television stations. In recent years, however, the typical *ban* consists only of 5 reporters who represent the "big five" newspapers. At times, they are joined by 2 other reporters, each representing one of the wire services. Depending on the political climate and the development of domestic and international events, the *ban* can grow to include as many as 15 reporters, representing all the major newspapers and TV stations in Japan. The objective of such a group is to cover—closely and constantly—one leading person whose activities are of great significance to the political, economic, social, and all other spheres of the nation's life. The *ban* follows this person all day (and even after regular working hours) to observe his activities and meetings with other people and to write stories (or report on television) about him with special reference to the question of how this person's activities affect a given matter.

There are several such *ban* and some of the most important are those connected to *Nagata kurabu*. Among them are the *kanbôfukuchôkan-ban* (the *ban* of the deputy chief cabinet secretary); the *kanbôchôkan-ban* (the *ban* of the chief cabinet secretary); and, perhaps the most important, the *sôri ban* or *shushô ban,* the one that covers the *sôri* (prime minister). The *sôri ban* is important for two reasons. First, it is the first assignment of a reporter who joins the political desk. A reporter will serve in this *ban* from one to one and a half years, at the longest for two years. During this time, the reporter's ability to gather information and write stories is carefully examined and judged by the captain of the team, the desk members, and the political editor. Once reporters are evaluated as fitting to serve on the political section, they will be given their next assignment, usually for one or two years, to cover the activities of one of the political parties (first the LDP and then one of the opposition

---

4. The questions were: "Under what circumstances, and how frequently, do you meet your sources of information?"; "What is the best way of obtaining the most valuable information?"; and, "Where and when do you obtain the most valuable information?"

parties) or a government agency, such as the Ministry of Foreign Affairs or the Ministry of Home Affairs. This is the main reason why reporters are so competitive and determined to do their best to seek information and to excel during this crucial period of their career. Second, the *sôri ban* is important because it covers the activities of the nation's top leader, who is concurrently president of the ruling party. Thus, this *ban* watches the activities, which are of significance at the national (and international) level, of the person who holds the leadership position in the dominant party in Japan.

The *sôri ban* has some distinctive features. First, the structure of this *ban* differs from any other *ban*. Two reporters from the news agencies—*Kyôdô News Service* and *Jiji Press*—follow the prime minister and cover all his movements from 7:00 A.M., the time he usually leaves home, until late at night, around 1:00 A.M., when he returns home. When the prime minister enters his office (on the second floor in the prime minister's official residence) at about 9:00 A.M. each morning, until the moment he leaves the building at around 8:00 P.M., the *sôri ban* consists of representatives of all the major newspapers and other news media affiliated with *Nagata kurabu*, who cover the activities of the prime minister while in office. During the day, the *sôri ban* of 15 or so reporters sits near the stairs on the first floor of the prime minister's official residence in a chamber called *ban-ko-ya* (waiting room of the *ban*). To cover all activities of the prime minister, including meetings and contacts with important persons while at his office, each of the captains of the major news media at *Nagata kurabu* assigned three or four reporters to the *sôri ban;* they alternated among themselves every few hours and at least one reporter from each news agency was always in the *ban* chamber to observe the prime minister's movements.

In recent years, however, only the reporters from the "big five" national dailies can be seen in the prime minister's official residence when the prime minister is there. Reporters often wait on the second floor, in front of the prime minister's office, to observe any developments. As soon as the prime minister leaves his office, the entire *ban* rushes after him, hoping to hear him say something that can give them an idea for a story. When the prime minister leaves the building during working hours, the *ban*'s members follow him to his car, and see him off. Only the two reporters of *Kyôdô News Service* and *Jiji Press,* by agreement between all the newspapers, will stick with him wherever he goes by following his car. They are obliged to later inform all the newspapers about the prime minister's activities, their location, and results. The entourage of the Japanese prime minister, while moving in his car through the streets of Tokyo, therefore often consists of the car he is sitting in, with his bodyguards in front, and the representatives of the press in cars behind.

The main task of the *sôri ban* is, of course, to cover the routine work of the prime minister, reporting on who he meets with, and on the purpose and nature of these meetings. No less important, however, is another task of this *ban*, namely, to identify the people who visit and meet with the prime minister or with one of his aides. Having identified these people, the *ban* reporter must telephone the news agency teams at other press clubs and let them know about such a meeting. In most cases, the teams at the press clubs are expected to try to obtain some details that will explain, from the viewpoint of the agency they are covering, why a certain person has visited the prime minister. For example, when reporters at the *sôri ban* identify a bureaucrat from the Defense Agency entering the prime minister's office, they must immediately inform their colleagues about this meeting, not only in the press club at the Defense Agency, but also their colleagues at the Ministry of Foreign Affairs, the ruling party headquarters, the opposition parties headquarters, and sometimes even those at the Ministry of Home Affairs' club. Several reporters jokingly referred to the work of those in the *sôri ban* as "more the nature of a messenger than of a reporter." Informing their colleagues about the latest movement of the person they are covering is a task that is not peculiar to the *sôri ban*. When reporters from any other club see one of the key persons in the agency they are covering—such as a minister or vice minister or one of the LDP leaders—leave the building, they immediately rush to find out where the person is going and inform their colleagues by telephone at a place near the destination about the intended visit. Such activity not only keeps a steady flow of communication between the various clubs, but gives reporters in different locations the feeling that they do not work in isolation from each other, and that they are part of a big family working in the same news agency and guided by team spirit for the same purposes.

Faction Reporters

The *ban kisha* is closely related to and often mentioned with the activities of reporters at the *Hirakawa kurabu,* the one that covers the ruling LDP. The structure of the *Hirakawa kurabu* and the activities of reporters assigned to it deserve special attention because of the importance of this club in providing political information to the public. As with any other club, each of the major news media, the national newspapers, and the news agencies regularly assign a number of reporters to the *Hirakawa kurabu.* Generally, each of these media agencies sends between three and eight reporters to this club. The intent is for at least one reporter to cover one of the five main factions in the ruling party. A few newspapers, such as the *Nihon Keizai,* because of its emphasis on economic matters, assigns only four reporters to cover the activities of only four party factions. In times of necessity, however, such as when Kaifu Toshiki emerged in August 1989 from a small faction as the most likely candidate for the prime minister post, a paper like the *Nihon Keizai* will mobilize a reporter from another press club, e.g., from the one covering the Ministry of Foreign Affairs, to cover the activities of such a small faction.

Perhaps the most important reason why the same reporter could not simultaneously cover rival factions is related to the fact that a faction reporter keeps constant and close relations with the faction members, becoming familiar with their top secrets (e.g., the strategies the faction intends to use and various personal affairs), and if one has frequent contact with rival members there is the possibility of information leaks.

While some news agencies struggle with a situation in which one reporter must cover more than one faction, several of the national newspapers, for example, *Asahi* and *Yomiuri*, which have more interest in providing political coverage, even assign an additional reporter to cover the LDP. Such a reporter usually covers the party members who do not belong to any faction (*muhabatsu*). Until recent years, an additional reporter of the national newspapers covered the activities of the former NLC, which after the 1986 double elections joined the LDP. Including the reporters at the *Kantei* and *Hirakawa kurabu*, 12, or 13 reporters of the national newspapers and news agencies cover the LDP activities in general and its factions in particular. By comparison, only about 4 reporters are assigned to cover the activities of all the opposition parties. This, of course, reflects the great importance journalists attach to the ruling party because of its significant status in Japanese politics.

The importance—and thus the coverage—the media attaches to a given LDP faction is, of course, dependent on the dynamics of the faction, its power, and influence. At times, one faction is more highly evaluated by the press than another; but the faction regarded as the most important—the one from which the prime minister comes—is not always perceived as such by the press. This was the case for Prime Minister Kaifu, who came from one faction of the LDP (the smallest one), whereas the press attaches greater importance to the faction led by former Prime Minister Takeshita Noboru. Another example is that during the 1980s, although Nakasone Yasuhiro was prime minister and a faction leader, the faction led by former Prime Minister Tanaka Kakuei was the focus of attention of the press. Because its large number of members enabled the faction (and later the faction headed by former Prime Minister Takeshita) to have much influence, the large news agencies assigned two, sometimes three, reporters to cover this particular (and Takeshita's) faction. On the other hand, the bloc newspapers and commercial television stations assigned only one reporter each to cover this huge faction. Each news agency tries to assign at least one reporter to cover one LDP faction. Reporters from different news agencies who cover a certain faction of the LDP form one unit to make up the *habatsu kisha* (faction reporters). National newspapers such as *Asahi* have at least one reporter who belongs to each of the *habatsu kisha* units that cover the different factions of the LDP. The work of these reporters enriches their agency's political desk with a detailed picture of every event or trend that takes place in the party faction and thus in the LDP as a whole.

Because of the several functions of the *habatsu kisha*, it can be regarded as the most important group of journalists in Japanese politics. *Politics,* in this context, means the activities of Diet members within the Diet, and in and among the different political parties and factions. In essence, reporters affiliated with a specific party faction and assigned to cover its activities must in fact focus their attention on the activities of the leader or a few leading persons during a certain period of time. From this viewpoint, the faction reporter's task is similar to those of the *ban* reporter. Usually, the *ban* and the *habatsu kisha* not only have the same tasks, but also consist of the same reporters. Thus, for instance, if a reporter covers the faction that the party secretary-general is from, they belong to the *kanjichô-ban* (secretary-general's ban), in which main contact is with the secretary-general of the LDP. At the same time they must cover the activities of the leader and other important persons of the same faction. This is also the case for reporters from the *somukaichô-ban* (those who cover the chairperson of the LDP's executive council) and *seichôkaichô-ban* (the chairperson of the LDP's policy affairs research council ban). Reflecting the power and concession abilities of each of the faction's leaders, the two chairpeople of the councils and the secretary-general of the party are usually from three different factions. This facilitates the work of reporters and enables one reporter to cover the overall activities of the faction and one of its members holding a key position in the party.

There are a few exceptional cases in which the *ban* that covers a specific leading person in the party functions simultaneously with another group of reporters covering the activities of this person's faction. One example is the case of former Prime Minister Tanaka's faction. At one time more than one hundred Diet members belonged to this faction. In fact, after the 1986 double elections, it had 140 members; and some of them served in high positions in the LDP. To effectively gather information about the activities of this particular faction and about each of the LDP's leading members belonging to this faction at the same time, there was a need to differentiate between a specific *ban* covering one member holding an important position in the party and reporters covering the activities of Tanaka himself and the faction as a whole. This example explains why some of the national newspapers have assigned more than one reporter to cover this particular faction. Because the faction of former Prime Minister Takeshita also had more than one hundred members, some holding top positions in the party such as secretary-general, the media faced a similar situation. Thus, several newspapers and the wire services assign one reporter to cover the activities of this faction and its leading members and another reporter to the *ban* covering the functions of one of the faction's members holding a key position in the LDP.

A reporter belonging to the political desk hopes for an assignment to cover a specific LDP faction. In fact, most reporters see the assignment as the "flourishing season" of their career. To cover one of the factions means associating with leading Diet members and the leaders of the nation, and collecting interesting information while practicing exceptional news-gathering methods. It means proximity to a specific group having its own special dynamic activities, rules, and vibrancy. Each LDP faction has its own headquarters with its formalized organization including regular meetings, a known membership, an established structure, firm discipline, and a systematic hierarchical-leader-follower relationship in which the leader dutifully serves members of his faction by providing political funds, party and government posts, and election support (Fukui 1978). These special characteristics assure a reporter a much more interesting experience and exposure to more fascinating information than is available when covering, say, the work of the Ministry of Post and Telecommunications. Not every reporter can serve as a faction reporter, however. Editors are well aware that much of the success of a reporter in obtaining information—and thus enriching the desk with political coverage—depends on the reporter's personality and ability to adapt to the special characteristics of a particular faction. From an editor's viewpoint, each faction resembles a *mura* (village), or a family, in which one must adapt to certain rules typical of this group to function efficiently. A person's character and ability to get along with other people play an important role in a reporter's skill in establishing good relations with the faction members and obtaining significant information. For this reason, members of the political desk and editors attach much importance and give serious consideration in assigning a certain reporter to cover a specific faction.

Informal News-Gathering Methods

There are several significant characteristics of the faction reporters, as well as of any other *ban,* and the way they gather information. The internal structure and activities of any of these groups is like the press club itself; thus it might rightly be regarded as "a press club within a press club." A *ban* (or *habatsu kisha*) consists of the representatives of the major news agencies that are permanently in the clubs. This means reporters from 5 to 15 channels of the news media: 8 newspapers, 2 wire services, and 5 television networks. Each *ban* has a secretary who arranges meetings with the Diet members that the group is covering. Usually, a *ban* has two or three secretaries appointed for a term of two months. One of these is from a newspaper and the other is from a television network unconnected to the newspaper.[5] Like the press clubs, reporters work as a group, meeting with their information source(s) to gather

---

5. As noted, each of the major national dailies has "friendly" relations with a television network: the *Yomiuri* with *NTV;* the *Mainichi* with *TBS; Sankei* with *Fuji; Asahi* with *ABC;* and *Nihon Keizai* with *TV Tokyo.* These tie-ups are mutually advantageous.

political information. Ordinarily, the *ban* groups make their base in the offices of the persons they are covering, either the secretary-general of the LDP, the chief cabinet secretary, or the chairperson of one of the councils of the ruling party. They gather at that office when the person they are covering enters the office in the morning and they leave with the person at night. For most of the workday they wait for hours in the room nearest to the person's office, which is the secretaries' room, trying to observe the person's activities and to pick up any hints that will lead to a story. They follow the person wherever they go, whether to a committee meeting, to the Diet, to the party's headquarters, even to their private meetings with friends or family. In fact, the *ban* is a shadow to leading Diet members, to the extent that a reporter who followed the secretary-general of the LDP for a long period of time gradually began to walk like him (Odawara 1987).

Two practices in particular are perhaps the most prominent characteristics that distinguish the *ban* group from any other form of newsgathering. One is that the *ban*'s reporters can meet the leading person(s) they cover, not just in a press conference, but also, and mainly, at the person's offices for a friendly chat (*kondan*). In contrast to a press conference, in which a Diet member briefs tens or hundreds of reporters, they hold intimate talks in their own office with a limited number of reporters. Because these reporters cover their activities constantly, from morning until evening, the Diet members get to know each of them well, including their names and the news agency they work for. This kind of meeting with reporters enables a Diet member to provide information more openly, to explain issues related to their work in more detail, and even to disclose data that they will not reveal when meeting many reporters in a press conference. Nevertheless, such an informal manner often encourages the information source to ask reporters not to refer to them directly as the source of specific information or even not to publish certain data that they prefer to keep from the public eye for various reasons. Because the meetings are held with a small group of reporters, any information source can immediately detect who did not respect such a request just by glancing at the next day's newspaper or watching television. This concept and its implications are broadly discussed below.

As a method of news gathering, the *kondan* enables reporters to obtain broader and more in-depth information and further details about information obtained in press conferences held by these Diet members. Through the *kondan,* members of the *ban* are also able to verify information gathered at other places and from other information sources. In many cases the *kondan* is conducted on a daily or weekly basis. For example, the chief cabinet secretary meets with the *ban* for a *kondan* almost every day after the afternoon's press conference; this *kondan* is known as *kanbôchôkan-kondan* or, for short, *bankon* (a friendly talk with the chief cabinet secretary). For this reason many of the press conferences with the chief cabinet secretary do not last more than three or four minutes; and immediately after a press conference, the *ban* rushes to the chief cabinet secretary's office to hear details and ask open questions. The LDP's secretary-general (*kanjichô*) is another person who holds a *kanjichô-kondan* very often, almost daily.

Notably, in recent years the *kondan* has been frequently used by other persons having contact with the press, not only those who are covered by a special *ban*. In fact, the *kondan* is practiced so often that many reporters, politicians, and bureaucrats perceive it much more as a formal rather than informal method for transmitting political information. Ministers, vice ministers, section heads in each government agency, and party officials inform the press through a *kondan* more—in terms of quality and quantity—than through official press conferences. For example, the minister of foreign affairs conducts a formal press conference once a week in *Kasumi-kurabu*, but meets representatives of the club in their office for a *kondan* at least another two times. The administrative vice-minister in the same agency holds a *kondan* twice a week on a regular basis; usually they are held a day before cabinet meetings (which are on Tuesday and Friday). Other high-ranking officials hold a *kondan* with reporters especially before an important international meeting or while preparing for a foreign visit of one of the leading Diet members. A *kondan* is held on a daily basis in most government agencies during the period of budget deliberations in the Diet, enabling reporters to sense the "real" mood in a given ministry toward an issue put on the committee's agenda or to hear reactions of a ranking official in the ministry following the latest developments in the committee.

Not all the *kondan* are of the same nature. In journalistic jargon, two kinds of *kondan* can be distinguished. The first is the *naisei* (domestic affairs) *kondan,* and the other one is *seikyoku* (political situation) *kondan.* The former is centered on domestic policy and politics. New policies of the cabinet, issues that the LDP intends to put on the agenda of the Diet or the cabinet, and the reaction of one (or all) of the opposition parties to the ruling party initiative all fall into this category. The latter is concerned with general political circumstances and trends within parties and factions; questions related to the struggle over leadership in the ruling party, the attitude toward supporting the new approach the secretery-general intends to take, or, more recently, issues concerning political corruption and bribery. Predominantly, the latter type of *kondan* is held by the three leading officials of the LDP, heads of factions, or their closest aides, depending on the nature of the political situation. The domestic affairs *kondan* is held mainly by the chief cabinet secretary, and in some cases related information is gathered during *daijin* (minister) *kondan.*

The *kondan* is only one of the news-gathering methods and privileges reserved for the *ban* group. There is another privilege that the *ban* enjoys.

Reporters can meet the persons they cover outside their workplace, especially before and after work hours, using another method of gathering information, namely, "night attacks" or "night rounds" (*yo uchi* or *yo mawari*) and "morning visits" (*asa gake*). Morning visits refer to the gathering of the *ban* early in the morning, around six or seven o'clock, in the private residence of a Diet member whose activities or faction they cover. Similarly, "night attacks" refer to the gathering of this group of reporters at the Diet member's home after working hours, around 8:00 to 10:00 P.M. Meeting in a leading Diet member's living room provides an intimate and relaxed atmosphere for the reporters and the Diet member to converse with each other. Very often, during this very friendly visit that may include drinking whisky or eating snacks served by the Diet member's wife, information essential to the press is provided to the reporters. Reporters view such an association as the best opportunity to gather, in the words of a veteran reporter, "the real information, the *honne,* beginning with the way politics are conducted and ending with the 'stories behind the stories.'"

Another reporter added: "All that a Diet member cannot tell in a press conference, they tend to tell us in the late hours in their home. At this time, we can also verify and fill in the details about many other items we collected during the day."

Several aspects are related to this method of gathering information. First, the "night attack" is practiced much more often than the "morning visits." This is because the deadline for submitting stories for the evening edition of the newspapers is 1:00 P.M., and long before this time reporters can meet the Diet members they cover in their offices, hear briefings from the chief cabinet secretary, and even get a word in with officials of the bureaucracy. From this viewpoint, meeting a Diet member at 7:00 A.M. is of little use. On the other hand, "night attacks," which begin at about 8:00 P.M., give reporters three or four hours to write stories before the morning edition deadline. Night rounds can also serve as a method of squeezing information for a reporter who finds himself without any item of news at the end of the day. Second, there is a significant dichotomy between the Diet members who are the subjects of the morning or night visits. Whereas in the "night attacks" reporters visit leading Diet members—such as the secretary-general of the LDP, the three leading officials of the LDP, the chief cabinet secretary, and faction leaders—in the "morning visits," reporters concentrate on meeting the LDP faction leaders who play a role in decision making within the party. This concept carries significant weight in reporters' activities, as will be discussed later. As a rule, however, visiting the homes of one of the LDP leaders is a natural phenomenon, but reporters rarely visit a Diet member from the opposition parties. In fact, a leader, such as the secretary-general of the SDPJ, meets members of the press at home approximately once or twice a year, following exceptional events in the opposition parties.

Another significant aspect of the "night attacks" and "morning visits" is that, as in the press conferences in the clubs and the *kondan,* all the reporters meet their information source together. This means that when visiting any official's residence, all the reporters from the various news agencies enter the house and leave together; they chat with, ask questions, and receive answers from the Diet member in the presence of their colleagues from other news agencies. There are cases, however, in which a reporter, having significant objectives in mind, some of which are discussed below, would prefer to meet with a "second-rank" Diet member (that is, not one of the leading persons in a party or faction) in privacy and talk without the presence of other reporters. Like the *kondan,* the necessity for the visits or "attacks" is especially dependent on the political climate and the need for additional information to supplement that collected during the day. Consequently, contact with Diet members before or after work hours does not take place everyday. There may be several days when a reporter goes without meeting a Diet member, followed by several days in which reporters meet daily with a Diet member in their home. Likewise, while the Diet is not in session or when there is nothing important on the political agenda, and thus no need to obtain urgent information, reporters rarely gather at the Diet member's home to get political information.

Usually, each of the methods reporters use to gather information is prearranged with the information source. In a political climate like Japan's, in which political crises are very rare, reporters may reach the conclusion during the day that it might be useful to meet the Diet member they cover after the workday because of some events that occurred in the morning or due to events that are on the agenda for the following day. In such a case, the *ban* secretary(s) must talk with the Diet member and obtain approval for the visit. Because the "night attack" often involves reporters visiting not one, but several Diet members' homes, the secretary must arrange the approximate time for each visit. Sometimes, however, sudden developments encourage reporters to urgently meet with a certain Diet member. In such cases, one of the *ban* secretaries can telephone a Diet member's home without previous warning on behalf of the *ban* and request a meeting for discussing the particular development.

As was described earlier one of the reasons for the meetings between reporters and Diet members is to maintain a friendly relationship. Thus, when the *ban* initiates a meeting with a leading Diet member it does not necessarily mean that there is a need to obtain information. It might be linked to the reporter's wish to meet with information sources in order to keep agreeable contact with them. From this viewpoint, the nature and the characteristics of the "night attack" are an ideal environment for both parties to socialize in a relaxed atmosphere, while exchanging views on many issues and strengthening their relationship. Noteworthy is the fact that not all Diet members like reporters hanging around them all day. Moreover, when some of them come home after a hard day and want only to rest, they get angry when they find several reporters waiting to hear more of their opinions about the political situation. Generally speaking, as Diet members climb the political ladder and, as a consequence, are surrounded by more and more reporters, they feel more like captives of the press. Reporters escort their information sources from early morning to late evening, and some leaders, especially those of the LDP, feel that they cannot do anything without being watched by the reporters. At times they prefer their privacy, at least at home. Thus, reporters are prohibited from entering these Diet members' homes and must wait near the gate if they want to see and talk to the information source.

Together, the *kondan* and "night attacks" seem to be the most useful methods of gathering information in Japanese politics. Reporters believe that the "night attacks" in particular provide them with the kind of information they can rarely obtain in regular press conferences. When asked to evaluate the amount of information they gather by each of their methods, the reporters I spoke to stated that press conferences provide them with about 20 percent of the information concerning a given issue, and the *kondan* and the "night attack" provide them with the other 80 percent. In the view of the political editor of one of the national dailies:

> All of the information reporters use when writing their stories is based solely on data they have collected during the *kondan,* totally ignoring the information they obtain in press conferences.

Reporters as a whole noted that receiving information through direct contact, especially while meeting their information sources in an intimate atmosphere, is considered in their eyes more reliable, more accurate, and much more trustworthy than information issued during press conferences. For these reasons, the *kondan* and "night attack" methods are preferred by Japanese reporters. Political editors and desk members also view these methods as the best way to gather useful information. One implication of this attitude was reflected in this reporter's words.

> The information that I bring to the desk, claiming it was obtained at a *kondan* (or "night attack"), will be evaluated more highly than information obtained at regular press conferences. Editors tend to publish such information without hesitation or further verification.

The second implication is that newspapers give reporters from the *ban* free use of the companies' cars and drivers to facilitate their transportation from one information source's home to another during the "night attack." Several of these cars are equipped with portable telephones to enable reporters to maintain constant contact with the desk. They can call the desk following a visit to a Diet member's home and report the news items they have gathered. The desk, in turn, may ask them to either write a story based on this information or to obtain further details from any other available information source. The desk members may even contact reporters from another *ban,* or those covering other Diet members, to obtain more details about a given issue. Because of the important and significant role LDP factions occupied in the process of news gathering employed by reporters in Japan, several of their characteristics deserve special examination.

Part 3
Communicating with News Sources: Dimensions of Competition, Customs, and Dependency

CHAPTER 5

Variables in the Gathering of the News

The Era of Handouts

As a means for gathering political information, the Japanese press clubs, through their associated activities, greatly facilitate contacts between news sources and reporters. They also serve as a major channel through which the press is informed in detail by officials of political parties, party factions, and government agencies on many social, economic, and political activities occurring anywhere in Japan. Frequently, however, these officials and Diet members endeavor to use the efficacy of these press clubs as a means for transmitting an endless amount of information.

In recent years, a growing number of government agencies and leading Diet members have shown an increasing tendency to disseminate more and more information through the organized system of the press clubs. This is expressed in the increased number of press conferences held by the various agencies and the number of handouts they provide to reporters. Several of the government agencies hold up to 170 press conferences and distribute nearly 420 handouts per year; which averages out to more than 1 handout per day. This tendency has led many observers and communications researchers to view present-day Japanese journalism as *happyô jânarizumu* (announcement journalism) or *kôhô happyô no jidai* (the era of handouts) (Hirose 1986; Nishiyama 1988). That many agencies hold frequent press conferences and provide reporters with several handouts does not necessarily mean that this information is of great significance or that the contents vary. On the contrary, because of the short interval between press conferences (or handouts), there is often not much to update; i.e., it seems that the same ideas are expressed in different words in several successive handouts. Repeatedly emphasizing a particular topic perhaps enables the news source to focus the reporters' attention on a particular issue. This, in turn, might lead to such continuous coverage and treatment in the press that it may be placed on the public or political agenda.

Moreover, because so many press conferences and handouts are handled through the press clubs, reporters are discouraged from looking for news by themselves. Many reporters that I spoke to feel indeed that the handouts are sufficient for accomplishing their job successfully; this is to the extent that the so-called *toku ochi kyôfushô* (the phobia of not writing/missing what everybody else writes) is common among reporters in the different press clubs. Thus, it is not surprising to often find that when writing their stories, reporters tend to depend more on using some of the handouts that are distributed to them than on inquiring directly about the latest developments in the agency they cover. But, as suggested in the previous chapter, the Japanese press clubs are more than a mere channel through which information is transferred to the general public. They contain and reflect several important variables that shape and determine the nature and scope of political communications in Japan: the functions of the print media versus other channels of communications, the role of reporters vis-à-vis their colleagues, and the content of the information gathered and made known to the public. The objective of this and the following chapters is to examine the variables associated with the press club system and to detail the extent to which it affects the reporter's work. These variables are analyzed in light of the keen competition that exists between the various news media and in the context of the cultivation of contacts and interactions between small groups of reporters and one or very few news sources.

Press vis-à-vis the Press

Perhaps the most dominant feature that characterizes journalistic circles in Japan is the numerous newspapers, television stations, magazines, and weekly publications that keenly contend with each other to deliver the news. As previously mentioned, there are more than 120 daily newspapers in Japan (including the national, bloc, and local newspapers) and at least 6 television broadcast stations that transmit information throughout Japan. In addition, there are several hundred weeklies, monthlies, and professional magazines, many of which have a circulation exceeding five hundred thousand copies and, like the daily newspapers, they provide their readers with feature stories about ongoing events and detailed coverage of social, economic, and political activities. Because the number of political news sources is limited, as was detailed in the preceding chapter, a situation has developed in which there is obvious and intense competition between reporters to obtain political information. To a considerable extent, this competition not only affects the contacts that reporters have with news sources, but with Diet members in general, as well as their relations with their colleagues from other news media channels.

Newspapers Versus Newspapers

Before discussing how competition between reporters is reflected in the press clubs, a brief outline about the nature of the competition in the Japanese media is in order. This is because much of the competition between reporters derives mainly from the competition between the national and local (and bloc) newspapers, between the national newspapers and the wire services, and between the national newspapers themselves, concerning in-depth coverage. The competition between the various print media is much more significant than that between broadcast stations. This is mainly because, while endeavoring to attract as many readers as possible and to provide the widest coverage possible, newspapers overlap each other's coverage domains.

A national newspaper in Japan, for example, usually publishes two kinds of stories: major stories of national interest, which will get the same placement throughout Japan, and stories that vary by prefecture or local community. The latter are published either in the local editions (*chihô-ban*) of the national newspapers (each newspaper devotes two or three pages to each prefecture) or in a special weekly edition for the entire prefecture, which handles news of wider common interest. Although until recent years the regional bloc newspapers concentrated on news in their own regions, they are now devoting space to national and even international news. On the one hand, each of the bloc newspapers endeavors to provide their readers with a wide variety of national and international news and analyses, resembling the national newspapers. On the other hand, however, the bloc newspapers attempt to be as local as possible and to cover events in their own immediate areas. To provide their readers with local news, each bloc newspaper usually devotes two pages to each prefecture in its region and divides each prefecture into districts, with one page of local news covering each district.

In addition to local news, the local newspapers (*chihô-shi*) also have an interest in national and international coverage. While providing local news, each local newspaper also devotes a growing amount of coverage to national and international news. The news agencies, such as the *Kyôdô News Service* and the *Jiji Press,* provide the local newspapers with related stories, background material, and commentaries. Thus, local and bloc newspapers can now provide their readers with national and international coverage that is competitive with the national newspapers.

Moreover, there is competition between the national newspapers themselves, each with its own target. They compete on every level, including prestige and status, sometimes to a point beyond financial concern. The determination of each newspaper to successfully compete with its rivals is reflected in its wish to report every event that takes place anywhere in Japan or abroad. This tendency has occasionally led to extreme behavior and sensationalist coverage of specific events. Using the excuse of freedom of the press and the right of the people to know, reporters often ignore matters related to human rights, such as the right to privacy. Particularly, during the 1970s and 1980s, newspapers often reported the arrest of and charges filed against citizens before they were tried by a court of law. Reporters from the national dailies (and, more significantly, the representatives of television stations, especially those from programs aired during the afternoon hours) were dispatched to the homes of people who had been arrested to obtain comments from family members or neighbors. This sometimes caused social isolation and even suicide by the alleged criminal or a family member.

Not wanting to miss any detail of any event, the daily newspapers, especially the "big five," dispatch an inordinate number of reporters to cover the routine activities occurring near the press clubs. Consequently, a huge network of reporters constantly covers government offices, the work of the bureaucracy, and political parties. As outlined in the preceding chapter, some of the national newspapers have about 9 reporters assigned to one beat; at many locations they have at least 5 reporters covering the activities of certain government agencies or political groups. For example, when the Diet is in session, each newspaper assigns reporters, usually those from the political section who work at the press clubs in the Diet and the *Hirakawa kurabu,* to specifically cover daily routine affairs. Reporters from other press clubs, e.g., those in the Ministry of Foreign Affairs or the prime minister's official residence, but from the same newspaper, can be also seen surrounding Diet members in the Diet building in an effort to obtain some tidbit of news that will lead to a story. At the same time, colleagues—not necessarily from the political section, but from the same newspaper—can be seen covering events in the same building. They may be, for example, from the economic or social section, trying to follow the latest economic or social developments related to the Diet as a whole or to some Diet members. Thus, in many cases, 10 or more reporters from the same news company can be seen at one location. Simple multiplication of reporters of the "big five" national newspapers alone gives more than 50 reporters at one place.

With so many reporters in one place (all of whom usually having similar deadlines for submitting their reports), the work occurs not only under the obvious pressure of time but also in physical and psychological competition with reporters from competitive newspapers. Reporters often feel they are even competing with reporters of their own newspaper from another section. Indeed, rivalry also exists between the various desks of the same news agency over the ability of a particular desk's reporters to gather a greater variety of information (especially exclusive information) than reporters from other desks. Obviously, the competition between reporters is not just to obtain information from Diet members, but also to gain their attention and to establish—or maintain—contact with them, a tendency that makes the competition constant and ongoing, as will be discussed below.

To obtain political and other information, news channels spare no efforts, especially the daily national-newspaper companies. Each of these companies provides its reporters with all the necessary tools for obtaining information. They give reporters a free hand in going to and from the press clubs; when a reporter needs to go from one place to another, the company car and driver are available. Moreover, a news company will even pay hotel and restaurant bills if a reporter could not go home while trying to obtain information until late at night and had to spend the night away from home. To compete successfully, some of the daily newspapers even use "tactics" to ensure that they obtain more important and more interesting news than the other newspapers. Needless to say, family relationships with politicians, for instance, can play an important role in a reporter's accessibility to certain Diet members and obtaining political information. This notion led one of the national newspapers to assign a particular reporter to cover the prime minister's activities. Because the reporter was related to the prime minister, this reporter could enrich the newspaper with stories and interpretations concerning the political world, the LDP, and the prime minister himself. In an interview this journalist noted:

> When all my colleagues from other news agenc[ies] were going home late at night, I used to come back to the prime minister's residence and ask to see him, to talk and obtain much more information than the other reporters.

Another example of this tactic was the assignment of a reporter from a national newspaper to cover one of the LDP factions in which the reporter's father was a member. Because of this relationship, the door was open to this reporter, allowing him not only to obtain a large amount of information but to eventually become a Diet member himself (and to join, of course, this same faction). Another noteworthy example of such a tactic is when editors assign reporters to cover the activities of leading Diet members who are from the same town, city, or prefecture as the reporter. This is perhaps in the belief that a Diet member and a reporter from the same place can communicate more smoothly. According to one political editor of one of the dailies: "A Diet member might feel more relaxed while conversing in his unique prefectural accent and tend to give much more information."

The tendency of editors to take advantage of this is reflected in their assignment of reporters to cover the activities of leading Diet members, such as leaders of factions, the LDP secretary general, and the chief cabinet secretary, who are from the same district, especially during election campaigns. At such times, reporters are assigned to cover the activities of such leading Diet members 24 hours a day and to report about their meetings with voters, their speeches, and other activities. Under such circumstances, the reporter often becomes a promoter for the politician. Escorting the candidate from one meeting to another, the reporter will often be asked by the Diet member to tell

supporters and other audiences about the Diet member's work, its significance, his or her contribution to domestic and international politics, and
especially about efforts to promote issues for the benefit of the home district.
Because of the rivalry between newspapers, each news company's editors and
desk members are, in some respects, rather strict with their reporters, expecting them to report every event. A newspaper company will not tolerate another newspaper publishing information or covering a topic that does not
appear in its own newspaper. Editors believe that a reporter assigned to cover
a specific political group is responsible for obtaining complete information
concerning that group. If one of the other newspapers prints something that
the reporter from their newspaper did not report, this is usually not taken
lightly. Thus, the efficiency of a newspaper is seen by the editors as dependent
on having good contacts. And the maintenance of a satisfactory relationship
with these contacts makes for the desired predictable flow of information. To
the editors and the desk members that I spoke to, the ability of a particular
reporter to provide the desk with information is compared with other newspapers. One desk member said:

> Deskmen do not always know what is happening and we expect the
> reporter to tell us. If a rival newspaper publishes a news item that the
> desk did not receive, this is good indication that a reporter is either lazy
> or does not have good access to news sources, which is an essential
> factor in a reporter's work. Under such circumstances, we often take
> such things into account when thinking about a reporter's next assign-
> ment.

This concept compels reporters to bring information to the desk daily by
all means. To fulfill the desk's expectations, reporters at the various press
clubs often write about the existing political mood in the agency or political
group that they cover or, when they have no access to further news, just
rewrite a few of the many handouts provided to them at their workplace. At
times, reporters try to dig up "underground" information to satisfy the desk;
and the notion that "when in doubt it is better to overplay a story than to
underplay it," has frequently led reporters to write stories that were later
proven to be groundless. Some examples of this are introduced later in this
chapter.[1]

---

1. False reports presumably submitted under the same circumstances have also occurred
concerning matters in which the public was highly interested. For example, it was reported that
several suspects in the kidnapping of the president of *Glico*, a confectionary company, had been
caught by the police (*Mainichi*, 1 June 1989, evening edition). It was also reported that a hideout
used by Miyazaki Tsutomu, the suspect in the kidnap-murder of four small girls, had been
discovered by the police in a mountain area near his home in western Tokyo, and that several
pieces of evidence had been confiscated (the *Yomiuri*, 17 August 1989, evening edition).

The competition between the various news media is also reflected in two other aspects of the press clubs. Perhaps in each newspaper's endeavors to attract an increased readership, political editors and the political desk of all the newspapers attach much importance to the activities of leading Diet members, such as the leaders of the LDP factions: to what these Diet members do, say, and think. Conspicuous in this regard is the importance editors allocate to the prime minister, with the prime minister increasingly becoming the central focus of national news coverage of government. The tendency toward a major emphasis on a nation's political leaders is not new and has, in fact, been noted for many years in the case of the president of the United States (Cornwell 1959; Baluthis 1977). A study of national media coverage of the U.S. presidency in the *New York Times,* in *Time Magazine,* and on CBS television news noted that the frequency of stories related to the presidency rose steadily throughout the 1950s, 1960s, and 1970s, and that the president represents the single most important story that the news media follow on a continuing basis (Grossman and Kumar 1981, 254–58).

In this regard, the Japanese case does not differ much from the American one. Nevertheless, there is an important difference between the top leaders of these two countries. In comparison to the U.S. president (or, more significantly, to any other leader of a Western country), the Japanese prime minister has less real power to establish new priorities for the nation or enforce important measures. The reason that the Japanese prime minister gets considerable coverage thus has nothing to do with his real power, but with the belief held by members of the political desk that the public understands the human side of politics easier than it understands topics such as government decision-making processes or the work of the bureaucracy on a specific bill. Newspapers, thus, report less about processes, background, current facts, analyses of issues, and reviews of alternative policy proposals and more about what Diet members in key positions think and do. The reader presumably feels closer to events if they are presented through the activities of political leaders and more readily assimilates the functioning of government and movements within the LDP factions as these events are created and managed by leaders of the ruling party. The political climate in Japan is thus reflected more than in any other type of coverage in stories such as how and why political leaders create, manipulate, and solve certain issues.

To successfully compete with other newspapers has another meaning for the editors, i.e., to publish news items *before* their competitors. Editors thus see that newspaper's capability to enhance its reputation rests in their ability to provide vivid and interesting coverage as well as piquant information in the form of scoops (*tokudane*). There is an interesting aspect to the exclusive information in Japanese journalism. Because most of the dailies' editors and desk members regularly receive copies of rival newspapers as soon as they are published, they can immediately detect a story about an event that their own newspaper did not report. In many instances they quickly contact a reporter at a particular press club and request that a related story be written. In an extreme case, one of the desk members will write such an article. This kind of activity ensures that the next edition of all the other dailies will include a story or feature article about an issue that was previously provided in only one of them. Since the daily national newspapers publish morning and evening editions under the same name as a set, virtually all scoops by a particular newspaper last no longer than half a day; i.e., until the next edition, when related stories will appear in all the other newspapers.

Reporters Versus Reporters

The previously described competition between the national, bloc, and local newspapers has a great deal of influence on the daily activities of reporters, including the process by which they gather news. They are in the vanguard, living and breathing this competition day after day, competition that is evidenced throughout the system—from obtaining information to personal interaction—and particularly in the press clubs. The press clubs assure reporters that they can easily fulfill the editors' expectations. Through this system, they have daily access to political information, either through handouts or through briefings provided by a high-echelon bureaucrat or Diet member in their respective club; and they can write stories based on these. Moreover, since all of the reporters meet a certain leading bureaucrat or Diet member and are exposed to the same information, this ensures that an editor will not call one of them and ask why they did not write a story that appeared in another newspaper. Nevertheless, the press clubs in fact have more the semblance of a pressure cooker. Reporters from a variety of newspapers meet their colleagues from other newspapers for extended periods of time, day in, day out, and they all know each other quite well. They frequently lunch together and even meet colleagues from other news agencies after work and drink together. On vacations or weekends, some of them even play golf together or meet for other sports and amusement activities. It would seem, on the surface, that they are friendly and have rather profound relationships, but they actually are keenly competitive. Beginning in the morning hours, when they gather at the press club, everybody is constantly monitoring their colleagues' movements, trying to discern whether someone else, from another newspaper, managed to obtain news that they missed. In the words of one reporter, "No one in a press club must demonstrate any out-of-the-ordinary behavior. . . . they are all under constant scrutiny by the other members."

Precisely because of this phenomenon, a reporter will occasionally put on a poker face in the press club, especially when he believes he has obtained some information that other reporters did not, and he does not wish to let them know about it. Or, a reporter (most notably those from the wire services) may keep a certain item of news that he believes is a scoop to himself until all the other reporters have left the building. Only then will he send it on to the newspapers.

Keen competition is an integral part of the daily work of reporters belonging to a particular *ban*, who cover the activities of specific leaders of the ruling party's factions. This is because of the significance and constant need for information about the LDP and also because of the relatively close association between reporters and their colleagues from other news media and with their news sources. The *ban* also quite conspicuously reflects some reporters' eagerness to initiate and to succeed in obtaining some additional information, or scoops, that the other reporters do not have. The motivation of a reporter to gather exclusive information may come from several sources. The motivation might be the wish to prove ability; or to stand out in the eyes of colleagues. Another important motivation concerns the reporter's promotion. Whether a reporter will be promoted depends on the ability to work hard, to work seriously, and to collect important news. It is well known by journalists that if reporters do not provide "hot" news, that is, scoops or exclusive information, within about 10 years after assignment to the political section, the desk will not evaluate their work highly. Under such circumstances, they may be assigned to work at one of the outlying offices of the newspaper rather than in Tokyo.

On the other hand, if a reporter provides hot news, he or she may win a prize from the president of the newspaper, which is considered an important step toward promotion. A reporter who excels in news-gathering work can serve as a captain at a certain press club, especially in one of the most prestigious ones such as *Nagata* or *Hirakawa,* and may be called upon to later serve as a member of the desk. A news agency can also show its gratitude to an excellent and devoted reporter by an assignment as the agency's correspondent to a foreign country. Thus, it is safe to say that to a certain extent a reporter's determination to gather exclusive information stems from the will to avoid exile from the center of events in Tokyo and to assure eventual promotion to a position more beneficial in terms of prestige and money. For these reasons, reporters will do their best to obtain exclusive information. They may telephone the home of a Diet member, a bureaucrat, or a party official late at night and ask questions. A reporter may even call and consult with the private secretary of a Diet member to obtain some information about recent developments. Others may try to obtain exclusive, inside information by contacting Diet members who are past employees of the same news company. This is particularly true of the *Yomiuri,* the *Nihon Keizai,* the *Mainichi,* the *Kyôdô*

News Service, and NHK, where some politicians have worked. The Diet member may continue to show gratitude for past kindness shown by the company by offering assistance and information.

Many reporters, especially those who covered a specific faction of the LDP two or three years in the past, try to obtain information from this faction although they have been shifted to another press club, far from the party center. These reporters maintain their contacts with the people they used to cover and continue to meet and obtain information from them. This tendency is especially apparent when there is an urgent need for information, such as at the time of a cabinet reshuffle or during intense negotiations between various party factions. Editors and desk members occasionally try to take advantage of the old connections of former faction reporters for the benefit of gathering information and encourage reporters not to limit themselves to covering only the activities of the agency to which they are assigned.

To obtain exclusive information, a reporter may even risk breaking the informal rules of the *ban.* The following example illustrates this attitude. As previously explained, when the *ban kisha* decides to meet a specific Diet member, all the arrangements—including the time and place—are made by the secretary of the *ban.* At the arranged time, all the reporters of the *ban* meet, but one is missing. After waiting for some time, the *ban* will proceed to the meeting with the Diet member without this reporter. In fact, while the *ban* is meeting with the Diet member, the missing reporter is having a private meeting with another Diet member, and more than likely obtaining some information not to be shared with colleagues. This phenomenon is outlined in the preceding chapter and is an exception to the "night attack," in that one reporter—rather than a group—meets a Diet member. While engaging in this practice the reporter's objective is, of course, to obtain exclusive information; and to do so, a reporter may even turn to second-rank Diet members, such as the heads of committees or even vice ministers. Meeting these Diet members alone, even if the latter is not one of the top national leaders, may sometimes result in obtaining hot news. Nevertheless, as one editor noted:

> It is clear to all reporters that a great risk is taken by engaging in this practice. If a colleague of a reporter discovers that the reporter did not join the *ban* because they had a private meeting with another Diet member, they may forfeit their trust and be subjected to *mura-hachi-bu* (ostracism). This means that the erring reporter will be boycotted and will lose their right to participate for some time, usually one week, in the *kondan* or "night attacks" with the Diet members the *ban* is covering.

The eagerness for scoops influences not only the way a particular reporter functions, but the overall news-gathering process as well. Take the "night attack" as an example. At times, the "night attack," the method regarded as the most effective for gathering detailed information, becomes an arena that reporters use not only to gather news, but to keep an eye on their colleagues from other news media to prevent them from achieving private scoops. Thus, the "night attack," as a group-oriented tool for gathering news, becomes an effective means for, more than anything else, watching the other reporters and making sure that nobody gets more than the others. Consequently, a reporter may sometimes participate in a "night attack" more for listening to gossip stories than for obtaining any actual news. To avoid spoiling the chance of a later scoop, reporters may intentionally refrain from asking hard questions, but monitor their colleagues' questions to analyze how much they know about specific issues, observe the reaction of the Diet member, and attempt to determine whether there is something in the answers that may warrant further investigation. The outcome of such a situation is that the "night attack" is conducted openly and smoothly in a congenial atmosphere, during which reporters place more importance on reading their colleagues' minds and observing the behavior of the Diet member than on collecting and writing stories. To many reporters, thus, a news-gathering method such as the "night attack" provides an opportunity to keep track of the other reporters. But to a reporter driven by the wish to get far beyond the dry information, participation in a "night attack" is often perceived as a waste of time, since scoops are rarely obtained there.

Personal Contact with News Sources

An editorial writer of one of the dailies has explained:

> There is only one precondition for obtaining scoops from a Diet member; that is personal contact based on longtime association. During the years that I have worked as a reporter, I have learned that there is some information that a reporter cannot obtain from a Diet member, even at gunpoint. But after years of meetings, when strong, close relations are cultivated, a reporter can obtain any information they want from a Diet member up to the latest words of the prime minister expressed in the most closed meeting of the ruling party. Thus, the ability of a reporter to gather information is a reflection of their ability to establish solid contact with Diet members.

A captain at one of the clubs said:

> The longer I know someone else, the better we can clear the way to develop personal relations expressed in such terms as *shinyô* (trust, confi-

dence), *tsukiai* (social obligation to another) and *ninjô* (human feelings), all of which have special significance in Japanese culture. Longtime association is the basis for cultivating mutual trust and mutual understanding to the extent that a mutual feeling will occur, strengthening our association.

Cultivating news sources is thus a matter of energy, persistence, and attitude. Generally, the existing environment in Japan is rather conducive to developing close, longtime relations between reporters and Diet members. One reason for this is the press club system and the generally easy accessibility of reporters to Diet members from all of the political parties. Moreover, the political climate in Japan contributes to such an environment; it is a political atmosphere characterized by stability, in which only gradual changes occur in domestic policies and leadership (to the degree that one can predict with certainty who will emerge as the new leaders or the neo-new leaders). The organization of the ruling party itself, with its several factions, also provides an opportunity for reporters to be in constant contact with Diet members, mainly in light of the system adapted by the news agencies, in which one reporter from each news medium covers a specific faction and is thus inevitably in regular daily contact with its members.

The fact that a Diet member is slowly advanced in Diet activities, gradually assuming more political responsibilities and taking a more active part in decision-making processes, enables the Diet member and a reporter to establish their contact on a firm and solid ground, based on years of contact. During this time, Diet members gain experience as politicians on the national level; broaden and deepen their knowledge in a particular area; and strengthen their personal contacts with other Diet members, bureaucrats, party officials, and members of any other group they have contact with. These experiences help the Diet member to be better informed and to function smoothly during daily political activities. As has been illustrated, with political experience, a Diet member tends to be involved in more activities of greater importance on the national level and to fulfill more significant posts in the Diet and the government. Reelection for three or four times seems to be the turning point in a Diet member's career; from this point on, in the case of the ruling party, for example, a Diet member begins to take an active role in one of the party's or the Diet's committees or to assume vice minister posts. They have more frequent contacts with some of the reporters they met previously and their contact is strengthened from this point on.

In line with this concept is another important feature related to the newspapers' employment system. A political reporter serves in this section for a long time, actually from the first day of work at that newspaper's headquarters, and climbs the ladder—a process of at least 20 years—until becoming a member of the political desk or editorial section, covering a variety of political activities during the process. Part of the process, as mentioned, is working at several press clubs for a few years, which enables a reporter to maintain years of contact with many Diet members.

Junior and Veteran Reporters

In reality, any Diet member having regular contact with the press will have frequent meetings with reporters who differ from each other mainly in their experience. Through this experience, a reporter learns how to maintain contact with news sources, how to successfully compete with a colleague to fulfill an assignment, and develops different views toward the type of contact and the various objectives in meeting Diet members.[2] Of the many reporters who meet Diet members on a daily basis, some have just begun working as political reporters in the press clubs close to the prime minister's office, in contrast to veteran reporters who have worked in *Nagatachô* for the last 12 to 15 years and know every room in the Diet building. In many instances, one can even meet the staff of the political desk, the political editors or the editorial writers, who have worked with Diet members for 20 to 25 years and still maintain contact with the Diet members with whom they had daily contact when they were gathering information as reporters.

Members of the political desk, political editors, and editorial writers have longtime experience in covering political activities and longtime associations—more than 20 years—with Diet members. They have climbed the corporate ladder at their newspaper companies at the same time the Diet members, whom they used to meet, climbed their ladder. Most of these newsmen regard the Diet member's offices as their second home; and they see Diet members, (especially those in key posts who function as news sources, such as the prime minister and leading members of the ruling party) as, naturally, their old friends. Very often they talk about these leading politicians in a nostalgic way, recalling past events in which the reporter and a particular Diet member were involved. The experience they have gained during their work enables them to understand any political movement and even to successfully predict the next steps that will occur by way of analysis and interpretation. Their work experience and their longtime association with Diet members give them an open door to meet any Diet member they wish, at any time and place. Nevertheless, since their work is now at their companies' head offices, their duties no longer require direct and constant contact with Diet members, at least not for the purpose of gathering information. The work of

---

2. The questions asked here were: "What are the main characteristics of your work?"; "Do you feel that you work under pressure? If yes, what kind of pressure and how do you cope with it?"; "How frequently do you meet Diet members in general?"; "What is the nature of your contacts with Diet members?"; and "How would you describe your connections with reporters from other newspapers?"

members of the desk is mainly concentrated on issuing instructions about which items are to be treated as newsworthy; consulting with the captains of various teams; and deciding how to compose the political page, revise news stories, or request a rewrite when a story is inadequately developed (Kim 1981, 64–65). Editorial writers, on the other hand, concentrate more on expressing reflections on a certain situation in politics, based on published material and according to their experience and knowledge of the political arena. Although these journalists need not go outside and meet Diet members to fulfill their work, they are often seen in the Diet building or in Diet members' offices to verify information received from the press clubs or just to pay a visit to old friends.

Veteran newspeople, who have covered the political environment for 10 or more years, have already experienced work in four or five press clubs and have longtime contacts, not only with Diet members, but with party bureaucracies and the bureaucracy in general. They have already become captains in a particular press club, and some of them will soon be promoted to desk positions. The political labyrinth is very clear to them—to the point that their perspectives of political activities and Diet members have been firmly shaped. Through their extensive experience in *Nagatachô,* the veteran newspeople know all the Diet members; and even if they have not met some of them directly, they know their backgrounds and can easily differentiate a promising Diet member who has the ability to succeed from one who has only a slight possibility of being reelected in the next election. Sometimes they look at a Diet member as a news source and sometimes as a friend. Their experience tells them who is worth meeting to obtain the latest detailed information on any current issue, and who might give them only vague ideas. They can easily distinguish those who have genuine stories from those who are cranks and troublemakers who only want to attract press attention to themselves or their work.

Young reporters do not have much work experience. Their assignments to press clubs usually do not exceed five or six years; that is, they have had experience at one, two, or three different press clubs, usually the one that covers the prime minister's office and the one near the headquarters of the ruling party. Their contacts with Diet members on the national level are limited, meaning that they have not yet developed deep connections with Diet members but are eager to do so. The young reporters I talked to expressed the view that their daily contacts with Diet members contributes much to their understanding of how the political machine works, how the LDP succeeds in initiating bills, and about the weak points of the opposition. One of these reporters noted:

> For me such a contact is more useful for studying politics than any politics related course that I took in my graduate days. The Diet members

and officials telling me about their daily work are my best teachers of politics, and I study a lot.

One essential point distinguishes junior and veteran reporters. This is related to the notion that apart from those Diet members who comprise the source group, other Diet members cannot disclose any more than crumbs of information related to their own activities as a member of one of the Diet or party committees. Junior reporters, however, do not take this concept for granted. For them, a prominent difference exists between the group of information sources and other Diet members that stimulates contacts with a much wider range of Diet members. This is rooted in the fact that direct access to the main sources is not always available due to their hectic schedules. Other Diet members, generally speaking, have more time to meet reporters; in fact, they are eager to meet the press and feel more free to give reporters speculative views, opinions, rumors, or gossip that they have heard and to disclose hard information that the source group will not disclose. The recognition that even other Diet members, in reality a wide range of Diet members, can serve as news sources plays a major role in news gathering, especially when there is an urgent need for political information (as on the dead days—such as Saturdays and Sundays—when the political coverage is not sufficient for the political desk); and to fulfill this need junior reporters turn to Diet members who do not belong to the source group.

Establishing and Maintaining Contacts

One factor common to all reporters, junior and veteran alike, is the constant striving to establish and maintain contacts with Diet members. On the one hand, indeed, the competition between numerous reporters who represent many newspapers in competition with one another, obligates each reporter to establish close and reliable contacts with Diet members, knowing that rival reporters will also try to do so. And, on the other hand, as was cited earlier from one Diet member, "rapport precedes cooperation . . . attention has to be given to maintaining the affective as opposed to the instrumental side of the relationship." In fact, to the reporters, veteran and junior alike, the first task in news gathering is forming a system of contacts from which they can obtain information. A reporter wants information on a given story and will go to a contact that is known to be appropriate. Every time a contact provides information that helps to create satisfactory stories, that source is flagged as a "good contact," whose information is regarded as reliable, which in turn makes it more likely that the reporters will return for more information from the same source.

Reporters try to establish and maintain contact with Diet members in several ways. Most notably, reporters tend to visit—uncounted times—the private offices of Diet members. This tendency partly explains the previously discussed high frequency of meetings in one week between reporters and Diet members. To members of the desk, who expect reporters to write stories, these frequent meetings are, in the words of one desk member, "Mainly aimed at killing time rather than gathering news, considering the fact that the number of news sources is limited."

To the reporters, however, these meetings are, as one reporter noted:

> . . . To keep in touch with the Diet member to let them know that I exist a little bit more than other reporters. . . . relationships that I have with Diet members who I see almost daily differ from relationships that I have with Diet members whom I meet or talk with only once or twice.

The idea of establishing and maintaining contact with a Diet member is an important reason for a reporter to initiate meetings with them. Thus, they try to visit Diet members' offices often, chat with them, and even exchange words with their secretaries. Generally speaking, reporters will do everything they can to gain the good will of Diet members and to establish connections. Consequently, reporters tend to feed Diet members—quite intentionally—soft questions concerning a specific issue, trying not to pressure them, seeking more to agree with them as much as they can rather than trying to confuse or trouble them with irritating inquiries. They also—as will be discussed in the next chapters—provide many Diet members with a great deal of information, advice, feedback, and suggestions concerning various issues.

An important indicator of the extent to which a reporter has succeeded in establishing a close relationship with a Diet member is, obviously, the ability to obtain exclusive information. This is also the ultimate proof that both actors have developed a very solid friendship that goes beyond professional contact. In Japan, such a matter is reflected in the extent to which a reporter can enter a Diet member's home. One who has just established contact with a Diet member can visit the latter's home for obtaining information, but is allowed to enter only the living room. Here, a reporter can meet the Diet member, for example during a "night attack" of the *ban,* but can not go anywhere else in the house. They thus belong to the so-called *ôsetsuma-gumi* (living room group). As contact with the Diet member continues for some time and both get to know each other better, the relationship reaches a stage in which the reporter may enter the kitchen, and even take some of the Diet member's food and eat there freely. The reporter then belongs to the *daidokoro-gumi* (kitchen group). The closest stage of contact is when a Diet member feels close enough to a reporter to let the reporter move freely throughout the house and even share the most hidden secrets in the back parlor. This is the stage in which the reporter belongs to the *okuzashiki-gumi* (back-parlor group) and can meet the Diet member face to face in the most private part of the house.

Longtime association with a Diet member not only clears the way to obtain information, but also serves to develop a better rapport. It is extremely important to a reporter, from young to veteran, to understand the Diet members' behaviors—the way they think, their values, interests, and attitudes—to maintain smooth and understandable communication with them. This is particularly true for two interrelated reasons. First, when writing a story, most Japanese reporters are focusing on understanding the news source's viewpoint and transmitting his thoughts to the public, rather than quoting the source; in fact, direct quotation is extremely rare in newspaper stories. Reporters usually refer to what their sources say in indirect speech. This puts the reporter in control of focusing the story, combining information and wording from scattered parts of an interview, and trying to present the ideas and opinions of the source. For this reason, when meeting with Diet members, reporters tend to hold free talks with them concerning certain issues about which they want information. This kind of talk is designed for reporters to express their opinions about a certain topic, expecting Diet members to then express *their* opinions in an open atmosphere in which there is a further exchange of ideas, opinions, and thoughts, rather than questions and answers. In the broad sense, thus, in Japan the information sources produce stories, not statements. Second, some of the main news sources in Japanese politics generally speak in such a way that their words can be interpreted in several different ways. If one knows how a news source thinks, however, it is easier to extract the ideas and real intentions and the *ura* (behind) meaning of their words. Moreover, longtime face-to-face meetings enable a reporter to correctly read the facial expressions and fully comprehend the news source's opinion on most matters.

To veteran reporters, longtime contact with Diet members is a vantage point in their attempt to establish solid interaction with many of them. During this time, it is common for a reporter to establish a strong relationship with one, two, or three Diet members. This is, indeed, true of most Japanese reporters who usually rely on only a few news sources. As one editor opined: "If you find the reporter, you find the news source of the newspaper."

To be sure, the effort to build and sustain good relations may not be limited to reporters: it also includes Diet members. Diet members know that maintaining friendly relations with reporters can also help them, perhaps in the form of favorable stories and associated publicity. Meeting with reporters for reasons such as maintaining good relations was claimed by close to one-fourth of the Diet members, as outlined in chapter 3. As a matter of fact, reporters often stated that Diet members periodically invite them to restaurants or bars, and through this interaction the Diet members try to maintain regular contact with them. This is particularly true for reporters of various *bans* and for editorial writers who are invited to receptions hosted by political parties or LDP factions. One of the new leaders in the LDP described an invitation to socialize with reporters as "part of my job." Maintaining good relations with reporters is also expressed by the gifts Diet members often give reporters, especially during certain seasons of the Japanese calendar: *Ochûgen* (in the summer) and *Oseibo* (at year's end). On occasion, reporters also receive a bottle of liquor from a Diet member, especially after being elected head of a ministry for the first time. They will usually send a gift, such as liquor, to members of the press club close to their office. Referring to this attitude, one reporter remarked: "These presents are intended perhaps to create a more friendly atmosphere between members of the two groups."

Customs and Informal Rules

The privilege of entering a Diet member's back parlor, to meet face to face, and to obtain exclusive information, is not an easy accomplishment for a reporter. A reporter must compete daily with many colleagues for years to gain the attention and trust of a Diet memeber to attain such a privilege. Moreover, to obtain exclusive information from a Diet member means not only succeeding in the struggle with other reporters but also with the system itself. This system, which consists of many informal rules and customs, discourages reporters from looking for scoops. It encourages reporters to conform to various practices that prevent them from easily obtaining private information, and it forces them to cooperate with colleagues who are all looking for political information. In fact, without respecting and observing the various rules, some of which result in cooperation with other reporters, reporters would not be able to fulfill their assignments.

Informal Rules in the Press Clubs

Many of these rules, adopted a priori by members of all the press clubs, are often criticized by scholars (for example, Koyama 1982) and media personalities as opposing freedom of expression and free competition between the various media and as being detrimental to the ethics of reporters. Because of the common and frequent use of these rules, they have long been regarded by reporters as well as by political news sources as quasi-formal, or the "common sense" (way things are done) of *Nagatachô,* to be respected and observed by all involved. Should somebody break the rules of the press club, they may be punished for damaging the press club's friendship and honor and be required to make compensation. Such punishment may be what is called *tôin teishi* (prohibited from entering the house) in journalistic jargon, which means to boycott or ostracize a reporter from the press club.

Different types of rules exist in all the press clubs, and each club has its own characteristics and goals. Invariably, the rules have two objectives: to maintain good contact with the news sources and to smooth the flow of information from these sources to the reporters. In other words, the rules are intended to prevent friction between news sources and reporters and to avoid situations in which the news sources will feel uncomfortable or become confused by the activities of reporters or their coverage. Some of the informal rules are practiced more frequently, almost on a daily basis. One example is related to the so-called *kokuban kyôtei* (blackboard agreement). Each press club has a blackboard that contains information on coming events for the particular agency, on scheduled press conferences, and announcements about the topics to be discussed. It is agreed that reporters are not supposed to write stories based on data that is written on this blackboard. They cannot write, for example, on planned activities of the agency or on the fact that the minister (or a bureaucrat at a certain level) will explain, in a few days, a particular issue relevant to their workplace. Another example is related to the identification of the news sources in the news media channels. Not all Diet members wish to see their names appear in the context of a particular item of information or to be referred to as the source of this or that information. This is due to the fact that even a veteran Diet member who serves as a party or faction leader cannot always correctly predict the impact of a published story. Because of the understanding that a certain story can place a Diet member in a delicate situation, reporters and news sources distinguish between information that can be openly attributed to a particular news source and information that cannot. Information received from news sources is thus classified into categories *omote* and *ura* (front and back, or visible and invisible).

Omote is when a news source, such as the chief cabinet secretary, holds a formal press conference (as may be recalled, this official holds such meetings with the press twice a day) and the remarks made there can be attributed in a story. In fact, most political news reportage aired by television stations in the late afternoon hours (5:00 P.M. for news of NHK and 6:00 P.M. for news of commercial stations) refer to information regarding the government with phrases such as "according to the chief cabinet secretary," "the chief cabinet secretary's views are," etc. Under the same circumstances, the press will openly report the views and opinions of the prime minister or one of the cabinet ministers. As previously discussed, however, most political news sources almost invariably hold closed press conferences (*kondan*) in their offices or homes with a small group of reporters, and this information is of the *ura* class. A story based on information obtained through *kondan* will rarely divulge the name of the news source; instead, it will mention, for example, that the information was obtained from a general authority, such as *shôsoku suji* (a well-informed source). Commenting about this attitude a Diet member said:

This custom allows me, as a news source, to talk openly with repoters, to reveal my real thoughts and feelings about a given issue, without the fear that their words will be attributed to me in tomorrow's newspapers.

Thus, information disclosed by the chief cabinet secretary will appear in the morning editions of newspapers as attributable to *seifu shunô* (a senior government official); information obtained from one (or all) of the three key officials of the ruling LDP will be attributed to *jimintô shunô* (top-level LDP official); vice ministerial remarks during *kondan* will be attributed to either *gaimushô shunô* (top-level official in the Ministry of Foreign Affairs) or *tsûsanshô shunô* (top-level official in the Ministry of International Trade and Industry); and, news obtained from bureaucrats at the level of division chief (*buchô*) or chief of section (*kachô*) of a certain ministry will be attributed to *gaimushô suji* (a source in the Ministry of Foreign Affairs) or *mombushô suji* (a source in the Ministry of Education). The identity of all of these news sources is known to everybody in *Nagatachô* and is only concealed from the general public.

Other rules of the press clubs are rarely exercised and reporters are requested to observe them only on special occasions or in conformance with certain events. One example of this is when a new cabinet is inaugurated after an election or a cabinet reshuffle. Reporters traditionally give the prime minister and the new ministers the so-called *goshûgihyô* (literally to offer congratulations, or to give a tip or gratuity). In other words, there is a honeymoon period of two or three months, during which reporters are expected to lend their support, and refrain from criticism of the cabinet, giving the new government and the prime minister time to set the tone of the administration.

How Sources Control Information

Another custom of reporters is that they pool their questions before important press conferences, such as those held by the prime minister, which are broadcast live over television and radio. Indeed, from the prime minister's viewpoint, the best scenario is to know in advance the precise questions that reporters are going to ask. These questions are given to the prime minister in advance by the secretary of the press club. The secretary is often consulted by the prime minister himself or by one of his private secretaries about the nature of some of the questions. Reporters may be asked to omit sensitive questions, or to change a certain question because of a lack of available details, or, more significantly, because answering it might embarrass a colleague, a bureaucrat, or a party official.

Similar practices are observed in the so-called *burasagari* (hang down), a frequently practiced custom of the *sôri ban*. When the prime minister concludes an important meeting with a visitor and leaves his office in his official residence, reporters of the *sôri ban* often stop him and ask questions regarding the meeting, its nature, and its consequences. Surrounded by television cameras and many reporters who hang onto each other's shoulder in order to hear the prime minister's words, the prime minister answers the reporters' questions one by one in a rather spontaneous fashion. In fact, however, the custom dictates that reporters have already let the prime minister know, usually through his private secretary, what they intend to ask him when he leaves his office. The direct implication of this practice is that at a press conference or *burasagari* the questions and answers seem to flow naturally because the prime minister, or other news source, knows exactly what will be asked. Another method used to control the reporters' questions during these press conferences is to keep the press focused on a clearly defined set of issues. For example, before the prime minister leaves for important international meetings, reporters are "advised" to limit their questions to those about the coming trip.

By influencing the news agenda, the prime minister and his advisers are able to anticipate questions and limit the risk of the prime minister being pulled into uncharted water. Once the questions can be anticipated, the prime minister can study the issues and be prepared for the news conference. Even if a member of the press asks a question with an unexpected angle, the prime minister can steer the question directly into one of these prepared responses. Reporters are very aware that press conferences have become another staged event and that they are nothing more than props for the performance. Despite this knowledge, they continue to participate, because this is what they are expected to do, but, as mentioned, they prefer to employ other methods while looking for the genuine news in Tokyo.

Another example is the *embâgo* (embargo). *Embâgo* has two meanings: one refers to the general agreement between the news media agencies and the news sources not to publish a specific item of information before a certain time, even though the news agencies have received the information beforehand. This category includes speeches by the prime minister. Copies of the speech are regularly distributed to the editors of all the newspapers before it is delivered. The editors are not permitted to publish it until after the prime minister has delivered the speech. The second meaning of *embâgo* is when a news source knows that a reporter (or sometimes even a group of reporters, such as an entire *ban*) has certain information and asks the reporter not to submit it to the desk. The news source may prohibit publication of such information for several reasons: because it may confuse or embarrass a colleague, political party, government agency, or even a foreign country; because it may interrupt the process of negotiation or decision making between parties or within the government; or for personal reasons, which is the most prevalent reason for Diet members to ask reporters not to publish certain information. In practical terms, the *embâgo* limits the reporter's freedom to publish information, notably exclusive information, obtained from other news sources or through private investigation of a certain issue. But for the sake of maintaining good contacts with news sources, reporters tend to honor requests not to publish certain information.

Another example illustrating the extent to which customs prevent reporters from seeking and publishing exclusive information is related to one of the privileges of political reporters; namely, to join a leading Diet member and to cover their activities outside Japan. A political leader, such as the prime minister or the foreign minister, often travels abroad to participate in important international meetings. These may include meetings of the leaders of the industrialized Western nations and occasional meetings with heads of states. The political leader will be escorted by many reporters assigned to cover the trip. The tendency in recent years is for up to three hundred reporters, the so-called *dôkô kisha* (companion reporters), from different news media channels to travel on the same charter flight as the prime minister (or cabinet minister). These reporters are not only from different news media agencies but are mobilized by their respective companies from several press clubs, such as *Nagata, Hirakawa,* and *Kasumi.* Moreover, for some important international events, such as a world summit, they are even from different sections, such as the foreign, political, and economic sections of each news media channel. These reporters constitute a team of their company, just like the team in each of the press clubs, with each reporter contributing several parts of any given story. A reader can thus enjoy a broad range of detailed stories that cover and analyze every activity and event of the leader's travels abroad.

Sending reporters to foreign countries to cover even a short visit of a leading Diet member is, from an economic viewpoint, not an easy matter for the various news media companies. Some of the media channels, such as the bloc newspapers, cannot afford it and have to rely on the wire services—*Kyôdô* and *Jiji Press*—for detailed information. Other news companies spend a huge amount of money to send their representatives on such an assignment. For this reason, news from this group of reporters usually receives more attention by editors; it receives more space—particularly on the front page—and larger headlines. In addition to coverage of the routine activities of the leading Diet member, each company expects their reporters to send reports describing remarks and ideas expressed about general political issues or policy. Any leading Diet member who travels abroad refers to aspects of domestic politics (through *naisei kondan*, focusing on domestic policy and politics) and many other issues outside the scope of the current trip during their briefings to the press or *kondan,* all of which desk members and editors expect the companion reporters to write stories about.

Reporters who accompany a leading Diet member on such a trip are usually not experts on foreign affairs or international politics. Partly because of this, before departing Japan they usually receive guidance briefings from officials of the Ministry of Foreign Affairs about the nature of the particular trip, i.e., its purposes and schedule. During these briefings they are also told what is expected of them during the trip and how they can contribute to its general success. Reporters are told that they are not allowed to transmit information except that issued by officials of the Foreign Ministry, one of the aides of the Diet member involved, or the Diet member. This is especially true for important international meetings, such as a meeting of the leaders of the industrialized democratic nations. On such occasions, several representatives of Japan, such as the prime minister, the foreign minister, and the finance minister, will participate. While having the privilege of traveling with and covering the activities of the Diet members involved, reporters are expected to write stories based solely on the particular Diet member or one of their close aides. Officials of the Foreign Ministry instruct and "advise" reporters not to pay attention to rumors spread by their counterparts from other countries and not to look for items of news by themselves.

Instead, during such a trip, the Foreign Ministry officials spare no effort to update reporters about all matters so they can complete their assignment in the best possible light. These officials provide the reporters with news releases, announcements of briefings, and copies of every document regarding meetings or summit declarations, even before the official release time. They translate many documents into Japanese and give reporters full information about the mood and details of the talks that took place behind closed doors. The Foreign Ministry expends a great amount of energy and money for reporters and, perhaps as "a reward" for those who followed the instructions mentioned above, will even organize a special trip for the reporters to see attractive locations in the area and to do some shopping.

Cooperation between Reporters

The work of reporters involves practices that discourage them from looking for exclusive news items by themselves, force them to conform with their colleagues, and, contrary to the keen competition that characterizes reporters' work, encourage cooperation between reporters. Of particular relevance are the practices of the *ban* group. As mentioned, the *ban* group of reporters operates as an organized unit. All the reporters meet their news sources together and talk, ask questions, and receive answers in the presence of reporters from other news media. Moreover, sometimes reporters of the *ban* cannot gather information without the cooperation of their colleagues. The routine work of one of the *ban,* say, the *sômukaichô-ban,* which covers the activities of the chairperson of the executive board of the ruling LDP and the meetings of the board itself, will serve as a good example to illustrate this concept. Members of the *sômukaichô-ban* usually sit close to the chairperson's office in the party headquarters. When the executive board of the LDP meets, however, the reporters move close to the meeting room. Because they cannot enter the room in which the meeting takes place, reporters gather in an inner room adjacent to the meeting room. As a gesture of good will from the chairperson and other members of the board, the door between this room and the meeting room is left slightly ajar, to an extent that one reporter can peek inside the meeting room and listen to what is going on. At intervals of five minutes or so, each reporter of the *ban* sits near the door, peeks in, and listens. Upon returning to the group, the reporter tells the other reporters what was heard and they all jot it down on their memo pads. Before reporters write up these stories, they usually confirm the gathered information with one or more of the board members with whom they are acquainted. Generally speaking, the reporters of this and other *bans* can accomplish their work only by cooperation.

Another example, also related to the work of the *ban*, is the so-called *memo-awase* (matching memo). The *ban* group of reporters will often surround a key Diet member, usually a faction leader or the prime minister, who is entering or departing the office or meeting place. They do this in an effort to obtain a comment regarding a certain issue. Since all of the reporters cannot clearly hear what is said, those in the inner circle, close to the Diet member, tell the others what they heard, and all of them confirm what they have written on their memo pads by matching it with their colleagues' memos. A final example is that when a "night attack" is concluded and the reporters from various news agencies leave the news source's home, it is customary to hold a short discussion about the contents of the meeting. They usually discuss and interpret the important points of the meeting and the significance of the ideas or information the Diet member expressed. This enables the reporters to reach a consensus as to the relevance of some issues to the public and on the value of emphasizing one point or another raised during the meeting in a related story.

To what extent do such customs and practices of the *ban* affect reporters' work? As previously suggested, these and other customs greatly influence political coverage, as well as the nature and related interpretations of all press coverage (political, social, and other). This is reflected in one of the main characteristics of the Japanese press discussed in chapter 2, namely, the great deal of uniformity (*kakuitsu*) in the angles used by reporters and the degree of emphasis given to a particular news item in all newspapers.

Uniformity in Coverage

Much of this unison in political stories can be explained by the "pack journalism" phenomenon, also exhibited by American journalists (for example,

Crouse 1974), of the Japanese press. Several common factors can be observed: there is generally a large pack of reporters who face the same demands and share the same access and facilities; all journalists witness the same event and are exposed to their news sources at the same time, either during formal press conferences, *kondan,* or "night attacks"; and they all receive the same briefings and handouts, describing what is to take place on a particular day. For some press conferences, only a small number of reporters actually cover the event and later return to "pool" the information with other reporters, who will write the story as if they had witnessed the event. This is the so-called give and take, epitomized by the adage "you scratch my back, and I'll scratch yours," a phenomenon called "information trade off." One reporter said:

> When a press conference is held and I must attend another meeting, I will ask a reporter from another newspaper, but not one from the wire services that sends stories to my newspaper, to attend the particular press conference and provide details later.

All reporters are told when to publish certain information and what sources to attribute it to. Reporters rely on very few news sources for gathering political news: the chief cabinet secretary, the prime minister, the three leading officials of the LDP, and the five LDP faction leaders almost all of whom are members of the ruling party. The reporters discuss the stories among themselves, collectively composing the sketch of the story they will all file. This uniformity in coverage is especially beneficial to reporters, mainly because all newspaper companies like to get the same information that is published in other newspapers. Pack stories seem thus to be quite acceptable to editors. They may not always be the most exciting brand of journalism, but they are safe. The news agency does not run the risk of being the only agency to run a story that may prove to be incorrect. By following the pack, editors assume that if a reporter happens to be wrong about interpreting a certain trend, they will share the error with the other media.

The uniformity in coverage is easier to understand if the role played by the wire services is understood. As previously stated, the representatives of the wire services—*Kyôdô* and *Jiji Press*—escort the prime minister all day long and provide information to all the news media channels about his activities, such as with whom he met, what he talked about, and his schedule for the next day. In addition, the wire services, especially *Kyôdô,* regularly transmit stories about the political world (including routine events in *Nagatachô* and *Kasumigaseki*) and feature stories interpreting several of the most significant recent events, to 64 print media agencies (which publish 86 newspapers) and about 141 broadcast companies. *Kyôdô* sends political reportage to all the local newspapers and recently even to the bloc newspapers. Due to time limitations or a lack of enough stories to fill the entire paper, the print media usually do not rewrite these stories, but publish them in almost the same way they are received. Thus, they contribute to the similarities in the political information published by the media on the national, bloc, and local levels.

Uniformity in coverage, the result of pack journalism, can also have a dangerous implication, particularly in a country like Japan. As discussed in chapter 2, the Japanese are avid readers and tend to revere the printed word and accept the content of articles as accurate and trustworthy. If all the newspapers (and other news media channels as well) publish the same information with the same interpretation of a certain political event, it is natural to believe that they portray reality, more so than if some of them printed different information. This uniformity in the Japanese press is often highly misleading, and on several occasions the press has unanimously reported items that were later found to be false. One important example occurred during the no-confidence motion made by the opposition parties to the Ohira Cabinet on May 16, 1980. At that time, all of the news media channels reported absolute rejection of the no-confidence vote in one voice. In fact, the motion had actually passed when 69 LDP members absented themselves from the voting. These members were mainly from the factions headed by former Prime Minister Fukuda Takeo, former State Minister Komoto Toshio, and some from the former Nakagawa faction, all objecting to the connection that then Prime Minister Ohira had with the Tanaka faction as well as to various tax policies of the government. Their absence from the voting forced the prime minister to dissolve the Lower House and call for elections. Another example occurred in May 1986, regarding the reporting of upcoming elections. Whereas all the newspapers were unanimously stating that there was only a slim chance for double elections, simultaneous elections were called for and duly held.

The answer to the question of why such mistakes simultaneously occur in all the newspapers has already been discussed. Nevertheless, it is relevant to question the origin of such false information. Why, and from where, did reporters receive such information? The answer is not simple, and further elaboration of several variables is needed. Two general factors can serve as a framework to explain such a phenomenon. The first is that events and activities are sometimes speeded up, and unpredictable developments do occur. Even for the most experienced politician, it is difficult to guess what might happen in tense political situations. Attitudes and perceptions can change 180 degrees in a matter of a few hours from what had been reported to the press by the most reliable source. Rapid changes in the political climate, and thus in the activities of leaders who must adjust their tactics to these changes, is one of the reasons why it is difficult to correctly predict what the next step of leading Diet members will be. Another explanation can be put forth, however. This is not directly related to the work of reporters, but to the assumption that, for various reasons, some Diet members do not provide full details about a given event or may even provide false information to reporters. One reason for this attitude, for example, is the wish to test the reactions of other factions or political parties toward a certain issue. Or, the Diet member may wish to promote personal business. These two concepts, among others, are discussed in detail in the next chapter.

CHAPTER 6

Controlling the Press: The View from the Diet

Information and Information Sources

Information Sources' Domination

The nature of their work requires that each reporter covers the activities of only one agency or political group. Reporters, thus, are not able to have knowledge of every activity that takes place everywhere. During lulls in the domestic and international political arenas, reporters in a given press club often do not fully know what is happening in other government agencies, political parties' headquarters, or LDP factions. Conversely, because they are assigned to cover a limited scope of activities, the reporters' perspective of events often tends to narrow and to focus on activities directly related to their particular workplace. Quite understandably, then, for the reporters, the agency or political group they cover constitutes the "center of the world," in which each occurrence is perceived as being of great importance and warranting a broad related story. In fact, a reporter who covers a certain agency even for just a few months or days often loses his sense of which activities are most important and would have significant implications for the public, and therefore, are worthy of attention and coverage. This is particularly true today with the ever increasing number of activities in all government offices, political parties, and party factions. Under such circumstances, reporters' work becomes more complex because they have to cover more and more events. When several reporters from the same media channel are assigned as a team to cover the activities of a certain agency, they can divide a number of "worth-coverage" events among themselves, each reporter covering one event. At a certain time during the day all the reporters meet and, with the supervision of the captain, write a story containing details of several events that occurred in the agency, based on the information gathered by all the reporters.

Several reporters from the same news agency are not always assigned to one beat, however. Many press clubs have only one reporter from one newspaper to cover all activities at that location. Typical is the case of the reporters of the *ban* who cover the many activities of leading Diet members in a certain political faction. The *ban* consists of several reporters, each representing a different media channel. Each reporter must cover the routine activities of the leading Diet members; participate in press conferences, *kondan,* and briefings organized and presented by the leaders; and gather information while visiting the leaders' homes late at night. Because they report to different media channels and cannot cover more than one event at a time, reporters often must choose among several events occurring at the same time and write about what they consider to be the most important events.

In many cases, a group of reporters, such as the *ban,* from different media channels covering a specific political party or party faction, decides among themselves which events are more important and which deserve less attention. Very often, however, reporters are unable to decide the full nature of events, in which direction one event or another might develop, or the real implications of a certain event in comparison to another. Because reporters tend to see things at their workplace from a rather narrow viewpoint, focusing mainly on the agency or political group they cover, they usually depend heavily on a reliable Diet member (or government official) who, in addition to identifying stories for them and providing the information necessary to write stories, also tells them which events might have more significance on other government agencies or political parties; which activity is more crucial and important to the overall work of the Diet, bureaucracy, or other groups; which events are of more interest; and which might have more influence on the general public.

Information sources are fully aware of reporters' dependency on them. They are also aware of the pressures reporters work under, such as external pressure from rival reporters competing for information and internal pressures for reporters to write stories in a certain way and meet deadlines. Being aware of these circumstances, information sources sometimes try to take advantage of the situation to suit their own needs. And information sources can indeed take advantage in several ways to "dominate" the news. First, the information source decides on the most convenient time for passing information, in terms of handouts, speeches, press conferences, and, more notably, *kondan,* to meet the deadline (or broadcast time) of the media channel they consider most desirable. Some information sources prefer to pass specific information to reporters through press conferences organized in the press club or in handouts distributed to reporters in the morning hours of the workday. Others, in fact most information sources, prefer to pass information to reporters at their homes when reporters visit them late at night. Such a practice assures them that a related story will appear in the morning edition, which means that it will receive the attention of more readers than those of the evening edition and perhaps other Diet members and bureaucrats as well. Other information sources prefer to pass information to reporters at a time when they believe that exposure to a larger segment of the public is likely.

An example is that almost all important press conferences with leading

Diet members, such as the prime minister, are organized and broadcast live on television (and sometimes on radio) in the afternoon, usually between 5:00 and 6:00 P.M. This ensures that at least the most important points will be detailed or summarized on the 6:00 and 7:00 P.M. news of the commercial stations and NHK, respectively. As another example, the prime minister announces, with only a few exceptions, cabinet changes and the names of the new ministers at night, usually around 9:00 P.M. This information is broadcast nationwide by NHK during the 9:00 P.M. news or soon after the news in an extended addition to the news when the viewing rate is rather high. Moreover, information sources often pass detailed information to reporters after a certain problem has been solved, after a decision has been made, or even before the decision is made, according to his convenience. Last, an information source can use the embargo method and pass certain information (e.g., a speech) to the press in advance, but prohibit publication until a certain time.

Second, the information source can often decide which reporters to pass information to, or, more significantly, which ones will receive more information and scoops than the others. This concept is especially important because of reporters' growing inclination in recent years to write stories based on information gathered during face-to-face interaction with the information source. Although information sources cannot control which reporters will be assigned to cover their political party's activities, or their own activities, they may favor one, or some, of the reporters and pass more information to them than to others. An information source can decide which reporters to admit through the back door (at home or office) for private meetings to pass on more explanations about many issues and which reporters' telephone calls to answer late at night to pass on scheduling details for the next morning. If, as is claimed, a reporter's value is determined by the ability to obtain exclusive information, the information source can make it easier for a reporter to attain a better reputation. By granting a reporter individual scoops, an information source can help, even determine, the reporter's promotion and, thus, career. Third, an information source can control the nature of the information given to reporters. In other words, although sources of information may not determine the news, they may still be able to influence the perspective from which it is viewed (Gans 1980, 145). A source can encourage discussion of and promotion of those issues he or she favors, and, on the other hand, can put less emphasis on or withhold information about those issues he or she does not wish to promote.

More importantly, through long experience in political activities within their political party and the Diet, and because of extensive contact with reporters, information sources in Japan are keenly aware of two things. First is that it is easier to pass a certain type of information to the public through a political reporter from one of the daily newspapers than through a television reporter. As may be recalled, not all television stations have sufficient staff to constantly cover the activities of all political groups and all leading Diet members. In the case of the *ban,* only the reporters of the "big five" national newspapers constantly cover the activities of leading Diet members on a regular basis, whereas television reporters come to gather information only if there is some important or exceptional activity. Second, every information source knows that reporters trust them almost blindly; that if they give reporters some information along with explanatory background material to make a story, reporters will rarely turn to others for additional information, will not bother to check out the story to see if they can find a better angle, or, more significantly, to verify the information received. In many cases, because of their scoop-consciousness, reporters feel that verification might lead to a public announcement. Thus, reporters tend to forsake verification and send the news they have gathered from reliable information sources directly to their companies.

Trial Balloons

The reliance of reporters on Diet members of a specific rank for information gathering tends to work in favor of those Diet members who tend to use this dependency for achieving certain goals of their own. Sometimes even reliable information sources try to use the media as a trial balloon in an attempt to test the reaction of a certain group of readers and to learn whether a specific idea or program will be acceptable. For this reason, a reliable information source may choose to pass a particular item of information to a reporter. The tendency to pass this kind of information is perhaps less prevalent among the prime minister and party faction leaders and more prevalent among those Diet members identified as "close to the LDP leaders" (*sokkin*). Some Diet members in this category try to advance not necessarily their own interests, but those of their political party, by using this trial-balloon (*dashin kikyû*) technique of news manipulation. Six LDP Diet members, all with lengthy experience in the Diet, admitted during a discussion about this technique that they had each passed an item of information that could be regarded as a trial balloon to reporters at least once in recent months. When asked to be more precise about the nature of such information they pass to reporters under such circumstances, they commented on items of information aimed at testing the reactions of government officials from various ministries; in particular, to observe the extent of reaction specific bureaucrats give to a particular policy issue. The LDP Diet members in particular—and all Diet members in general—do not believe that they can test the reactions of Diet members from rival political parties or party factions through newspapers. One of the LDP Diet members explained:

Diet members, especially those who meet reporters most often, tend to verify information through their contacts with reporters. Any senior colleague, who takes part in the decision-making process and has the authority to decide or to influence the decision, can easily verify any information they read in the newspapers through their contacts with the many reporters surrounding them, and thus identify any attempt made by another Diet member to manipulate them through the press.

Nevertheless, the press often serves as a useful tool for LDP Diet members trying to manipulate or to determine the reaction of the bureaucracy through trial balloons. Since LDP Diet members, especially those who participate in the decision-making process, are in constant contact with the bureaucrats, one may wonder why there is still a need to use the press to advance certain goals concerning the bureaucracy. A leading LDP Diet member emphasized the need for such a practice to take place before the process of negotiations concerning a specific issue begins between the LDP (or one of the party's committees) and the representative of a certain government ministry. Sometimes a few, or a group of, LDP Diet members decide to take measures related to a specific issue. For example, the group of Diet members that supports the interest of farmers would like to introduce a bill that would limit the import of vegetables from foreign countries. Those who want to see this bill realized and those who participate in the decision-making process within the LDP and support the proposed bill have no idea of what the reaction of the bureaucracy will be on this issue. The bureaucracy may immediately reject any initiative concerning this issue, or at least begin a long, subtle process of discussions among themselves, which may be quite time consuming. In such circumstances, as one LDP member explained:

> Because many of my colleagues at the LDP are committed to representing the interests of special groups, and we are under constant pressure from these groups to promote their business, we often feel that in order to lay a foundation for dealing with a certain issue more quickly, we must pass a warning signal to bureaucrats. This should work as a catalyst for them to begin preparations for negotiation on a certain issue. These bureaucrats may then start consultations involving the different departments within their specific government office with perhaps the intention of examining the possible implications of existing laws; or in an attempt to channel some manpower to do further investigation on the matter in order to facilitate the proposed bill into becoming a bill; or, they can even think about the possibility of consultation and collaboration with bureaucrats from other offices. We can even receive a call or an indirect communication from bureaucrats asking to delay the proposed bill; or, unoffi-

cial advice from them to think about specific revision. LDP Diet members, particularly those who participate in the decision-making process may thus intentionally drop a hint to reporters that a certain policy is being considered.

In this way, Diet members can take great advantage of the predisposition of officials in the bureaucracy to be very sensitive to what is written in the newspapers about their agencies (Kim 1981, 102). Knowing this, LDP Diet members may tell reporters that the party has decided to take certain measures concerning a specific policy. The reporters who greatly depend on these information sources, and in many cases do not know their true intentions, write the story. When the information is published, the government officials at a particular office try to perceive the real intentions of the LDP and then begin their own preparations by studying the issue and the possible legislation with real concern. To learn about the effectiveness of this technique, I was advised to talk with LDP Diet members, especially former bureaucrats, who have some experience on both sides of the coin. All of the Diet members with such experience were of the opinion that this is indeed the best way to expedite things and to motivate officials to meet the needs of the LDP. Moreover, in this way, Diet members of several committees within the LDP can also test reactions to policies initiated by the LDP. Thus, the LDP can use the reactions of government officials to either modify a certain bill they intend to introduce or to look for another plan to overcome criticism. Based on their past experience, LDP Diet members condoned this strategy for quickly achieving their objectives. In the views of some opposition-party Diet members, the trial-balloon technique is not exclusively aimed at bureaucrats. A leader of one of the opposition parties stated:

> The LDP even uses this technique to stimulate individual cabinet members, or the cabinet as a whole, to pay attention to a certain issue. Such a tendency can be observed especially when LDP Diet members are brought under pressure by certain segments of industry who want to promote their own interests and would like these Diet members to flex their political muscle in the ministerial decision-making process in a way that will benefit their industry. In these cases, LDP Diet members who are closely supported by certain pressure groups—such as the *zoku giin* ["tribe" of Diet members]—will seek to pass some information through the newspapers to stimulate a certain minister or the entire cabinet to look at a certain issue or to reconsider a certain policy for the benefit of their supporters.

The trial balloon is one of the techniques Diet members use to provoke the press into publishing intentional information. There are, however, other instances in which Diet members try to control the nature of the information they pass to reporters. This is actualized in the following two ways: first, when an information source puts pressure on reporters to publish certain information; and second, when an information source passes information to reporters but pressures them to not publish it. In the first case, even if an information source encourages reporters to write stories of a certain nature, that does not necessarily means that an article will be published. Every article is screened and evaluated several times between the press club and the political desk, where the final decision of whether to publish it rests with the editor. Nevertheless, even if a story is published, all information sources are not always satisfied with the way things are presented or with the way a story is written. In the second case, even if an information source prohibits publication of a certain item of information, it is possible for related information, in part or in whole, to find its way to the public through other channels. Or, it may be transformed and reach other political participants through personal communication. On a daily basis, reporters are constantly faced with requests to publish or not to publish certain information. Thus, reporters constantly wander between these two opposite requests, which symbolize their contacts with Diet members. A detailed discussion of these situations follow.

Behind the Published Stories

Invited Articles

One of the best ways to illustrate how Diet members "encourage" reporters to write certain articles is through "invited articles," known in journalistic jargon as *yarase* (literally, make someone do something), *kakase* (make one write something), or *chô-chin kiji* (a lantern story). In general, *yarase,* a "set-up," refers to a simulation portrayed as a real event. It may grow out of a staged event. To Japanese reporters, especially to political reporters, it means an article that a Diet member asks a reporter to write, usually about the Diet member's own activities or, in some cases, the activities of a political group, such as the member's party faction. What leads Diet members or, more importantly, information sources to ask a reporter to write about their political activities? Primarily publicity. In the words of a reporter: "All Diet members want to give the general public an idea about their work, the things they are promoting, and the people they associate with during their workday."

The reason Diet members tell a reporter what they have done recently is obvious to the secretaries of the Diet members. One of them said:

My boss is a politician who usually works from morning until late at night; he regularly meets more than 30 different people representing pressure groups, voters, bureaucrats, and other officials every day; attends Diet or party committee meetings and talks with hundreds of people on the telephone. At the end of the workday he feels that his voters should know that he devotes himself to public work. So what's wrong if he asks a reporter to write something in the newspaper about the hectic schedule he keeps? After all, all Japanese Diet members like to see their name in the newspapers. It is the best way to inform the voters and supporters that they work.

Through invited articles an information source also wants to let the public know about the nature and scope of the activities of their political party or party faction. But more than just informing the public about the functions of the group, party or faction leaders seek to gain public understanding and support for the issues they try to promote. Furthermore, leaders who seek press coverage about the activities of their group wants to boost group morale and to consolidate group unity against rival groups. Coverage of their activities can serve as a great reward and a source of pride and encouragement for the group's members to continue their activities as a united group and to achieve more and more of the groups' objectives. In the long run, it might even encourage new members to join the group. For example, a potential political candidate may identify with ideas the group promotes, or with the hard work the group does, or with the collective work done by the group's members, as reported in the press, and express intention to join the group.

Not only leading Diet members, such as the leaders of political parties or party factions, ask reporters to write about their own or their groups' activities. It is not rare for party officials serving as directors of divisions in their parties' headquarters, or for government bureaucrats, motivated by the same reasons that drive Diet members—namely, to let the public know how hard they work and to see their names in the newspapers—to turn to reporters with such requests. Actually, the tendency to ask reporters to write about their activities is prevalent among almost all Diet members, from junior ones to veterans with more than 20 years in political activities. Meeting and talking with various groups of Diet members reveals that, without exception, all of them believe that they have the ability to update reporters, broaden their knowledge, and help them to gain more insight and background about political events, especially those in which the Diet member personally participates. This attitude is reflected by the fact that 206 of the Diet members (out of a total of 402) claimed that they meet reporters to give them information. This tendency, outlined in table 3-4, contradicts the fact that the number of information sources is far below this figure. Study of this apparent contradiction reveals that the tendency to meet reporters to give them information is particularly prevalent among two categories of Diet members: junior ones who have been elected three times at most and those who may have long service in the Diet but do not belong to the ruling party.

Junior Diet Members and the Press

Junior Diet members are particularly conspicuous. Almost all of them have extremely low news appeal to reporters, though they can expect the local media to pay attention to their activities in their own districts or prefectures. But it is unlikely that any of the national dailies will cover their activities or ask their opinions about a particular national-level issue. Two groups are exceptions, however. The first group consists of former secretaries of Diet members who resigned those positions and were subsequently elected to the Diet. Noteworthy in this group are the former secretaries of leading Diet members such as former Prime Ministers Ohira Masayoshi and Nakasone Yasuhiro. Because of their previous position, many former secretaries have established prolonged contacts with reporters and members of the political desks of all the leading newspapers. They were the people who updated these reporters about many aspects of their bosses' work: their activities; their public speeches; their talks behind closed doors at party or faction meetings; and their schedules, thoughts, feelings, and general moods. Thus, they are well-versed in Diet, cabinet, and LDP procedures and activities; and because they have, either through their former bosses or by personal charisma, built strong relationships with many other influential Diet members, reporters approach them, even as junior Diet members, to obtain information, views, and observations.

The second group of junior Diet members who attract reporters are the second- and third-generation Diet members, that is, those who succeeded a close relative (usually a father) who died, or those who were elected to fill the Diet seat of a retired relative.[1] Because this group of Diet members has ancestral merits, most of them enter the political world with such great advantages that they have better chances of acquiring cabinet portfolios or other important positions within the ruling LDP. In fact, during the late 1980s, 9 of the 20 members of the Takeshita Cabinet, and 12 in the Uno Cabinet, were sons of Diet members. Six such persons were in the Kaifu Cabinet, in addition to the LDP Secretary General (Ozawa Ichiro). Perhaps reporters turn to junior Diet members from this group to establish long-term contacts, looking to the

---

1. Most of these are elected after inheriting their relative's three legacies: *jiban* (supporters' organization), *kanban* (the relative's fame), and *kaban* (relative's cash-filled attache case). Most of these Diet members belong to the LDP, but some are from the SDPJ and CGP. In 1990, for example, about 40 percent of the LDP House of Representatives' members, 130 Diet members, were so-called patrimonial politicians. Among them were the eldest sons of former prime ministers Suzuki Zenko and Fukuda Takeo, who were elected to the Lower House for the first time after they inherited their fathers' constituencies. A son of former Prime Minister Nakasone Yasuhiro was a member of the House of Councillors. The increased number of hereditary Diet members in recent years is well reflected by the growing number of cabinet positions occupied by these Diet members.

time when one of them will occupy a leading position, rather than for gathering current information.

Junior Diet members from these two groups are a minority in the Diet. Although the other junior Diet members do not have sufficient experience to attract the attention of reporters, this does not mean that they sit and wait for years until somebody turns to them for information. On the contrary, they constantly do their best to gain the attention of the national dailies' reporters and, through this, publicity. Diet members use several techniques to gain the attention of reporters. The first, which is reflected in the tendency of junior Diet members to meet reporters frequently (as outlined in chapter 3), is to initiate meetings themselves and attract reporters to their offices by proffering information. Knowing that they cannot attract reporters who are experienced in covering political activities because such reporters have established contacts with veteran Diet members and thus do not need the limited information they can provide, a junior Diet member turns to reporters who do not have extensive experience or to reporters from the local newspapers. Interestingly, the fewer times a Diet member has been elected, and thus the less experienced, the greater the tendency to feel that he or she has information of value to pass to reporters. In some cases, junior Diet members may be overwhelmed by or wary of their new environment, much more so than a veteran Diet member, and apt to direct the attention of reporters to a particular issue considered trivial by veteran Diet members, but considered worth covering by the reporters. When meeting with reporters, junior Diet members pass along hearsay they have picked up during their daily activities and to drop statements such as, "yesterday in the prime minister's office, I heard . . . ," statements that usually provoke reporters to at least try and obtain more information from higher up.

A second technique is that, in their determination to gain publicity, some junior Diet members give reporters advance information about their forthcoming activities, especially about participation in events on the local, national, or international levels. Whether a Diet member is invited to make a speech about a certain issue to a certain group of local citizens in their district; to participate in a symposium with other participants from other prefectures; or to leave for a short trip abroad as a member of a delegation, they find it necessary to give reporters full information about these activities, their locations, the contents of their speeches, a summary of the main ideas they advocate, and a detailed schedule of their meetings with public figures and other people abroad. Junior Diet members and Diet members of the opposition parties may give a reporter details about the type and content of questions they intend to ask a minister or bureaucrat in one of the meetings of the committee they serve on. They do this in the hope that a reporter will be interested enough to monitor the meeting and write about the Diet member's activities or at least write a story about the fact that this Diet member introduced a certain issue in the committee.

Junior Diet members may even try to attract the attention of reporters through distinctive activities—sometimes innovative and imaginative, sometimes dangerous and risky—and continue to update the reporters about the developments of a particular activity. One example is the action of Diet member and professional wrestler, Antonio Inoki. In late September 1990, in the midst of the Gulf Crisis following the invasion of Kuwait by Iraq, Mr. Inoki went to Iraq on his own initiative and met the second-in-rank to President Saddam Hussein in an effort to arrange the release of Japanese citizens detained in Iraq as hostages. This deed attracted media coverage, resulting in a large number of newspaper articles and television stories. Junior Diet members and Diet members of the opposition parties also try to attract reporters by identifying with popular issues. For example, in 1989 several Diet members of the opposition parties used the so-called Geisha Affair, an incident involving former Prime Minister Uno Sosuke who allegedly had a sexual relationship with a geisha, to call for the establishment of an ethical government. They also used the public protest against and dissatisfaction with the LDP in the wake of the so-called Recruit Scandal to call for the resignation of those Diet members involved in the scandal, and also used the clamor against the unpopular consumption tax to call for its abolishment.

Because it is rather difficult for junior Diet members or Diet members of the opposition parties to achieve nationwide attention as individuals, junior Diet members often form groups to call attention to their existence or to specific causes in which they are interested. Examples of such groups include the *Heisei no kai* group, formed at the beginning of April 1989 by 41 dovish LDP Diet members. Led by Morita Hajime, the group consists of junior Diet members from all the LDP factions who have been elected not more than four times to the House of Representatives and not more than three times to the House of Councillors. The group's platform includes campaigning for clean politics, disarmament, and peace policies. Another group, led by Kamei Shizuka, consists of 36 junior LDP Diet members who formed the Liberal Reform League in April 1989. This group demanded that those LDP Diet members who were implicated in the Recruit Scandal take responsibility for their roles by resigning from the Diet.

Junior Diet members and Diet members from the opposition parties are well aware of the "soft stomach" of the press and the weaknesses of reporters, and a number of them have successfully developed several techniques to gain the attention of the press. One of these Diet members remarked:

> I often call one reporter, suggest that the reporter write a story about a certain issue or meeting in which I participated by passing some information, then adding that this item of information "is just for you as a scoop." After the reporter leaves my office I then call another reporter and tell him the same thing. Referring to certain information as a scoop

increases the likelihood that the information will be published in one newspaper or another.

Another technique that such Diet members use to gain attention and, ideally, coverage, is to pass information to reporters on specific days; for example, on Saturdays and Sundays. As previously discussed, few political or legislative activities occur on weekends, resulting in a scarcity of political stories to fill the political pages on Sundays and Mondays, making it more likely, in theory at least, that almost any information Diet members pass to reporters on those days will be published. Nevertheless, veteran reporters are unlikely to fall into this trap, so they appeal mainly to less-experienced reporters.

Diet Members' Expectations and the Reporters' Views

Reporters are fully aware of the situation in which Diet members, juniors and veterans alike, request that they "write a few words" about themselves, their activities, or their party faction, and provide them with detailed information for this purpose. Some Diet members even explicitly express their hope for favorable reportage. Many reporters claim that the bias in the information they receive from these or other Diet members is extremely clear; and, in the words of one reporter, "Any reporter can obviously identify the motive behind such information; and I can completely understand the position of the person who tries to convince me to write something about what he does."

Even so, reporters sometimes accept the situation at face value, without trying to "get behind" the presented information, and they tend to acquiesce to Diet members' requests to put their names in the newspapers. The *yarase* article, which is written as a result from a direct request of a Diet member and whose content reflects a message that the Diet member wants to deliver, appears in the political page like any other story. In most cases this type of story is shorter than a regular story and occupies less space; it is not a fictitious story but is based on a real event, such as a meeting between a certain Diet member and a constituency delegation to discuss local affairs; or a meeting with several visiting government officials from another country to exchange opinions on possible cooperation. The center of such *yarase* articles is usually focused on one Diet member (although it may focus on a group of Diet members) who would not probably have a regular chance to attract reporters' attention; thus, the probability that a story on that member's activity would appear on a regular basis is rare. To be sure, the *yarase* articles do not appear every day. They can be found most commonly on weekends, for the reason mentioned above. They appear most often also in a "dead season," e.g., the summer vacation, when *Nagatachô* is deserted of almost all Diet members. In such periods, when most of the Diet members are back in their constituencies and only a few Diet members remain in their offices, Tokyo reporters are more vulnerable to writing stories based on "requests" of Diet members.

To some reporters, then, the *yarase* is used just to fill up space in the newspaper. It helps to "close the paper," as one editorial writer claimed. From another viewpoint, reporters also take advantage of this technique and use it as a tactic to successfully confront their colleagues and to gain the attention of Diet members; to show that they are ready to offer assistance, "a kind of service to the Diet member," in the words of a reporter, and to demonstrate that they want to establish or maintain close, solid contact with them.

During interviews, a number of reporters agreed that Diet members prefer the *Asahi* for *yarase* articles. One reporter from the *Sankei*, said: "Because the *Asahi* has a large circulation, a good audience, and is an influential newspaper, Diet members put much effort into influencing the *Asahi* reporters."

At the same time, however, all the reporters expressed the general view that rival newspapers publish invited articles more often than their own newspaper. Reporters from the *Sankei* said the *Mainichi* does it more often, and those from the *Asahi* claimed that the *Yomiuri* does it every day. *Nihon Keizai* reporters said their newspaper does not have much space for political stories, and for that reason nobody can blame them for publishing *yarase* often. In the view of some reporters, the style of *yarase* is very popular, especially on commercial television, and a few even mentioned that NHK sometimes introduces such coverage. Whereas each reporter criticized rival newspapers for publishing invited articles, Diet members pointed to rivals from other political parties or party factions as attempting to create an advantage through such publicity. One Diet member from the LDP faction led by Prime Minister Miyazawa said that "Takeshita faction members are particularly skillful at getting *yarase* articles published, as a means of influencing the public and other Diet members, including those of the LDP."

Another Diet member from the Democratic Socialist party pointed to Clean Government party Diet members as experts in appealing to reporters and "making them write about their own activities." A Diet member from the SDPJ said:

> It is difficult to get reporters to write what I want, and sometimes they even write about issues I do not want them to write about. I try to explain things in such a way that an article will result in a style which I find appropriate, but it does not always work. One reason might be extraneous influence from other sources, LDP Diet members perhaps.

The view of another LDP Diet member was:

> Some reporters write *yarase* as an indication of their support of the opinions held by the party faction they cover. . . . After all, we expect a reporter who is covering our faction for years, day after day, to show some sympathy toward us.

That reporters write about Diet members' activities does not necessarily mean that the Diet members are always happy with the coverage. In fact, Diet members are very often dissatisfied with the way they are represented in the newspapers. A complaint usually follows. In some cases, a Diet member is so dissatisfied and angry that he may even call a desk member, the head of the political section, or an editor in a newspaper company, and register a complaint about a published story. Through their contacts with Diet members, several reporters have found that if they write articles criticizing a Diet member of the LDP faction they cover, that Diet member or, more significantly, the faction leader, gets back at them. This has happened over the years, and some Diet members have even terminated the relationship because of what reporters wrote about them. Afraid of losing the contacts they have with Diet members, reporters do their best to avoid conflicts and often tend to consider how a certain story might affect their relationship with Diet members. They pay close attention to the way an information source may react. To maintain contact with their current information sources and those they are trying to cultivate contact with, reporters tend not to confuse "their" Diet members by what they write. Thus, a reporter always weighs any potential story with the need to supply information to the desk against the relationship with the Diet members involved. And when a reporter must weigh certain information, the tendency is to tilt to the Diet members' side.

The concern of reporters to deeply consider the stories they are writing is based on the realization that, although their relationships with Diet members are strong or getting stronger, they are simultaneously very fragile and delicate. Thus, reporters will do anything not to jeopardize their contacts with Diet members. Reporters feel that they cannot be "a broken reed" to any Diet member or ranking official at a government agency who counts on them, by writing about some topics the latter will feel uneasy about. All reporters know quite well that there are "other reporters behind the door" who look for mistakes in order to gain the information source's trust and to obtain more attention and exclusive information. The reporters' viewpoint was expressed in the following way by one reporter:

> All that I have constructed for years, all the confidence and trust that Diet members have in me, I am not going to sacrifice for the price of one scoop, though I know everybody will praise me; I am not going to write about something that may cause embarrassment to a certain Diet member, even if it would make the headline in tomorrow's paper.

Off the Record

Daily contact with information sources and other Diet members, government officials, and political party officials enables reporters to obtain a great deal of information. Some of this information, such as details about new government policies, plans to introduce a new bill, or plans to dissolve the Diet and call for general elections, is of interest to the general public. Other information, such as foreign-aid support, investments the Bank of Japan is considering in third world countries, or visits of the prime minister to other countries, is also of interest to foreign countries and to international organizations. Items of information may also be of interest to specific, or limited, public groups such as the voters in a certain district or a certain interest group. Whether an item of information has narrow or broad implications, is of interest to a wide or limited segment of the public either in Japan or abroad, or whether it warrants immediate publication or can be delayed, newspapers cannot publish all the information reporters obtain from their information sources. This is partly due to technical reasons (such as space limitations), or the relative importance of other news items that the desk members evaluate as more worthy of publication, or the need for more details. There are other reasons for not publishing certain items of information, however. These are related to a source's request, sometimes prohibition, to not write stories about a certain issue or to not disclose specific details about a certain matter.

One type of publication prohibition in Japan—the *embâgo*—has already been discussed. As may be recalled, the embargo refers to the source's request not to reveal to the public certain information acquired by the reporter. The off-the-record (*ofureko*) tool is another technique that information sources use for prohibiting or partly limiting publication of certain information. In essence, this refers to information a source passes directly to reporters while asking them not to publish it or not to attribute specific items or stories to them. The off-the-record technique has several characteristics in Japan. First, it is practiced frequently by almost all information sources. It is not unusual for a leading Diet member to talk openly with reporters, such as the *ban* group of reporters, and tell them later not to disclose any details of the talk. This occurs so often that every reporter readily expressed the opinion that much of the information Diet members pass to reporters is off the record and remains unpublished. One editor said that 80 percent of information received is off the record, in comparison with information that can be published. In other words, only a small percentage of the information reporters receive from Diet members is published. Because the off-the-record technique is practiced so often, to many journalists the concept has partly lost its original meaning. It is true that reporters who receive the off-the-record information tend to acquiesce to the information source's request and do not publish it. Although an information source prohibits publication of certain information, it might spread by word of mouth all over *Nagatachô* within hours. Thus it can reach the ears of reporters who did not hear the information directly from the information source and are not prohibited from writing a related story.

The practice in recent years of passing certain information to reporters and asking them not to publish it may have become popular among many Diet members as a means of attracting reporters to them. In the view of several desk members, in many cases a request not to reveal certain information is only intended to impress reporters into thinking a Diet member knows something about a certain issue. Usually, however, this kind of information has no significance and is not at all important. Such information is of no more value than a cheap gossip story that no reporter would consider worthy of publication. But since an information source has requested that it not be published, the information suddenly becomes more valuable and the information source is regarded as more knowledgeable. Since many Diet members want to be considered important and knowledgeable, they often use the off-the-record ploy for these reasons.

The second important aspect of the off-the-record device is that it is often practiced during the private small-group talks that information sources conduct with reporters, such as during *kondan* and "night attacks." Clearly, a Diet member or a government official who conducts press conferences with tens of reporters from various news media channels would never ask them, in front of many television cameras, not to cite their comments in regard to a certain case or not to refer in a story—in whole or in part—to what they just said. Technically, of course, it is easier for an information source to make such a request to a small group of reporters, such as the *ban* group of reporters who meet information sources face to face. The limited number of reporters in the *ban* group makes it rather easy for an information source to determine who did not respect their request just by glancing at the morning edition of the newspapers the next day. Moreover, an information source can talk more freely with a small group of reporters in a meeting that may last for an extended period of time. Even without explicitly suggesting which information reporters should or should not reveal in their stories, an information source can rely on reporters to distinguish, based on prolonged contact, what can be published and what is off the record.

Certain categories of Diet members, more so than others, tend to place tighter restrictions and limitations on the publication of information given out to reporters who cover their activities. These include the leaders of the LDP factions and the so-called new leaders. The faction leaders are afraid that other members of the faction may misinterpret their comments in the news media, which might lead to an embarrassing situation within the faction they lead. In some cases, such a misunderstanding might result in an open conflict between the leader and other members of the faction. The "new leaders" may ask, sometimes vigorously, for an explanation or clarification about what was published. In other cases, it might cause a conflict with a rival faction over a certain policy issue or over sharing cabinet positions such as cabinet minister or vice minister. The up-and-coming new leaders, who strive to attain the support of as many Diet members as possible in an attempt to translate this support into party leadership, perhaps have another reason for asking reporters not to publish certain information. Because they seek the sympathy of members of various groups who often have opposing opinions about many issues, it is important to each of the new leaders to be perceived as one who does not identify or advocate a certain issue or idea. They want to be liked by everybody and thus need to keep a neutral image concerning various issues. To avoid making anybody angry or provoking criticism from other Diet members, these Diet members may ask reporters not to mention their names in connection with certain information in their effort to maintain a low profile.

For these reasons, most of the information that leading LDP Diet members pass to reporters is off the record. Sometimes all information is completely restricted, not only from being published, but also from being communicated verbally by those who attended the meeting. Thus, reporters are not only restricted from writing a story but also from telling their colleagues or even their own desk members and editors about the contents of their meeting with a certain information source. This is because many information sources know that even if a reporter would not personally write a story, the information can be communicated to the desk, and one of the desk members can write a related story. Or, more interestingly, to avoiding embarrassing a certain information source, jeopardizing the long-term contact, or provoking termination of the relationship with the political reporter in the relevant *ban,* the desk members may ask another desk, such as the social or economic desk, to write a story based on this information. Therefore, to prevent publication of such information in this way, the information source forbids reporters to give even their editor an idea about the contents of their comments.

To what extent do reporters follow such requests? Almost all reporters interviewed stated that they always respect the requests of an information source and do not reveal, even to the members of the desk, what they have been asked not to disclose. One reason for this is probably because many information sources are so influential that they can, sooner or later, determine whether anyone, such as a desk member, knows something about a matter that a reporter was asked not to reveal. This might result in the end of the contact the reporter has with this particular information source and, as has happened in many cases, the reporter might lose the trust of many other Diet members. Another reason for this is perhaps because their superiors, when they were reporters, respected their information source's requests and did not tell their bosses on the political desk everything. Perhaps the most conspicuous reason for reporters to respect the Diet member's request is that some information sources are so sensitive that they look every morning to see what was written about them. Others even assign one of their private secretaries to scan the morning editions of all the daily newspapers to see which reporter wrote about them and what was written. This secretary also checks who, of the *ban* group, did not respect the request not to publish certain information.

One example of this practice is related to former Prime Minister Tanaka Kakuei and his private secretary, former political reporter Hayasaka Shigezo. One of the most important daily tasks of Mr. Hayasaka was to check all information published in the newspapers about his boss. If he found any of Mr. Tanaka's off-the-record comments in a newspaper, he would summon all the *ban*'s reporters and scold the reporter who published it. Moreover, at times he even prohibited that reporter from attending some meetings with his boss. Sometimes several reporters were denied this privilege, and only two or three reporters attended the private talks with Mr. Tanaka. In this way, Mr. Tanaka, through his secretary, achieved total control over those rep)rters who covered his daily activities. Since Mr. Tanaka was an important leader in Japanese politics and the information he passed to reporters without publication restrictions was very rare, information from him was highly valued among reporters in general and *Nagatachô* in particular.

There is another important aspect related to off-the-record information, however. Since information sources can look at the daily newspapers and easily determine which reporters did not respect their request, much of the information obtained from Diet members cannot be published in the national newspapers. Instead, it is relegated to the weekly and monthly magazines. These magazines have become an important channel in recent years and a useful source for detailed information, especially intriguing news items not usually carried by the daily newspapers. For example, the weeklies (and some of the monthlies, such as *Bungei Shunjû* and *Chûô Kôron*) exposed political corruption and wrongdoing in government to the general public during the 1960s and 1970s (most notably, *Bungei Shunjû* exposed the Lockheed affair concerning former Prime Minister Tanaka). These magazines reported pollution problems caused by the petrochemical industry to the public during the 1970s and 1980s. They also reported visits to Japan of several U.S. ships allegedly carrying nuclear weapons, links between some Diet members and powerful interest groups, and the involvement of several Diet members in political scandals.

Some of the weeklies are published by the "big five" daily newspapers, such as *Sandei Mainichi* (published by the *Mainichi*) and *Shûkan Sankei* (published by the *Sankei*). The circulation of several of them, such as *Shûkan Posuto, Shûkan Shinchô, Shûkan Asahi*, and *Shûkan Gendai*, is between five hundred thousand and seven hundred thousand copies. In many cases, these weeklies and several of the monthlies seek to publish information that reporters cannot publish in the national dailies. In their attempt to attract readers with better and more interesting information, the editors of these magazines encourage reporters of the dailies to write about events that they cannot report in their own newspapers. Thus, while passing the dead hours of the day, especially while waiting for the late-afternoon briefings or news conferences in the press clubs, some reporters can be seen writing, as freelancers, about the talks they had with a certain Diet member. Since some of these reporters often feel that they have more freedom in this type of work than in their regular work, and because their stories are published without their byline, they usually tend to disclose more details and more interesting information in the weeklies than in the daily newspapers.

The last important dimension related to the off-the-record technique is that while it is essentially aimed at withholding information from publication, it gives special meaning to and maintains and encourages a strong interpersonal relationship between the information source and a reporter. By talking with a reporter and revealing certain information regarding the latest political events, and then asking that it not be published, an information source indicates the extent of the trust involved in the relationship, that is, believing that the reporter would not take advantage of such confidence and exploit that trust. Sometimes much more than trust is involved. A Diet member or any other information source who discloses true feelings and thoughts to a reporter (including the problems and pains existing at work or even in private life) directly indicates the degree of closeness with the reporter. When an information source asks a reporter not to tell anyone else those innermost secrets, this means that their relationship has reached the highest degree of intimacy. There may be something, perhaps an aspect of the information source's secrets, feelings, and thoughts, that only the two them know and share. These aspects of trust and closeness, which are strongly connected to each other, encourage an atmosphere in which reporters and information sources would like to see each other, even if there is no need to obtain or pass information. In this environment they talk freely, even have a heart-to-heart talk, and foster an atmosphere in which reporters feel that their words of encouragement or advice are needed to help the Diet member. And by communicating in this way with Diet members, reporters often assume an extremely important role in their work.

Good Words, Advice, and Suggestions

Diet members often obtain advice, suggestions, and personal counsel concerning many issues, e.g., party policies, party faction strategies, activities of a specific Diet committee, and even their own public image, through contacts with reporters. Any Diet member can exploit the advice or suggestions received from reporters, for promoting their own prestige or for promoting their constituency, to asking questions at meetings of a Diet committee. The experience reporters acquire in their daily contact with the political world's activities is often useful to Diet members and the advice they receive from reporters is an important factor that contributes much to their Diet work.

Many Diet members have continual close contact with various aides who give them a great deal of assistance and advice. For example, each Diet member has several secretaries, in their *Nagatachô* office and their home-district office, all of whom provide extensive assistance. They mainly serve as important channels of communication for the Diet member in linking their constituents' needs and wishes in general and their voters and supporters in particular. Secretaries attend various functions, such as political party or party faction meetings; and when the Diet member is unable to attend a meeting of a party or Diet committee, a secretary monitors it for them and relates the substance of the proceedings. Moreover, Diet members often assign secretaries to do research and to provide material and information they need in their regular work on a party or Diet committee. Thus, the secretaries must look for specific data in books or old newspapers and copy or summarize it for the Diet member, who will use it to present ideas or questions in the committee. Secretaries, especially private ones, escort the Diet members all day to give support, provide feedback and advice, and offer useful comments and suggestions about any problem their boss faces. Clearly, Diet members do receive a great deal of assistance from their secretaries, but most of them also prefer to hear opinions and suggestions from reporters before they take an action or adopt a certain measure. One leading LDP Diet member stated:

> Reporters know better than most of my close aides what is neccessary for me to do as a Diet member, when to do it, and how. Based on their broader knowledge and a keen ability to analyze any political trend or movement, their sense of judgment is uncanny.

Whereas a Diet member's aides may need time to check on a certain issue to obtain more details before advising them on how to deal with the issue, reporters provide the neccessary advice on the spot. And if time is the most important factor in Diet members' work, when they need quick advice to make the best decision they tend to turn to reporters.

Several influential Diet members consult with professional people about various issues. Notably, some LDP Diet members confer with university professors, but what they want from reporters is different. Scholars can provide theoretical knowledge, a basis on which to build a general stance or a special way to explain a certain policy and the motives to support or oppose a certain matter. Reporters, on the other hand, in the words of an LDP Diet member,

> are best suited to judge what influence a specific decision will have on any of the other political organs, i.e., political parties, party factions, the

bureaucracy, and on the public in general, and not less important, how voters and supporters in my district will react.

The significance of obtaining advice from reporters has been emphasized by many Diet members from all political parties. A leading LDP Diet member commented:

> When the party is preparing some specific party policy, Diet members tend to see things from a narrow point of view, and that's when it helps to consult reporters. They provide a different perspective, sometimes with the knowledge of other parties' opinions. They are very good as expediential consultants.

Some CGP Diet members also claimed that when they want to adopt a certain policy, they first consult reporters, and a SDPJ Diet member admitted: "My party often takes reporters' views very much into consideration when thinking about a certain measure."

Amazingly, Diet members of all levels want and need a variety of advice from reporters. To Diet members who do not have much experience in political activities, reporters are a valuable source of new ideas on how to promote their status in their parties or party factions. Reporters advise junior Diet members about which group of Diet members to associate with to acquire more public recognition. They even advise them as to which leading Diet members they should ask to accompany them to their constituencies to address their supporters and other potential voters, especially before an election, to signify their prestige and connections to their voters. Based on their experience, reporters even devise campaign strategies for junior Diet member candidates. Some reporters advise junior Diet members on what topics they should address in appealing to voters, with one Diet member admitting during an interview that a reporter even helped him to write speeches. Reporters also suggest what topics to introduce in Diet committees, how to introduce them, and when. They also provide suggestions about various issues they think Diet members should introduce on the agendas of their political parties or party factions.

To some Diet members, such as ministers and vice ministers, especially those who often meet reporters at press conferences, reporters are the best advisers about the press. Reporters give such Diet members advice about the best style in which to introduce their ideas; what to say first and last; which points they should emphasize and which ones not to mention; and how they can attract the press to gain more publicity for their suggested policy or for themselves as Diet members. To other Diet members, reporters are the best source for feedback about their approach to specific issues and are constructive critics who advise them how to do their work appropriately. One Diet member noted, "They advise Diet members of my party how to criticize colleagues from another party, on the most appropriate time to bring up a problem in the Diet, and when to confront the ruling or other opposition parties."

One minister, for example, admitted during an interview that when he holds a press conference with reporters assigned close to his office, he tries to obtain the reporters' opinions concerning the way he works. Reporters advise Diet members about when they should meet with the faction or party leader, what they should ask the leader, and what issue it would be best to delay until the next meeting. While observing one reporters' news-gathering methods and contact with sources, I witnessed a situation in which a leading Diet member asked him for his opinion of an election poster. The Diet member was worried about how potential voters would react to the color of the poster and to one of the slogans that appeared beside his picture. He was even ready to change it according to the reporter's advice.

Leading Diet members also need and get advice from reporters. In fact, even committee chairpeople, secretaries-general of political parties, and leaders of party factions receive suggestions and advice pertaining to policy, faction leadership, proposals, and public appearances. Diet members of this level often meet not only with the reporters who cover their daily activities but also with veteran reporters, such as desk members and editors. Some of those veterans revealed that when they meet a Diet member with whom they have had long contact, they hold something like a seminar to discuss various political issues on the agenda of political parties or the Diet and study those issues from all possible viewpoints. Even the prime minister consults re- porters about a wide range of political issues and highly values their advice. During the years that former Prime Minister Nakasone was in office, he occasionally met with 10 to 12 reporters from the *Nagata kurabu,* for what has become known as a *kare-raisu* meeting. Reporters who were selected by the secretary of the press club to meet the leader of the nation, would eat curried rice with the prime minister and openly discuss issues and offer him advice concerning his public apperances, the best way to appeal to the public, how to treat the leaders of the opposition parties, and even on the times to keep his mouth shut. It is not rare for the prime minister to consult with reporters before an election about the "whats, whens, and hows" needed to assure public support, how to improve the party image, or even the image of the prime minister himself. During an election campaign, the prime minister often asks reporters for their opinion regarding the LDP's chances. The prime minister even consults with reporters, and more significantly, one of the desk members or political editors, on cabinet matters concerning international events. One reporter for a national newspaper recalled that he once advised former Prime Minister Ohira, who was about to leave for an overseas trip to meet with President Jimmy Carter of the United States, to attend the funeral of Yugoslavia's late leader Marshal Tito first, advice that the prime minister followed. Another political reporter mentioned that he was consulted regarding a speech former Prime Minister Nakasone intended to deliver in the White House. And a political editor disclosed: "I am a very welcome visitor in the prime minister's office. Everybody there knows that when I want to meet the prime minister alone, that means that I have something important to tell him and it will be better for him to listen."

Reporters, desk members, and political editors revealed during interviews that the advice and suggestions they give Diet members may have great influence under certain circumstances. For example, if a Diet member is confronted with a given issue for the first time, has little experience, and cannot foresee the possible implications, a reporter's suggestions are heeded. Or, when a Diet member is confronted with a new subject but has not yet gained enough information to first deal with the subject appropriately, reporters are called upon—especially those with long experience concerning Diet activities—to acquire data about the related issue. Or when a Diet member, such as a committee member, wonders about the possible reactions of colleagues in other political parties, or the public, to a new policy proposal, reporters are able to supply the possible reactions on the spot and in the most neutral way. And when a Diet member has received many suggestions concerning a specific issue and cannot decide which to choose, a reporter's opinion and advice may be solicited and followed.

Newspaper companies are fully aware of the situation in which reporters function as advisers and provide endless suggestions to Diet members. Some members of the political desk have expressed dissatisfaction about it, though they themselves occasionally give advice to Diet members. They claim that they instruct their reporters, as much as possible, to keep a certain distance from Diet members, to keep the relationship a working relationship. One member of the political desk commented:

> When new reporters come to our desk, we instruct them to be in close touch with Diet members and, at the same time, remain neutral. But because of the keen competition with rival reporters from rival companies, they really need to have very close relationships with Diet members and provide suggestions and advice; otherwise, they will get no news at all.

Reporters not only provide useful advice and feedback to Diet members but also provide them with an endless amount of information, as will be discussed in the next chapter.

Part 4
Political Dynamics and the
Role of Reporters

CHAPTER 7

Information and Political Reality: Diet Members' Views of Political Communicators

Diet Members and Information

Information is an essential tool in the work of every public official and, as revealed by Allison (1971), Janis (1972), and Kennedy (1968), elected politicians are highly dependent on the process of communication. Deutsch (1963, 182–85), for example, noted that information is necessary to achieve government's goals, evaluate demands and support from the public and other political participants, and monitor feedback concerning their activities. In the case of British members of Parliament, as revealed by Barker and Rush (1970, 386), legislators require two types of information: facts about situations and knowledge of what the concerned people feel or intend to do regarding these situations. As a rule, the politician's primary concern will be related to information about his or her current purpose. In Japan, the existence of many political parties, party factions, pressure or interest groups, and various branches of the bureaucracy, all striving to achieve their various goals, turn the political world into an environment in which information is a precondition as well as the ultimate factor for all political activities.

For two significant reasons, Diet members in particular must be keenly aware of all details of the latest political events. The first reason has a cultural connotation related to the distinctive mode of Japanese ethics that places strong emphasis on harmony in the relationships between members of a group. The Japanese deem the individual to less significant than the group and value a group player more than a solo star. Emphasis is allocated to collective aspects and much importance is attached to group dynamism and collective decisions. Differences of opinion, the Japanese believe, can best be resolved, not by argument or voting, but by seeking a consensus in a slow, cumbersome way. To prevent open clashes of opinions, the Japanese prefer subtle ways of adjusting conflicts and achieving consensus. Leaders in Japan invest much time and energy in efforts to promote the collective interest by practicing a preliminary process, *nemawashi*, which consists of broad consultations in endeavors to enhance empathy and cooperation between all the disparate interests of all members of the group; of attempts to cool emotional conflicts;

and of constant efforts to achieve and maintain *wa ishiki* (harmony concious-ness) in relations with other participants and groups (Feldman 1992). *Nema-washi* has two goals. The first is to maintain harmonious human relations by giving full and emphatic consideration to others in a working situation. The second goal has to do with the general and ultimate purpose to be achieved and decision making. By careful personal interactions, which take place in intimate informal settings, the Japanese obtain complete support for a certain issue and the formal meetings proceed without controversy (Hashiguchi et al. 1977; Kato 1977).

Focusing on the political environment in this regard, because Japanese tradition and practice both place far less emphasis on individual leaders and leadership than do Western societies, one finds that Diet members, especially those in leading positions, exert much effort to first acquire sufficient informa-tion about their partners in the political game and then reduce the number of controversial bills introduced in the Diet and prevent public debate over issues. This is done on two different—but closely related—levels: one in-volves other Diet members, either in one's own party or party faction, in a rival party, or in factions within the same political party—all in the so-called *Nagatachô* circle; and the other involves bureaucrats from various govern-ment bureaus in the so-called *Kasumigaseki* circle.

On the first level, Diet members discuss various pending issues with their colleagues and endeavor to resolve them based on party unity and harmony. Several procedures concerning the routine work of both chambers of the Diet are usually decided by voting in a plenary session. In fact, however, such votes merely ratify decisions made before the session began by negotiations between representatives of each party. This type of negotiation takes the form of *misshitsu seiji* (political decisions made behind closed doors), or *machiai-seiji* (behind-the-scenes politics), which involve secret political consultations among the various partners in the political game. Through endless meetings conducted far from the public eye, members of various political groups, including ruling and opposition party representatives, quietly present to each other their opinions and stances on specific issues and express their support or objection to the views of other members on concrete topics. In such negotia-tions, they discuss how each party will be represented in the leadership posts, the duration of an extraordinary or special Diet session, and the seats of the party Diet members. Some bills introduced in the Diet are also first negotiated by representatives of the various political parties and are jointly endorsed by all the parties involved (Kishimoto 1981).

Perhaps more significant in this context are the constant contacts and negotiations that are held among the various factions of the ruling party. Historically, the intraparty factions of the LDP have been responsible for creating a competitive environment from which a prime minister would arise.

For this reason, faction leaders are always involved in maneuvering and bargaining, intensifying their scramble for power in their consuming goal to achieve the highest political offices in Japan; that of the prime minister (who concurrently serves as LDP president), of the cabinet ministers, and of the three top party executives (the secretary general, the policy affairs research council chairperson, and the chairperson of the executive council). The continued rivalry and intrigues among the leaders of the various factions have brought frequent change to government. For example, Prime Minister Miki Takeo was forced out of office in 1976 by other party leaders furious with him for permitting former Prime Minister Tanaka's arrest and indictment for his involvement in the Lockheed Scandal. Prime Minister Fukuda Takeo was forced out as a result of successful efforts by the Tanaka faction to implement a new presidential primary system to award Tanaka's ally, Ohira Masayoshi, the prime ministership. Fukuda and Miki betrayed the Ohira government in 1980 by keeping their faction members out of the Diet during a no-confidence vote sponsored by the opposition parties, bringing down the Ohira administration and, it is widely believed, causing the heart attack that led to Ohira's death 10 days before the election.

To maintain party unity and harmony there is a constant need for exchanging information between the various party factions. This need exists for two interrelated reasons. First, since the Diet members of these factions are elected chiefly for their personal appeal to the electorate, they arrive in the Diet without a fully worked-out party program (Reischauer 1978, 286). To establish general agreement among the Diet members of the various party factions, there is a need for negotiations to adjust opinion and achieve full and complete support for a certain issue. Second, there is no independent voting in the Diet and all Diet members vote according to the decision of the party (Krauss 1989, 52). This means that all the Diet members must communicate first to reach agreement. When Diet members are strongly opposed to the party's position, however, they may not attend a Diet session to avoid voting. This practice led to an unexpected result in May 1980 when, as mentioned, factional rivalry within the LDP kept many members away from the Diet and the opposition parties were able to win a no-confidence vote against Prime Minister Ohira's cabinet, thereby dissolving the House of Representatives.

Frequent negotiations also characterize the second-level relationship between Diet members and bureaucrats from the government bureaus. The bureaucracy is the center of political power in Japan. It is deeply involved in the political process and can engage in policy planning in an organized and systematic way. Although most bills originate within the government bureaus, preliminary negotiations and approval by the ruling and opposition parties is a necessary step in the process. To ensure smooth passage of bills, senior bureaucrats of various ministries present their bills to influential Diet members of the ruling party and explain their content and objectives. Through these contacts, some needed adjustments are made. To win complete support for a certain bill, Diet members of the ruling party and government bureaucrats then conduct informal meetings with the Diet policy committees of each of the opposition parties to discuss the manner and date for the introduction of a bill (Craig 1981).

The second reason for the great need for information by Diet members is related to the distinctive Japanese system for national legislative elections. In particular, the House of Representatives, the most important chamber in determining the reins of government, has a medium-sized electoral district system, electing two to six representatives per district (with one exception, i.e., a one-member district). Regardless of how many representatives are elected from a district, each voter has only one vote, so the winners are those who receive the largest number of votes. Similar patterns of multimember districts with single nontransferable votes also exist in elections for the House of Councillors. At election time, because of the number of candidates seeking office, a politician faces severe competition from many rivals, some of whom even belong to the same political party. One way to assure reelection is to be able, while in office, to produce benefits for the district. Consequently, Diet members devote much attention to and are more interested in individual or local cases—such as bridge improvement; building hospitals, railways, or schools; or broadening roads in the district—than in broad national issues. To be responsive to their supporters in the constituency, Diet members need information about the general mood, demands, and support. All of these help to decide whether to take action, what kind of proposals to put forth, and when and how to shape their activities to provide what their supporters want and need.

On a broader level, political parties as a whole are concerned about various aspects related to the general public. Public opinion polls, for example, are important tools by which Diet members of the ruling party measure public reaction to their policies. Diet members of the opposition parties use them as a vehicle for obtaining ideas about constructing criticism of the ruling party's policies. More importantly, information regarding public opinion enables Diet members to identify areas of lack of support for their party. This data is extraordinarily important, particularly just before an election. By identifying decreased support in a specific area, Diet members can take measures to gain more popularity for their political party. They may, for example, dispatch some leaders of their party to visit disaffected areas to make speeches or to talk with local residents to mobilize support.

Information, then, is an important factor for a Diet member to ensure reelection and function properly in the political labyrinth. To maintain political momentum, Diet members must achieve the full support of their counterparts. Through careful prearrangements, they strive to reach a predetermined conclusion acceptable to the ruling party, to the factions within this party, opposition parties, and government bureaucrats. This demands constant updating of information about what the other political parties or the bureaucracy have done, or their intentions, in order to consider the next feasible step or the most appropriate reaction. Information facilitates smooth functioning in Japanese politics. In other words, Diet members need constant, open access to a range of information about their rivals and partners in the political game to successfully coordinate matters dealing with policy and leadership and to prevent open confrontation. To receive the information significant to their work, several channels are available to Diet members. This chapter examines these channels, particularly the role newspaper reporters play as sources of information for Diet members. The significance of the role of reporters in this context is discussed by comparing Diet members' exposure to information obtained from reporters versus their exposure to the mass media channels in general and the perusal of printed media in particular.

Information from Newspapers

General and Preferred Reading Materials

Diet members are exposed daily to various electronic news media and monitor a wide range of daily and weekly newspapers, periodicals, and professional journals.[1] As many as 346 Diet members (86 percent, of 402 total members studied) regularly read at least one of the popular weeklies published by the "big five" newspapers (e.g., *Shûkan* [weekly] *Asahi, Shûkan Yomiuri, Shûkan Sankei*), other popular weeklies (*Shûkan Gendai, Shûkan Shinchô*), or the so-called intellectual magazines (*Bungei Shunjû*, and *Chûô Kôron*). In addition, 327 Diet members (81.3 percent) ordinarily read economic, social, and various cultural magazines either related to their work in the Diet as a whole or to committees on which they serve. These magazines deal mainly with matters such as agriculture, taxation, education, military, or international affairs, providing the reader with the latest information about, and detailed analyses of, specific issues, and providing many ideas about what to do regarding these issues. Similarly, 302 Diet members (75.1 percent) commonly read their own political party's publications (*tô kikanshi*) and similar material published by other political parties. Thus, as in the case of legislators in the United States

---

1. The questions employed here were: "Which of the following newspapers does the Diet member regularly read? The *Yomiuri;* the *Asahi;* the *Mainichi;* the *Nihon Keizai;* the *Sankei;* local newspaper; other _____"; and, "From which newspaper does the Diet member gain the most valuable information for his/her work? Indicate up to three of the following newspapers: The *Yomiuri;* the *Asahi;* the *Mainichi;* the *Nihon Keizai;* the *Sankei;* local newspaper; other _____."

(Dunn 1969; Weiss 1974), printed matter is a useful source of information for Japanese Diet members and covers a very broad range.

All Diet members place great emphasis on daily newspapers, especially the "big five," and on local newspapers. These are considered useful adjuncts to everyday political activities, depending on the issue of interest and the political climate. At times, the daily newspapers serve Diet members as valuable sources of information,[2] for acquiring knowledge about the activities and intentions of various political groups as well as the bureaucracy, for ascertaining public opinion, and for keeping a finger on the pulse of their constituencies. Figure 7-1 shows the preferences of Diet members for reading specific newspapers.[3]

As the figure shows, 356 Diet members (88.5 percent of those who participated in this survey) indicated a preference for at least one of the "big five," and the remainder indicated that they preferred to read local or bloc newspapers; only two Diet members indicated a prefererce for other newspapers. Looking closely at figure 7-1, two prominent preferences are discernible: 176 (43.8 percent) Diet members read the *Asahi* and 80 (19.9 percent) read the *Nihon Keizai* (or *Nikkei*), that is, more than 60 percent of the Diet members read only these two newspapers. Less popular is the *Yomiuri* (preferred by 11.4 percent), followed by local newspapers (9.9 percent), the *Sankei* (7.7 percent), and the *Mainichi* (5.7 percent). This tendency shows that preference by Diet members is not based solely on a particular newspaper's circulation. Although the *Yomiuri* has the largest circulation in the nation, the first preference is for the *Asahi,* followed by the *Nikkei.* As may be recalled, a parallel finding was also observed concerning Diet members' tendencies to meet reporters from these newspapers; that is, reporters from the *Asahi* have much more frequent contact with Diet members than do those from the rival *Yomiuri.*

That most Diet members read and heed a relatively small number of newspapers (such as the *Asahi* and *Nihon Keizai*) may have some significance in the way the Diet members interpret events. Presumably, the larger the number of newspapers Diet members read, the more ideas, viewpoints, and opinions they can have on particular topics and events; this, in turn, may enable them to evaluate and judge various events from a broader perspective. Nonetheless, the majority of Diet members expose themselves to only two newspapers. A possible explanation for this tendency is rooted in the concept (discussed previously) that contends that since the number of sources of news

---

2. The question was: "Generally speaking, what are your sources of information concerning your political activities?"

3. The question was: "Which of the following newspapers does the Diet member read most often and heed most closely? The *Yomiuri;* the *Asahi;* the *Mainichi;* the *Nihon Keizai;* the *Sankei;* local newspaper; other _____."

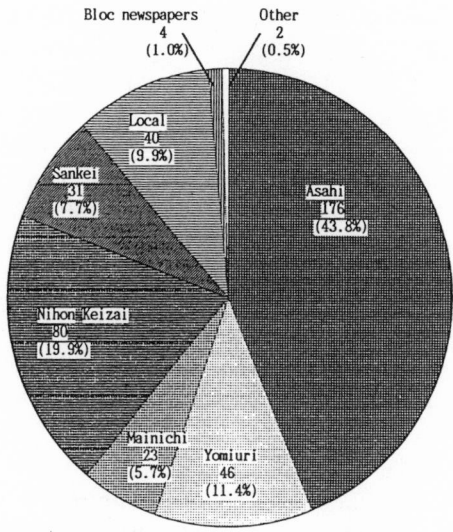

Fig. 7-1. Preferences of Diet members for reading specific newspapers. Figures indicate the number and percentage of Diet members who read a certain newspaper.

is limited, and because reporters gather the news together by following formal and informal customs, which results in the same stories in different newspapers, most published information is, more or less, of the same nature in all the newspapers and therefore there is no need to read different newspapers to acquire information about a certain issue.

The tendency of the majority to read the *Asahi* is possibly due to its image as the most prestigious daily newspaper in Japan. Nevertheless, it may be related to a more practical explanation. Comparatively speaking, the *Asahi* tends to present more detailed political coverage and analyses, some of which may be of use to the routine work of a Diet member. That the *Asahi* allocates more reportage to political affairs than any other national newspaper may reflect the tendency of its reporters to be in constant contact and to meet Diet members more often than reporters from any other newspaper. One explanation for why so many Diet members read *Nikkei* is that since it presents more economic and business news, Diet members use it as a source of information for their work on various Diet committees. This does not necessarily mean that Diet members read it only for this reason. Rather, many Diet members read the *Nikkei* because of its emphasis on economic affairs, and as a supplementary channel to the *Asahi* to obtain diversified political and economic information. Variance of emphasis in the coverage of issues by these two newspapers can provide Diet members with a complete picture of world affairs and recent business and political developments in the domestic arena.

Another prominent point in figure 7-1 concerns local and bloc newspapers. Since bloc newspapers can also be considered local newspapers, the exposure of Diet members to these newspapers is rather low, considering the important fact that most Diet members are elected from local districts. Diet members are usually kept away from their constituencies by their Diet duties in Tokyo, and the constituency's newspaper is one of the most common channels through which they can acquire information about the local electorate and voter demands and support. Only 44 Diet members (10.9 percent) indicated that they read local and bloc newspapers.

Selective Exposure to Newspapers

Diet members have a number of specific reasons that motivate them to monitor the printed media. These are correlated with several variables, such as personal interest, legislative work, and contact with interest or support groups. For example, several Diet members I spoke to tend to look in the newspapers to obtain information about the electorate and the general mood in their district. Reading local or bloc newspapers and, in some cases, the local pages (*chihô-ban*) of one of the national newspapers enables these Diet members to acquire information about tendencies and demands in their constituency. As previously discussed, junior Diet members have a propensity to monitor these newspapers but also admit that although the local newspapers are important, they are not their exclusive sources of information. Monitoring local newspapers can provide Diet members with useful knowledge about supporters' activities and needs, but even daily reading cannot provide fully accurate evaluations of the existing public mood. This partly explains the small percentage of Diet members who monitor local newspapers. Diet members thus evaluate the importance of local newspapers as parallel to the activities of their own offices in their districts, which regularly provide them with information, and as an additional source to the meetings they hold regularly with delegations or representatives of their constituencies who visit them in their offices in *Nagatachô*. This attitude is especially prevalent among Diet members elected from constituencies distant from Tokyo, who host—from time to time—representatives of their supporters. During these meetings they obtain information or detect trends existing within their constituences.

Diet members also read newspapers to obtain information about the actual state of political, social, and economic matters. Public opinion polls, regularly conducted by the national newspapers, are an important source of information about the general social or political situation. In fact, most political parties cannot conduct public surveys on their own. Even if they do, interviews do not always reveal the respondents' real intentions toward that particular party, whereas respondents do tend to reveal their intentions in the framework of research conducted by newspapers, which are considered politically neutral by the electorate. Thus, political parties, as much as individual Diet members, tend to rely on survey data to shape much of their regular daily activities, especially preelection strategies and tactics.

Diet members also read newspapers to obtain some insights about how the press reports wrongdoings of the government and about media opinions of the general functioning of the cabinet. This is especially prevalent among Diet members from the opposition parties, notably the SDPJ. Several of these Diet members regard newspapers as a long-lasting source for useful ideas about corruption of government officials, lack of leadership by the LDP, and wrong policy decisions. Special heed is paid by these Diet members not only to the regular political stories but, and perhaps more significantly, to certain columns in the newspapers. For example, some are attracted to the editorial columns published daily by every newspaper. Others tend to read daily feature columns written by newspeople or columns written by prominent critics, scholars, economists, or bureaucrats. By reading such columns, Diet members can get an idea and become acquainted with the interpretations, commentaries, and analyses of reporters, prominent persons, or specialists in a specific field. By scrutinizing the implications of a specific policy or focusing attention on the problems or difficulties that proposals have dealt with inadequately, these columns give Diet members a useful springboard for reaction, especially against the ruling party. They are useful sources to cite when appealing to their political counterparts. Finally, Diet members are motivated to read newspapers to find out how they and their political party or faction are exposed to the public. Among the Diet members who cited this as the reason that motivates them to read the national newspapers were upper-echelon Diet members such as the secretaries general and spokespeople from the SDPJ, DSP, and CGP; the heads of two Diet committees; the LDP vice-secretary general; and a leader of a party faction.

Surprisingly, Diet members do not usually spend much time reading newspapers.[4] As many as 283 Diet members (70.4 percent) spend only up to 15 minutes daily reading newspapers, which is less than the average time ordinary citizens spend reading them, as discussed in chapter 2. Another 91 Diet members (22.6 percent) read newspapers for between 15 and 30 minutes daily, and only 13 Diet members (3.2 percent) spend more than 30 minutes

---

4. The question was: "How many minutes a day does the Diet member spend reading the following newspapers? (Rank each newspaper by using the following scale. (1) = just looks without reading; (2) = 1 to 5 minutes; (3) = 6 to 15 minutes; (4) = 16 to 30 minutes; (5) = more than 30 minutes): the *Yomiuri;* the *Asahi;* the *Mainichi;* the *Nihon Keizai;* the *Sankei;* local newspaper; other _____; unknown."

daily reading newspapers they receive at their office. Coincidentally, all of them are members of the House of Councillors. Commenting on this finding a member of the Lower House said:

Diet members who belong to the House of Councillors have more time to read the papers than members of the other House. They are not as busy in meeting their voters, especially if one takes into consideration the fact that half of them were elected from a national constituency, which means that they were not elected by the direct electorate.

Fifteen Diet members (3.7 percent) considered as sources of information (as listed in table 4-1) by the press, who took part in this survey, spend the least amount of time reading newspapers. These upper-echelon Diet members tend to read newspapers for only up to 5 minutes daily, or they just glance at the headlines without reading the articles in detail. In other words, Diet members who are sources of information for the press do not spend much time reading newspapers. When meeting several of these Diet members and asking them to elaborate on this tendency, their views were almost identical, summarized by one LDP member who said:

These Diet members are fully active in all processes and policies in their political party, or in the Diet, and they are aware of all details to the extent that they inform the press. Thus, they have no need to read the information they have given to reporters.

That many of these Diet members are assisted by a secretary who marks relevant articles that the Diet member just glances at also explains why they do not need to spend much time reading newspapers. Another explanation is that time spent monitoring newspapers is correlated with the availability of and contact with other sources. With many other sources, the press is less necessary. This concept is discussed below.

Information from Reporters

Direct Sources of Information

Generally speaking, every Diet member is constantly at an information crossroads. Information flows nonstop between all the political groups, i.e., parties and party factions taking part in the political game at *Nagatachô,* and communications connect all these groups with the bureaucrats at *Kasumigaseki.* Individual Diet members may experience no special trouble in obtaining the latest information regarding any political or bureaucratic event from one of their colleagues. Diet members are in constant contact with their colleagues, especially those belonging to the same political party, or in the case of the LDP to the same party faction. Members of the same political group share a basic political philosophy and similar goals, so accessibility is less formal and an individual Diet member can talk with them more openly than with other colleagues. Nevertheless, Diet members also have constant contact with Diet members from other political groups who need to communicate and obtain information about various topics.

For reasons already discussed, Japanese culture encourages the establishment of communications between all political counterparts. As a result, the leaders of various political parties, or their representatives, meet often and negotiations are conducted during these meetings. The LDP and the opposition parties conduct endless political bargaining and discuss proposed legislation and the budget through informal organs such as the Diet policy committees. Constant contact also characterizes the relationship between the ruling LDP and the cabinet. This is partly because the LDP reviews and debates new laws and policies of the cabinet, including the budget, before they are introduced in the Diet. If the deliberation process on policy proposals of the cabinet is incomplete, the proposals will not be approved for introduction in the Diet (Craig, 1981).

Communication is the most important factor connecting the factions of the ruling party. As mentioned, in order to achieve complete support for almost every pending issue, there is a need to coordinate opinion among the members of the various factions. Each party faction regularly communicates with other factions within the party through meetings attended by all the faction leaders or their representatives. In some cases, faction leaders exchange views and opinions regarding an issue by telephone, but most contacts involving the faction leaders are in the form of face-to-face meetings. There are cases, however, known in journalistic jargon as a "political crisis," in which the gap between the basic viewpoints held by the factions' leaders toward an issue is wide and almost unbridgeable. There is slim chance of bridging the gap even if the faction leaders meet and talk to each other directly. In such a case, leaders are unable to access information easily due to their public standing. Thus, there is a need to lay the groundwork as fast as possible for the faction leaders to meet and to assure smooth talks between them. Under these circumstances, proper attention must be given to the selection of the person(s) who will do the *nemawashi*, the mechanism designed to promote group harmony. Such a person must have a knowledge of the disputed issue and be able to socialize easily to create the special "atmosphere" needed to establish smooth interpersonal transactions. He or she should not be, as Kato (1977) noted, too high in rank, but should know the desires of the top level as well as the rank-and-file. Typically, second-echelon Diet members of each faction consisting of six or seven veteran Diet members well versed in Diet activities, establish communication links. They go around the various factions, talk to their counterparts at length, and try to find out the true intentions of a rival faction leader. By presenting each other with their leader's opinion, they try to persuade and obtain concessions by which they will be able to achieve a mutual goal. As soon as a possible agreement is seen and the crisis situation seems to be resolved, the second-echelon Diet member's role is completed and the faction leaders can meet and talk directly.

Diet members also have contact with government bureaucrats and obtain information through several channels. Upper-echelon Diet members from the ruling and opposition parties, such as secretaries general, heads of committees, and faction leaders, can obtain a variety of information during direct meetings with government bureaucrats. Other Diet members can host and talk with bureaucrats at their party or faction meeting. From time to time they invite bureaucrats to their party's weekly meetings and receive information and updates about certain issues that these particular bureaucrats work on or about the activity of their bureau in general. In comparison to Diet members from the opposition parties those in the ruling party have more institutionalized, deep, and solid contacts with government bureaucrats, and therefore the LDP is better informed about these bureaus. Two reasons illustrate this point. First, many LDP Diet members (about 25 percent in the Lower House and 40 percent in the Upper House) are former bureaucrats (Pempel 1984).[5] These Diet members usually serve as members of the Diet committees corresponding to the ministries in which they previously served and often act as channels of communication to transmit ministry opinion predominantly to the LDP (and also LDP opinion to the ministries). Second, since the LDP and the bureaucracy share power and formulate policy together, they are mutually dependent. The bureaucracy depends on LDP influence to win budget allocations and have legislation enacted, and bureaucrats take special care over measures that may affect the interest of the LDP as a whole (Odawara 1984). LDP Diet members can thus obtain information from bureaucrats more readily than can members from the opposition parties.

In addition to the direct communications which yield updates on political parties, party factions, and the bureaucracy, there is still a need for information about these institutions from other sources. There are several reasons for this. First, even though Diet members have contact with other Diet members,

---

5. At the time of the present study there were 123 Diet members who used to work in government offices. In the case of the ruling party, for example, there were 113 such members. Of them, there were 34 ex-bureaucrats in the Tanaka faction, 30 in the Suzuki faction, 25 in the Fukuda faction, 7 in the Komoto faction, 7 in the Nakasone faction, and 10 Diet member ex-bureaucrats who did not belong to any faction. In the opposition parties, 5 were in the DSP, 3 in the SDPJ, and 2 Diet members from the CGP were also ex-bureaucrats.

they are always afraid of being led astray by their colleagues, especially by those from other factions of the LDP. Thus, they constantly look for a neutral source, one having, as one LDP Diet member disclosed, "No hidden motives or intentions to provide biased or selected information."

Second, even if a certain colleague can provide information, there is no assurance of their availability at every moment of the day because of their work engagements and commitments. Also, the information that can be obtained from a colleague might be limited in accordance with their political activities or personal interest. Diet members, especially those in the upper echelon, are in great need of wide-ranging and profound information about various topics from readily available sources. Thus, colleagues are not always the ideal solution. Another reason concerns the second-echelon Diet members in the LDP who have contacts with their counterparts in other party factions. These second-echelon Diet members—for some opportunistic reasons—do not always give the whole truth to the upper-echelon Diet members. The latter, for their part, cannot always access information easily due to the reason previously mentioned. Thus, they may find themselves in a situation where, to take action, they must verify information received from their aides.

Finally, through contact with government bureaucrats, Diet members, especially those from the LDP, can gather information. But they are seldom able to obtain information directly about the general mood and the real feelings in a certain bureau toward a specific matter, although such information is of special importance for evaluating the possibility of further legislation and implementation of related bills. Such information is also of great importance to the *zoku giin,* a group or "tribe" of Diet members who share interest in a particular area of public policy. They need this information to calculate their future activities while working for the interests of their client groups. For these reasons, Diet members search for other sources, preferring to obtain much of their needed information from reporters.

Reporters Versus Other Sources

Before discussing the nature and scope of information that reporters can provide to Diet members, it is worthwhile mentioning that obtaining information from reporters is stimulated by two main factors. The first is the easy accessibility—the open door—reporters have to most Diet members, and the second is the tendency of reporters to meet with Diet members frequently. These two interrelated factors enable reporters to obtain wide-ranging stores of information from the many Diet members they meet with; and, of course, to provide this to many other Diet members they have contact with. A reporter from the political desk of a national daily newspaper can (and many of them do) meet 10 or more Diet members or bureaucrats in one day, and obtain a significant amount of information from each of them. By afternoon, after participating in some press conferences, reading the handouts or other reports sent to their newspaper's desk at the press club, exchanging opinions (and information) with colleagues from their own or a rival news agency, and receiving some hints on certain political activity that the *ban* is supposed to cover at night, reporters may have detailed information about every current aspect of the political activities at both *Nagatachô* and *Kasumigaseki*. They now know what has happened during the day in every corner of Japanese politics and, even more significantly, what further implications may follow the latest event.

At the same time, Diet members at the end of the workday, may have met delegations from their district, lunched with representatives of labor unions or other groups whose interests they represent, talked with representatives of financial circles about ways to obtain political funds, held a meeting with their party's colleagues at the party headquarters, or sat in on one of the Diet's committee meetings (which meet two or three times a week) or a plenary session of the Diet.[6] In each of those activities, the Diet member must concentrate on different issues and devote much attention to different subjects, from local affairs, financial interests, and support groups, to party policy or plans for the next Diet session. But they have not had any opportunity to obtain information about, say, what the SDPJ or DSP leaders think about their party's proposals regarding liberalization of the Japanese market. They also do not know the latest general trends in the LDP factions and the general mood among officials from the Agriculture and Forestry Ministry as further developments stemming from situations that existed the day before. All this is essential information, particularly if one is on the party's or Diet's agriculture and forestry subcommittee.

For several reasons a Diet member may feel that a reporter, in particular, is a good source of related information (or a good channel for verifying information received from colleagues). In the eyes of most Diet members, reporters are sufficiently neutral, without any special opportunistic tendencies, to tell them the real intentions of their partners in the political game. Reporters are the easiest and fastest way to obtain information. At times when their colleagues are in a meeting or do not have time because of other engagements, Diet members can initiate a meeting with a reporter, or play host to a reporter who has come to their office in order to solicit information. Reporters' daily professional access to various domains assures upper-echelon Diet members that reporters can obtain the real information and readily pro-

---

6. When the Diet is in session, floor debate on bills is scheduled every Tuesday, Thursday, and Friday for the House of Representatives and every Monday, Wednesday, and Friday for the House of Councillors.

vide it to them, whereas second-echelon Diet members may keep certain information for themselves. In addition to information, reporters can also give Diet members good advice about what to do with this information. These factors elucidate the real situation: that many Diet members tend to believe more in what they hear from reporters than what they hear from colleagues, even from those in their own political party or party faction. This plays an important role in Japanese political life, as will be discussed later.

Diet members also obtain knowledge about various government bureaus through, and with the assistance of, reporters. The information that reporters can provide to Diet members is of special significance for several reasons. First, through the press clubs at the government bureaus, reporters, in general, have more constant, daily contacts with officials. These contacts are more frequent than those of most Diet members and, more significantly, more than those of Diet members from the opposition parties. Through frequent meetings, reporters can constantly update Diet members about the activities of bureaucrats in general, and in particular the function of certain bureaucrats the Diet member has a special interest in. Second, bureaucrats tend to talk with reporters more freely and openly than they do when meeting most Diet members. The fact that their job is to gather information enables the reporters to ask bureaucrats many questions and to obtain a considerable amount of data, whereas if a bureaucrat is asked the same questions by a Diet member, the bureaucrat may suspect the real intention of the Diet member and may not disclose all the details. As a result, bureaucrats tend to reveal much more information to reporters than to Diet members. Furthermore, like Diet members, bureaucrats also want to establish and maintain good relations with reporters. Through this relationship they strive to achieve favorable coverage. They also like to receive information about significant and decisive issues related to their work (e.g., reactions of influential Diet members to their current work on certain bills), to avoid antagonism and to alter these bills to ensure their passage. Because government bureaucrats want to maintain good relations with the press, they often tend to play host, chat with reporters from the press clubs near their offices, assist them, and tell reporters, as much as they can, about developments related to their work. Thus, a reporter can collect a considerable amount of information that Diet members have an interest in through informal contact with public servants.

Another significant advantage reporters have in dealing with bureaucrats is the fact that they can meet many bureaucrats from all levels and obtain information from all of them. They differ in this respect from most Diet members who can obtain information only from bureaucrats at a certain level, such as the head of a division or section, depending on their own position in their party or in the Diet. Thus, reporters may possess broader knowledge about a specific bureau and can follow the progress of a certain issue from its drafting stage until it gains approval by the upper echelon of the bureau. Diet members are unable to constantly follow such processes and the information they can obtain is limited and narrow in scope—according to the bureaucrats with whom they have contact. Reporters can meet bureaucrats anytime as part of their job, whereas Diet members usually must arrange an appointment beforehand to obtain information from them. Thus, information from the bureaucracy flows faster and in a more reliable way to Diet members through reporters. Finally, reporters can give Diet members the real mood, the *honne*, in the bureaucracy concerning a certain issue and the true reactions of bureaucrats to a proposed bill. Bureaucrats, in order not to intimidate or anger Diet members, may pretend that everything is going smoothly, but with reporters they behave naturally and tell the truth, even to the point of complaining.

The transfer of information from one Diet member, party faction, political party, or bureaucrat to another is not a simple process. First, as previously explained, reporters who cover specific activities, e.g., faction reporters, cannot easily meet Diet members from other party factions or political parties. Because each faction is like a "village" with its own rules and customs, each member of the faction is extremely sensitive to "outsiders," including reporters who cover other factions (as discussed later, they consider the reporters who cover their political group as "one of us"). Thus, when meeting with "outside" reporters, faction members will not disclose any information to them that might be considered important. Second, reporters who cover a certain government bureau do not usually have frequent contact with Diet members. As a result, they do not know exactly what kind of information the Diet members are looking for and when. Thus, the process of transmitting information is a rather complex network involving various reporters and deserves close examination. The discussion in this chapter is thus limited to the significance of the information reporters provide to Diet members, and the complexity of the transmission of information is discussed in detail later.

Generally speaking, the need for information from reporters is dependent on several variables. Most notable is the political climate at a given time. Information flowing back and forth between the ruling party and the opposition parties on routine days is essential for Diet members. Diet members' need for information from reporters is most crucial in a Diet session, especially just before voting on specific bills; at times of cabinet reshuffles; and at times of so-called political crisis when faction leaders cannot communicate directly. In these instances, political parties want to feel out the stand of the other parties, how the ruling LDP will react, and what impact can be foreseen on the bureaucracy. Thus, Diet members from the LDP want reporters to tell them about reactions in the opposition parties to a specific bill and under what circumstances they may support it. Diet members of opposition parties want to know how the other opposition parties will vote in the Diet concerning a specific issue. And Diet members of the opposition parties in general try to obtain data from reporters about trends in the various LDP factions and on interpersonal relationships between the faction leaders of the ruling party.

The need for certain information depends much on the political party or faction one belongs to. Significantly, Diet members of the LDP put much emphasis on certain information, whereas Diet members of the opposition parties would like to obtain other types of information. Careful study of the specific information needed by the political parties reveals that Diet members of the opposition parties constantly look for information concerning the other opposition parties, and their need for information about the ruling party is of less concern. This tendency derives from their often-used strategy to work against the ruling party in, for example, an attempt to use a certain technique to delay or obstruct the deliberation of a specific committee or the full house. Their need for information about the LDP is due to their eagerness to know what countermeasures or initiatives the ruling LDP will take as its next step. LDP Diet members would like to obtain information from reporters about the opposition parties, but are also interested in information about the other factions within the party. They want to know what tactics the opposition parties intend to use at a certain time and how the other parties evaluate some of the bills they intend to introduce; whether there is a need for minimal changes to satisfy a bill's opponents or whether they must push the bill through by sheer numbers of votes. At the same time, and even more significantly, Diet members of the ruling party also want information about the other party factions for the reasons discussed.

The different types of information a certain political group needs is reflected more significantly in regard to the bureaucracy. In the case of the ruling party, for instance, a party faction in which most Diet members are former bureaucrats, like the one headed by Miyazawa or Takeshita, regularly uses those Diet members' connections to obtain information about specific bureaus. These particular party factions, for example, have good contacts and corresponding interest in the finance, construction, and transportation ministries, while other party factions may have an interest in other bureaus. The former bureaucrats who are now Diet members in those party factions are the sources of information for their factions. From this point of view, these specific party factions do not need more channels of information about the bureaucracy. Individual Diet members and other party factions and parties who seek data from the bureaucracy but have no former bureaucrats depend heavily on reporters for such information.

Comparison among Diet Members

The need for information (and advice) obtained directly from reporters generally exists among all Diet members. The nature of the needed information differs by Diet member, however. It depends on the status and post the particular Diet member holds in a political party or faction, or in the Diet, in line with their personal interest and, of course, the nature of the contact they have with a certain reporter. In general, each Diet member is eager to obtain information and advice from reporters. Not all Diet members have frequent meetings with reporters, however. The Diet experience—and consequently the political post held—plays an important role in determining much of their contact with reporters.

Obtaining information from reporters, from this viewpoint, may also vary depending on the number of times elected to the Diet. In other words, the greater the experience (and position) Diet members have, the more active and responsible a role they play in the political process, thus, the more frequently they meet with reporters. Through these meetings reporters can serve as sources of information. Except for advice and suggestions related to their routine work, not all Diet members need the kind of information reporters can provide. Even if certain information is obtained by Diet members from re-porters, they cannot always make good use of it because of, say, the limited range of their activities and their inability to play any decision-making role in their party faction or opposition party. Thus, it is assumed that for Diet members who have less experience in the Diet, conventional channels for gaining general information, such as newspapers, are sufficient. Those who have been elected more times have already developed other channels—such as reporters—for obtaining specific information they need. Table 7-1 outlines the four main channels—newspapers, government bureaucrats, political party and party faction colleagues, and reporters—that Diet members rely on ac-cording to the number of times they have been elected to the Diet.[7]

Table 7-1 reveals that there is a correlation between the number of times a Diet member has been elected and the contact with bureaucrats. Three groups can be distinguished. The first group consists of those elected up to three times, and about 18.7 percent of these have contact with bureaucrats. The second group consists of those elected from four to seven times and about 50.2 percent of these have contact with bureaucrats. The third group consists of those elected eight or more times, and about 83.3 percent of these have contact with bureaucrats. The third group consists of upper-echelon Diet members who are prominent in the decision-making process of their party and the Diet, almost all of whom are sources of information. These Diet members particularly need contact with bureaucrats to carry out their work. Thus, the length of experience in the Diet and the positions that Diet members hold in

---

7. The question was: "Which of the following sources do you use most often to obtain the information you need for your regular, daily work as a Diet member?: newspapers; colleagues from other political parties or party factions; government bureaucrats; newspeople; your secre-taries. Check as many sources as you use."

their political parties, party factions, or in the Diet, determine contact with bureaucrats and dependence on them for needed information.

A second prominent factor outlined in table 7-1 concerns the use of newspapers. In this case, Diet experience can also play a crucial role. The more times Diet members are elected, the less they tend to depend on obtaining information from newspapers. Those elected five or more times do not usually use newspapers as sources of information. In contrast to the findings concerning newspapers is the attitude taken by Diet members toward colleagues from other political parties, party factions, and reporters, i.e., that the length of experience in the Diet determines not only their contact with colleagues and reporters but also their views of these people as information sources. Thus, those elected up to four times do not tend to consider colleagues or reporters as sources of information. There are two possible explanations for this attitude. First, junior Diet members do not have constant contact with reporters, and even if they do meet with reporters (mostly from the local newspapers) they have no need to obtain any information from them. None of these Diet members hold any key position in their party faction, political party, or in the Diet; and they are not involved in the decision-making processes in their party. Thus, the information that reporters could provide is outside their domain. As their main source of information, newspapers play an important role at this stage of their career.

Second, since these junior Diet members are not involved in decision

TABLE 7-1. Relationship between Using Certain Information Sources (Mean) Most Often and Frequency of Election to Diet (in percentages)

Number of Times Elected		Source			
		Newspapers	Colleagues from Other Party/Faction	Government Bureaucrats	Reporters*
1	(N = 10)	100.0	0	20.0	0
2	(N = 13)	100.0	0	7.7	0
3	(N = 7)	85.7	0	28.5	0
4	(N = 6)	50.0	16.6	66.6	16.6
5	(N = 12)	0	33.3	58.3	41.6
6	(N = 7)	0	28.5	42.8	57.1
7	(N = 6)	0	33.3	33.3	50.0
8	(N = 3)	0	66.6	100.0	100.0
9	(N = 2)	0	100.0	50.0	100.0
10 or more	(N = 4)	0	50.0	100.0	75.0
Total	(N = 70)	45.7	21.4	41.4	30.0

Note: Respondents were asked to check as many sources as they used.

*This column refers only to Diet members who meet with reporters at least three times a week.

making in their party, they have no need for contact with Diet members of other political parties or party factions or for negotiating with them as representatives of their own party. This brings about a situation in which most of them depend on colleagues in their own party or party faction as sources of information. Those who participate in negotiations between party factions or other political parties consist of upper-echelon Diet members, leaders of their political entity, and second-echelon Diet members (elected more than five times), who require contact with colleagues in other political parties or party factions for constant updating. This tendency is prominent in table 7-1.

Regarding reporters, Diet members elected four or more times do see reporters as sources of information, and this tendency increases in relation to the number of times elected. Concerning those elected 10 or more times, some of these Diet members do not need the specific information provided by reporters, partly because they have moved beyond the sphere of policy-making activities. Table 7-1 also discloses that, at a certain point, there is a clear shift by Diet members from considering newspapers as sources of information toward a new perspective of considering reporters for that role. As previously stated, being elected four times seems to represent a turning point for Diet members. From that point they begin to take an active role in Diet work. Regarding this sharp shift from reliance on newspapers to reliance on reporters, an explanation can be suggested: those middle- and upper-echelon Diet members who especially need information about the activities of other political participants to maintain political momentum cannot obtain it from newspapers alone. There may be several reasons for this.

First, newspapers do not publish related articles or do not publish them with sufficient details, often following a request of the source not to elaborate on certain information. Second, because these Diet members need such information even before it is published in the press, the fastest and the most reliable source available is reporters. Information from reporters can be obtained at any time during the day, from morning through work hours at the Diet member's office, to "night attacks" at a Diet member's private residence. Moreover, newspapers frequently present what some LDP Diet members termed "only vague information about general political affairs or attitudes." LDP Diet members need detailed information, and as one opined, "The only way we can obtain it is through other sources, and that means reporters."

Another Diet member from the same political party added, "On the surface there is a lot of *tatemae* (formal truth) in newspapers; we need the *honne* (real intention) and the sophisticated political information that we cannot obtain except through direct contact with reporters."

This tendency partly explains the limited exposure upper-echelon Diet members have to the press; they only look to see what was written about them and nothing else. Thus, when asked to estimate the amount of information obtained from newspapers, one leading LDP Diet member, with 20 years of Diet experience, answered: "Ten percent of my information." A vice-secretary general of the same party doubted that even that much information is obtained from the printed media. In short, if information can be obtained from reporters, there is no need to read newspapers.

Contact with reporters in this connection has a significant meaning to most Diet members in that they can obtain information before it is published. This means that they can react and their reaction will be expressed in the newspapers; or they can request a reporter not to disclose some information, requesting embargo for a certain purpose. Contact with reporters can also broaden the Diet member's knowledge concerning other information that was not published in the press, but which would be beneficial to know. Of special importance in this regard are public opinion polls conducted by the national newspapers. The results of these polls are usually published a few days, sometimes a month, after they are completed. Diet members frequently feel that they cannot wait for the results to be published and must know the general tendency as soon as possible, so they initiate meetings with reporters (or desk members) they know, and obtain a word or two from them about this data.

The fact that Diet members constantly obtain information that reporters have obtained in another Diet member's office poses the question of whether Diet members really trust reporters not to disclose to others what they provide to them. Diet members, generally speaking, are inclined to trust reporters in this matter. Reporters, though, tend to inform every Diet member of what they have learned from others, although selectively, depending on the nature of their relationship with specific Diet members. "Some get more, others get less," in the words of one reporter. A Diet member who does not have close relations with a certain reporter cannot expect to hear everything in full detail from that reporter. Many Diet members view this situation with a more jaundiced eye, and they even verify information they obtain from some reporters by talking to other reporters. This approach obliges a Diet member to be in constant contact with many reporters and is linked to the friendly relations they maintain, as will be discussed later.

CHAPTER 8

Consequences of Reporter–Diet
Member Interaction

Reporters in Politics

Reporters as Political Participants

As discussed in the previous chapters, the nature of the contacts between reporters and Diet members, including the motivations many Diet members have for meeting with reporters, poses several questions concerning the role that reporters play in political activities, particularly in shaping and influencing the behavior and attitudes of specific Diet members, political parties, and party factions. As I pointed out in chapter 2, in a previous study related to Japanese journalists, Kim (1981, 90–91) revealed that reporters do not see a role for themselves as participants in government policy-making. From the newspeople's viewpoint, Kim found that any attempt to exert an impact on government policy does not constitute real participation in policy-making. How then do reporters perceive their interaction with individual Diet members and political groups other than "government" groups?

To grasp the reporters' views, I asked them a broader version of the question that Kim employed in his survey, referring not only to government activity but also to the activities of other political groups.[1] In preliminary meetings, journalists were asked to refer to the question of whether reporters play any active role in politics at all. Almost all of the editorial writers and desk members answered in the affirmative. They believe that by writing stories about the political world and adding their own analyses and interpretations, reporters can be considered as playing an active role in political activities. This is because their stories can stimulate the readers' interest in political activities; and this interest, in turn, can encourage the emergence of an attitude, or shape behavior, or influence an existing tendency among the general populace (or voters in particular) toward political parties and Diet members

---

1. The main question asked here was: "Do you see a role for yourself as a participant in government, or any other political group—such as political parties and party factions— activities?"

and their activities. Later I asked the same journalists to particularly refer to the role reporters play vis-à-vis Diet members and political groups. In this case not all the desk members or reporters agreed on their influence on Diet members. Several reporters opined that through their direct and continual contact with many Diet members, especially with those in leading positions, they can exert a certain influence on the Diet members' work, on the way they see and evaluate specific political activity, and on their attitudes toward other political participants and the electorate. These reporters felt that under certain circumstances their influence is reflected in more than a few of the activities in *Nagatachô*.

Specifically, reporters believe that their influence on Diet members and political activities is reflected in two ways. First, by giving advice and feedback to those Diet members with whom they have continual contact, they often figure in changing the precedence and importance that these Diet members devote to certain issues in accordance with the reporters' ideas. Diet members often reject one or more of the issues on their desk, which they intended to handle urgently, and instead give another issue preferential treatment. Taking the views of a reporter into consideration, a Diet member may consult colleagues or other professional people whom he did not plan to talk to in the first place; and he may change his standpoint on a certain matter, or soften or harden his stance. Second, by transferring political information directly to Diet members and increasing their knowledge about issues related to other political participants, such as the activities of other faction or party members, reporters often introduce new factors to those Diet members. Thus, Diet members consider the consequences that may result from new information obtained from reporters and, at times, adopt new approaches or change some of their preliminary decisions.

Overall agreement regarding these functions is not unanimous for all reporters, however. Junior reporters, those who have worked at the political desk of their news agency only five or six years, and veteran reporters, desk members, and editorial writers have different opinions about the nature and scope of their participation and influence on Diet members. To the questions about their participation in political activities as derived from their contacts with Diet members, junior reporters do not report seeing any role for themselves in such a capacity. Their lack of experience impedes junior reporters from giving much useful advice or feedback to Diet members—though most Diet members often want to hear what they think about various issues. Because most of their contacts are new and they have not yet consolidated ties with many of the influential Diet members, junior reporters do not have the opportunity to obtain and thus transfer significant information between Diet members.

Conversely, veteran reporters, desk members, and editorial writers are those who tend to evaluate their function as "being involved" in political activities in the sense that they can influence Diet members' work. In the view of veteran reporters that I met with frequently, two main factors stimulate their role in political activities. The first one is their immediate environment. To most reporters, transmitting information between Diet members is nothing more than one aspect of the competition between reporters to win the trust of Diet members. By transmitting information, reporters do indeed gain the trust of the Diet members involved. One reporter commented on the functions of informing Diet members and serving as mediators between Diet members from various political parties and party factions. "This attitude did not start last year, and is also ascribable to our superiors, members of the political desk, and even editorial writers, all of whom performed the same role for the same reason when they were reporters on the beat."

Moreover, some of these superiors continue to do the same thing today. Thus, from the viewpoint of reporters, such an activity is perceived as part of the political (or journalistic) system, in which newspeople take an active role. Actually, most reporters often feel that the scope of their knowledge about many political activities is broader than that of many of the Diet members they meet; this is to the extent that reporters actually increase the Diet members' knowledge about many events. Due to the reasons outlined in the preceding chapter, reporters can gather more information during a regular workday—from various sources in different locations—than even a leading Diet member can.

Another, perhaps even more significant, reason for the perception that reporters have of their political activities is derived from their political orientations, which also have a certain influence on their functions in political activities. Several studies have pointed out that Japanese newspeople lean toward the left politically, and tend to be either centrists or moderate leftists. It is often claimed that Japanese newspeople in general do not like any of the political parties and that they criticize the LDP as well as the opposition parties, which they dislike as much as the LDP (Kim 1981; Brown and Lee 1977). Nevertheless, my meetings and interviews with a large number of newspeople suggest different findings. According to my data, except for seven reporters, all newspeople expressed sympathies toward the LDP, pointing out that they agree with most of the LDP's policies and programs. They view the activities of the LDP as "quite proper," "satisfactory," and "the best choice for Japan and the Japanese people," to cite only three of their views. Within the context of their work, reporters described their relations with LDP Diet members as the best and the most intimate, as compared to Diet members of other political parties or the bureaucracy. Are the political stances expressed by the reporters accidental? The opinion of several desk members was that they are not. The common view held by most newspeople is that their experiences working as political reporters have had considerable influence on the development of such an orientation. Some veteran reporters and editorial writers revealed that this orientation toward the LDP was quite foreign to them when they first went to work. One editorial writer said:

> The typical reporter, in his or her first years of work after graduating from university, brings certain ideas and an orientation toward his work that tend to be quite similar to those of some of the opposition parties, mainly the SDPJ. While working as a cub reporter in the press club close to the prime minister's office, then in the press club close to the head-quarters of the LDP, however, reporters have an opportunity to observe the activities of the LDP through the information they obtain and their contacts with LDP Diet members. Without doubt, this continual contact with LDP Diet members, the majority of them in leading positions, has a certain influence on reporters, which causes their sympathies to shift from the opposition parties to the LDP, especially when assigned to cover opposition parties' activities.

By that time, reporters have learned that the information they can obtain from the opposition parties is considerably less interesting than what they can receive from within the LDP. Most of them discover a lack of dynamism and of positive policy-making, and a much lower level of creative ideas. The opposition parties are obsessed with designing countermeasures to policies adopted by the LDP rather than formulating their own policies. Thus, most reporters show a certain loathing for the opposition parties and tend to have a high regard for the positive attitude taken by the LDP, which retains power yet is capable of compromise with bureaucrats and other political groups in order to reach decisions.

There is another factor that causes reporters to feel closer to the LDP than to any other political party. It is easy for most reporters to establish and maintain contact with LDP Diet members. This factor may be related to what reporters noted as the tendency of LDP Diet members to talk with them more openly about all issues, from political activities to private hobbies and interests, and their frequent efforts to satisfy the reporters' needs for information. Conversely, when meeting opposition-party Diet members, reporters get the impression that they are attempting to conceal much information about their party's activities and plans; that they cautiously select the information they give reporters; and that in their desire to transfer information to the public they forget the "humanistic" side of the relationship, making it difficult to establish trust and understanding.

The perception that reporters have of the LDP eventually leads them to play an active role in transmitting information from the opposition parties and the bureaucracy to the LDP. They become the main actors in funneling infor-

.mation to the LDP, spreading it among the leaders and, at the same time, transferring information between the various LDP factions. Thus, in general, reporters serve as an information channel to all of the leading Diet members of the LDP.

Diet Members' Orientations

When reporters were asked about participation in political activities, different opinions were expressed by junior and veteran reporters, and the same questions posed to Diet members[2] also revealed differences. Specifically, Diet members who feel that reporters can be regarded as participants comprise an overwhelming majority of the LDP Diet members. They see reporters as fulfilling an important role in their Diet work and emphasized that they can significantly influence party activities. Some Diet members believe that the reporters are participants because their stories do have a potential influence on the general populace, while still others view reporters as nonparticipants.

Diet members find many of the functions of reporters useful and helpful to the extent that many of them highly value the role reporters play. From the Diet members' viewpoint, reporters participate in political activities in three interrelated ways: (1) by giving a wide range of advice to Diet members, which in most cases the latter heed and follow; (2) by transferring information between Diet members, and thus serving as an important communications link between Diet members and between Diet members and bureaucrats; and (3) by acting as go-betweens for Diet members, political parties, and party factions.

Regarding the first factor, as previously noted, Diet members in leading positions who have frequent contact with reporters obtain a broad scope of advice from reporters during their meetings. Some of this advice enhances their Diet work. Based on the wide range of contact they have with Diet members of other political parties and the bureaucracy, reporters give Diet members feedback about their approaches to specific issues, comments about their ideas regarding a certain proposal, and other advice concerning their activities on one of the Diet's committees. Reporters introduce these Diet members to new ideas about how to promote a certain bill according to the mood in other political parties; they advise Diet members how to avoid confrontations with rival party factions; and they suggest to Diet members what kinds of questions to introduce (or what kinds of questions to be ready to answer) in their committees, and when and how to do so. In addition, they provide suggestions on various issues that they think Diet members should

---

2. The questions were: "Do you see newspeople as taking part in political activities? If yes, in what way? What kind of influence do reporters exert on Diet members' activities?"

concentrate on to achieve a certain goal. The influence of the advice and suggestions that reporters give to Diet members is remarkable. To illustrate: when asked about the participation of reporters in political activities by giving advice to Diet members, a veteran Diet member from the largest LDP faction commented:

> People tend to think that our faction consists of 120 members, but actually we have 125; the 5 others are the reporters from the "big five" newspapers who cover our faction. Taking into consideration their useful personal counsel and suggestions, it is only natural to consider them as members of the faction.

The second role Diet members perceive reporters as playing in political activities is their functioning as communication links between Diet members from different party factions and political parties, and as transmitters of information from the bureaucracy. Kim (1981, 92–93) noted that contact with reporters supplies Diet members with valuable intragovernmental information. Additionally, my own interviews reveal that Diet members see reporters as a link needed to facilitate the stream of information passing from one political participant to another. Although there is frequent contact between Diet members of the various political parties, there is still a need, for reasons previously explained, to obtain information from reporters that, in most cases, Diet members consider more reliable than information received directly from Diet members of other political parties or from bureaucrats. The concept of reporters as valuable information links, although it also exists among the opposition parties' leaders, is much more prevalent among LDP Diet members. The latter evaluate reporters as playing an important role in this connection, especially while transferring information between the party's factions.[3]

The tendency of Diet members to obtain information from reporters is perhaps one of the most striking phenomena in reporter–Diet member interactions. As outlined in chapter 3, 228 Diet members (about 57 percent) stated that they meet reporters for this reason. While the nature of the needed information and the reasons for obtaining it, especially from reporters, have already been discussed, three factors related to the tendency of many Diet members to obtain information from reporters deserve special attention. The first is derived from the tendency of Diet members to obtain information from as many reporters as possible. Whereas reporters tend to differentiate between

---

3. The questions were: "Is there a need in your political party (or party faction) for information concerning the LDP/other factions of the LDP/opposition parties/bureaucracy? If yes, why? How do you obtain such information? What role do reporters play in the above-mentioned situations?"

Diet members according to their experience in the Diet, the number of times they have been elected to the Diet, and the positions they hold in their political parties or party factions, and evaluate the information received accordingly, Diet members take another approach toward reporters. Diet members do not apply much of the criteria that are important to reporters concerning the need for information: reporters differentiate between Diet members who comprise the group of information sources and other Diet members, but Diet members consider almost all reporters as reliable sources of news, advice, and comments. Some Diet members, especially those with long experience in Diet activities and with extensive contact with reporters, have developed their own classification as to which reporters can give them more useful information than others. Some of them prefer the captains at the press club who receive all the news from reporters working under their guidance. Others tend to depend more on members of the desk staff who can tell them which stories will appear in tomorrow's newspaper and which will not be published; these desk members can also update them about general information, such as the results of public opinion polls that are still being analyzed and scheduled to be published a few days later. This information is of special value for leading Diet members who want to know it as fast as possible in order to take appropriate countermeasures. Not all Diet members are in regular contact with veteran reporters, however. From this viewpoint, most Diet members generally are not overly concerned about the experience reporters have in their work, as long as they can obtain information (and advice) from them. For both parties, of course, personal interaction, measured by the length of time of association and amount of trust developed, plays a major role. In many cases, the qualities of trustworthiness and understanding that Diet members look for in reporters are directly connected to the ability of the reporters to keep them informed.

The second factor in reporters providing information is related to the claim by many Diet members that they really meet with reporters more to exchange ideas and viewpoints than to obtain information. In fact, during interviews with Diet members, almost all of them noted that through such contacts their interaction with reporters has more of the nature of give-and-take rather than just take. "Give-and-take" was also the expression used by reporters to describe the atmosphere in which information flows back and forth while meeting information sources. At the same time, many reporters disclosed that Diet members often try to squeeze information from them, and while visiting a Diet member's office, they may be repeatedly asked about various issues. Some Diet members need to obtain a continual flow of information from reporters to fullfill their work. These include party faction leaders, secretaries-general, party whips, and those close to the leaders. To these leading Diet members, information about what other Diet members think about specific issues and trends in other political parties, which can be obtained from reporters, are always of importance to clear the way for negotiations aimed at maintaining the political momentum. These Diet members do not always wait for reporters to come by and tell them what has happened in a rival political party or party faction. It is not rare for Diet members in leading positions to initiate meetings with reporters and send them over to other groups to gather the detailed information they need.

In an in-depth interview, one of the leading LDP members commented on this tendency:

> In our faction we know the reporters who cover our activities very well, and usually we obtain word of the latest developments in the other factions from them. Occasionally we even send one or two of them to other factions to find out what's going on. Then, we consult with the reporters and ask their opinions, based on other connections and sources outside our faction.

To the question of why one faction sends reporters to other factions, another LDP Diet member added: "We can't send spies to find out what is going on in other places, so we send reporters instead."

Some Diet members explicitly stated that reporters have a special function within the LDP. A leading LDP Diet member said,

> One of the tasks of reporters is to bridge the gap between the LDP factions, even more so than between the LDP and the opposition parties—not to provide a balance, but to actually bridge the gap. The party factions all have a common goal, namely, power, through the prime ministership and cabinet portfolios. To achieve such power, they need information, mainly about the possible reactions of the other party factions to a specific decision. To us, gathering information means hearing it from the primary sources—through reporters.

The third significant factor in the flow of information is related to the question of why so many Diet members need information from reporters. As previously discussed, communications from reporters have particular significance in smoothing the decision-making process in political parties and party factions; in enabling consensus decisions to be reached by all the participants in a way that will satisfy all those involved; in knowing the real reactions of other participants to certain issues; and in considering further measures and strategies toward certain issues based on the atmosphere in other political parties. Not all Diet members are actively involved in the decision-making processes in their political parties or factions and do not directly negotiate with other political participants. In fact, only a few of them do, and they were identified previously as sources of information. Thus, to most Diet members, information such as the general mood in other political parties, the interpersonal relations between leaders of party factions or opposition parties, and what topics colleagues from other political parties have discussed with reporters do not have any practical meaning. Why then do so many Diet members try to obtain information from reporters?

Generally speaking, a Diet member is motivated to obtain information from reporters for several reasons, some of which are not related directly to routine work. For example, some Diet members want information for private use, such as to impress their colleagues with their knowledge of events that did not appear in the press. Young Diet members, in particular, who have less experience in the Diet, feel that the kind of information that reporters can give them is an important tool to prove not only their broad knowledge but also their connections and ability to gather information from sources other than the news media and colleagues from the same political group. They can show off that they know more than others, and know more details than what appears in the newspapers.

Diet members can use information they receive from one reporter to impress not only their colleagues but also other reporters. One Diet member admitted that this practice plays an important role in his contacts with reporters, and, in the long run, contributes to establishing solid relations. For example, this Diet member can meet a reporter from one of the newspapers covering his party faction and obtain information related to another party faction. Later, this Diet member may meet—or, more correctly, initiate a meeting—with another reporter from a different newspaper or from one of the television stations, who is also assigned to cover his faction, and proudly reveal the information he obtained from the first reporter. To prevent a situation in which the first reporter finds out that the Diet member leaked the information, the Diet member usually gives the information to the second reporter under two conditions: that the reporter will not talk with anybody about this information; and that he will not use it in a story for his news agency. And since the main goal is to impress the reporter, the latter may be indeed impressed by the Diet member's knowledge and may often approach this particular Diet member in the future to exchange information.

Diet members can learn from reporters what their colleagues actually think about them. By knowing the true opinions of their colleagues, a Diet member knows who to associate with and who could be an enemy. This attitude exists not only among young Diet members but at almost all levels of experience in the Diet. For example, a political editor remembered during an interview that when he was a reporter during the time of former Prime Minister Suzuki's cabinet, former Prime Minister Nakasone, who was then a minister, would ask him from time to time what Prime Minister Suzuki thought of him. This reporter said: "Since I was on good terms with both of them, I used to tell him what he asked me. Sometimes I would also tell Suzuki about Nakasone's opinion of him."

Veteran reporters mentioned that Diet members often ask reporters what their own faction leader's opinion is of them. Reporters revealed that some Diet members from the various LDP factions even want to know the opinions of other reporters from the *ban* who cover their respective factions, and what the political editor of their newspaper thinks about them. Thus, Diet members are eager to obtain a wide range of information from reporters.

No less important, Diet members believe that reporters are playing a full role in Japanese politics since they also function as go-betweens on behalf of Diet members, political parties, and party factions. This go-between role is part of the informal negotiations between political participants for laying the groundwork in order to achieve consensus and harmony. Because much importance is attached in Japan to collective aspects and collective decisions, Diet members in leading positions invest much time and energy by practicing broad consultations to achieve cooperation between the disparate interests of all members. Japanese reporters believe that in the leader's attempts to achieve consensus, their participation is essential for speeding up political processes, for facilitating the work of the Diet and political parties, and for facilitating communication between the different political groups. Because the Japanese concept of leadership values the virtues of a behind-the-scenes consensus builder, more than a strong, visible, and articulate leader, reporters and Diet members feel that Diet members in leading positions depend on reporters to continually provide them with information about all of the other political groups in order to facilitate the achievement of consensus. As one editorial writer noted:

Perhaps in another country, the prime minister can make a decision regarding any issue and that's that. In this country, however, the prime minister needs to achieve the support and consensus of at least, say, 70 percent of the members, otherwise he is not able to pass any decision at all. In order not to behave in an authoritative way, to be liked by everyone and to get the support of all the other Diet members, the prime minister, or any other members in a leading post, needs to know what the other people think about a particular issue; he thus depends on communication channels which the reporters can easily provide. Reporters do it because nobody else can function in such a role. They are expected to do it.

Perhaps the most common practice of reporters as go-betweens is related to the party factions. In many cases, faction leaders feel uneasy about communicating directly with their counterparts. Sometimes they are afraid of hearing negative reactions to their ideas or not getting a clear and definite answer. Or, when a delicate issue is on the agenda, the other faction leader may feel uncomfortable in a direct negotiation. Reporters are thus called upon to play this go-between role. In times of political crisis, the chances increase for political reporters to be asked by a member of the party faction they are covering to serve as a go-between for another party faction. They may be called by one of the leading figures in the faction (sometimes by the faction leader, sometimes by an aide), who explains the situation in detail and reveals the message that the faction leader would like to transmit to other faction leaders.

In such a situation, the reporters assume the role of empathic communicator. They begin by listening and collecting crucial information, as it is important to have a clear understanding of what the other side thinks about the problem in order to find out whether consensus can be achieved. The reporter must secretly meet with the leader or one of the other leading Diet members of the rival faction. Usually, such a meeting takes place either early in the morning or late at night, when a minimum number of people could witness it. The reporters then return to their own domain to pass on the received information. The reporter continues to move back and forth, transferring information from one leader to the other, until a probability for concession can be seen and the leaders can meet directly with each other to work out details of a solution to the disputed issue. In the process of transmitting the messages from one leader to another, information gets unintentionally distorted or omitted. In this way, it has a tendency to become inaccurate. Especially if the base structure is not firm enough, *nemawashi* (laying the groundwork for obtaining one's objective) invites misunderstanding of the issue rather than clarification. In this sense, the role played by reporters is an extremely responsibile one and influential to political leaders as well as to the political system as a whole.

Very often, however, a reporter who covers one party faction cannot meet directly with Diet members from another faction. As previously discussed, each party faction is like a village, a closed community that provides a roof and shelter for its residents, but it is not open to outsiders. Thus, a reporter who covers a party faction can feel at home and meet all the members of that faction, but in most cases that reporter will not be a welcome visitor to a rival faction. Under such circumstances, they must look for an alternative channel for transferring the messages they were asked to transmit to the second faction. In almost all cases, such reporters try to first communicate with one of their colleagues—notably from the same news agency—who covers the rival faction, and establish communications through this colleague. Otherwise, they turn to a colleague from other news media, and ask him or her to serve as a link in transferring the message. They may tell their colleague what their faction leader's position is on a certain issue, ask the position of the rival faction's leader, then transfer this information to the leader of their faction.

Three examples of the go-between role of reporters can be cited. The first is when the president of the House of Representatives sent a reporter to the LDP secretary-general to inform him of his intention to resign from his post instead of telling him directly (Sugiyama 1984). Another example was disclosed to me while interviewing a Diet member and concerns former Prime Minister Nakasone Yasuhiro. When Nakasone established his first cabinet, he asked a member on the editorial board of one of the national newspapers to meet this LDP Diet member, who belonged to another faction, and ask him to help the prime minister in his new position. This particular Diet member had past experience in fulfilling a special role in the prime minister's office, knew the full nature of a prime minister's work, and could offer much from his experience to assist the new prime minister. Even though the prime minister really needed the help of this Diet member and could contact him directly, he preferred to contact him through a reporter who the other Diet member knew well and to establish communication through that reporter. The prime minister presumably hoped that the appeal presented by this reporter would have more impact and would be more convincing than, say, if presented by one of his secretaries, aides, another leading Diet member, or even the prime minister himself. The last example of the go-between role was revealed to me in the following story from a reporter.

> Once I was asked by a former prime minister to talk with a certain person and convince that person to run for election as governer of Tokyo. Perhaps because I had covered the activities of the faction of this former prime minister for a long time and had good connections with the faction's members to the extent that they could rely on me, I was asked to negotiate on behalf of the former prime minister.

Generally, in the negotiations that occur among party factions, political parties, or the bureaucracy, Diet members believe that reporters are best equipped to function as information transmitters. Diet members view reporters as the only group having continual contact with them and access to all the political parties and even the bureaucracy; this makes reporters not only the best choice for such a role, but as the only choice. As one Diet member said, "They do it because nobody else can function in such a role."

This concept is similar to the previously discussed perception that reporters have of their function.

The ways in which reporters participate in political activities, especially the fact that Diet members obtain a variety of valuable information from reporters, shapes much of their perception of the role and functions of reporters in Japanese politics. Thus, for instance, when asked how they view reporters, the answers of Diet members were almost identical. Referring to his own experience with many of the reporters who cover his faction's activities, one leading LDP Diet member responded, "Reporters function as advisers to Diet members." Another LDP Diet member opined: "Reporters are like butterflies, transferring information from one party to another." Still another LDP Diet member described reporters as: ". . . secret agents employed by the ruling party to keep the party supplied with up-to-date information." And another Diet member summed it up like this: "Reporters are like antennae: the more such antennae I have, the better I can see the political mood in its reality."

How the Press is Perceived: Diet Members'
Orientations

Obviously, Diet members' views about reporters' role in political activities shape much of their perceptions of reporters. Answers to questions such as how Diet members evaluate reporters and by what criteria, and how Diet members view their relationships with members of the press help to explain Diet members' orientations toward reporters.

Most of the Diet members interviewed (59 out of 70, or 84.2 percent), favorably evaluated reporters and their work.[4] In most cases the Diet members viewed reporters as serious people who work under endless pressures to do their best in the most responsible way. These Diet members emphasized that they have a great deal of trust in reporters, believing that reporters will not disclose to others private matters and secrets they confide or will not report what they ask the reporters not to. Even the few Diet members who expressed criticism of reporters tended to smooth or blunt their criticism by referring to the pressures that reporters are working under, or to some common practice in the news-gathering process, as the cause of faults that reporters sometimes exhibit. Thus, for example, a leading LDP Diet member said:

> Since reporters have to collect information from Diet members whose ideas, opinions, and orientations are not always correct or complete, but always include the Diet members' hopes and expectations, some of these ideas permeate to the stories as a result of the time limits in which reporters have to submit their stories.

---

4. The major questions dealt with here were: "What is the nature of your contacts with reporters?"; "Do you believe that reporters maintain a neutral stand, or because of their contacts with Diet members do they try to influence public thinking in some way that Diet members may ask them to?"

Other Diet members opined that the fierce competition among the numerous newspapers cause reporters to rush after scoops and exclusive political information, in which they sometimes tend to exaggerate by emphasizing a particular aspect of a news item. In the view of one Diet member with more than 25 years experience in political activities, most reporters "have a unique sense of analysis and deep insight into politics." At the same time, many Diet members expressed criticism toward political stories in general and the manner in which they, their colleagues, and their political parties are reported in some of the daily newspapers. To most of them, most of the stories, as they appear in the newspapers "do not always reflect the reporters' sobriety and enthusiasm," mainly because they are instructed from above about how to write them ("above" referring to editorial writers and members of the political desk). In the words of one leading LDP Diet member:

> Reporters have one weak point in that they must follow their companies' policies and philosophy, thus they write articles in a certain way. . . . reporters are basically good and fair; but their superiors, editorial writers and desk members, guide them to criticize and stimulate them to express extreme opinions.

One LDP Diet member said, "They induce those reporters who gather the news . . . encourage them to look for unique information, and use that information to embarrass us."

In the words of one DSP Diet member:

> The desk members do nothing but sit far away, in their offices, far from the events, and based on the stories received and on their past knowledge, they analyze the present situation. In many cases they do not even bother to verify information they have received.

The distinction between regular reporters and desk members at the head offices of the newspapers is very significant among Diet members from all political parties. Diet members clearly distinguish between these two types of newspeople for three reasons. First, in the Diet member's eyes, a regular reporter is mainly covering a certain, limited issue, political event, or activity in one location. Thus, they tend to see things from a narrow point of view, which is sometimes good and sometimes bad, but almost always reflects bias derived from a particular information source's stance and attempts to promote a certain issue. Many of these reporters are in the first stage of their career, and Diet members believe that a word from them about their expectations of political reporters "will help much to improve their viewpoint and observations about politics." From the Diet members' point of view, editorial writers have more experience. They must consider issues from a broader perspective. Their task is to analyze specific trends in accordance with general affairs, with the stream of political events, and to judge them carefully. In the Diet members' eyes, editorial writers have more responsibility in their work than regular reporters. And when an editor writes something a Diet member does not like, they tend to consider it more seriously than if a reporter on the beat published the same ideas. Thus, although most Diet members favorably evaluate desk members and editorial writers, they also tend to criticize them more than they do reporters.

Second, Diet members distinguish between reporters and desk members because of their continual contact, sometimes for hours a day, with reporters rather than with the desk members. Through this long association, almost all Diet members see reporters as the most readily-available tool through which they can disseminate daily information to the public. Because reporters are in positions to broaden public, and especially voters', recognition and knowledge concerning the Diet member's daily activities, a Diet member will see a reporter, more than a desk member, in a positive light. Moreover, by constantly giving them a great deal of feedback and suggestions, and functioning as transmitters of information between the various political parties, the reporters who most often meet Diet members greatly facilitate their work. Diet members, especially those from the LDP, acknowledge that reporters help them to realize political and other aims related to their daily job.

Finally, since Diet members and reporters are active in the same political scene, living in and breathing the atmosphere of similar political activities and events, Diet members feel that they share a lot in common, so much so that many of them feel a close compatibility with the reporters they meet with frequently. During interviews, Diet members emphasized that they often view reporters as thinking almost along the same lines that they do, approaching various issues in the same way, and expressing almost identical opinions concerning any particular political topic. The reason for such an attitude may be the nature of the conversations Diet members have with reporters. A phenomenon that I observed while following meetings between Diet members and reporters is that reporters tend to agree with whatever Diet members say. In most cases, reporters know the stances and opinions of the Diet member they meet with, so they agree with them; and when the Diet member expresses ideas to the reporter, the reporter immediately expresses similar opinions. This attitude of reporters is aimed at maintaining and strengthening good contact with Diet members.

Diet members' belief that reporters' opinions are close to their own contributes much to the cultivation of close relations between the two groups. This climate of compatible association leads many Diet members to feel closer to reporters than to their colleagues from their own political parties or party factions. Many Diet members feel free and relaxed while meeting with reporters for the following reasons: because Diet members meet reporters more frequently than they meet their colleagues; because they can talk with many reporters openly and trust them not to disclose confidential information; and because with colleagues they meet to talk mainly about business, whereas with reporters they can enjoy a social atmosphere. In fact, for most Diet members, meeting with reporters is a pleasurable aspect of their political duties. Diet members admit that whereas they would never invite one of their colleagues to their home "to have a chat over a glass of whiskey," they do so often and willingly with reporters. Association with reporters in their home is beyond the realm of giving or obtaining information. Diet members just feel more comfortable with reporters. Furthermore, they believe that both sides can benefit from a relationship based on friendship. For the Diet member, of course, this means an easier way to transfer their ideas through a friendly reporter, and that may improve their public image. Thus, Diet members try to create an advantage, especially concerning the nationally influential newspapers, and spread some of their ideas, through a friendly reporter, to the general public.

When asked for the framework of their relations with reporters, most Diet members gave friendship (*yûjin kankei*) as the most important criterion. Many Diet members (60 of the 70 interviewed) value reporters beyond their political-coverage activities. One LDP Diet member disclosed:

> For me they are, of course, a potential channel to disseminate my ideas to the public; but first of all, they are my friends. And if any other Diet member tries to meet reporters from a purely business viewpoint, in the long-run they will never succeed in their contacts with them.

To most Diet members, the fact that both sides have things in common derived from the nature of their work—such as their mutual interest in politics—makes it easy to establish good relations. The question of image for many Diet members is closely related to the relations they can build with reporters. Of course, a reporter can help a Diet member a great deal in shaping the Diet member's image among the public and voters. More than that, if a Diet member has close contact with many reporters, his image, even among his colleagues, will improve. One Diet member expressed the view that, as long as reporters continue to visit, he feels self-assured and important; the fact that reporters want to visit contributes much to his positive self-image. To other Diet members, friendly relations with reporters means power. Diet members feel their influence in politics by their ability to attract reporters to their offices. One Diet member said, "I feel as if I am waging a war in which the reporter and I are shoulder-to-shoulder on the same battlefront; as long as they stick close to me and stay on my side, victory is mine."

Longtime contact with many of the same reporters enables a Diet member to establish close contact with reporters. And on this friendship basis, a Diet member can obtain advice concerning the newspapers, reactions and suggestions pertaining to policy, party faction proposals, etc. The contact with reporters is often so close that a reporter may feel unable to function properly at work and that a certain amount of loyalty and interest has shifted from news gathering to focusing on the Diet members' work. Under such circumstances, and with much encouragement from the Diet member, more than a few reporters have resigned from their work at newspapers and become full-time secretaries to Diet members. There are many cases in Japan of reporters who became private secretaries of prime ministers and of other leaders of the LDP.[5]

This compatibility between reporters and Diet members exists to the extent that Diet members—most notably those from the ruling LDP—believe that this relationship is basically characterized by mutual understanding, which inevitably leads to mutual dependency. In fact, several Diet members used the term *mochitsu-motaretsu,* mutual dependency, to describe their relationship with reporters. They believe that this mutual dependency between the two groups is the basic governing factor that encourages cooperation between them. This cooperation is most conspicuously reflected in those reporters who continually transfer information between political participants and give advice and feedback to many Diet members.

Regarding the political camps, Diet members of the opposition parties see reporters as more cooperative than members of the bureaucracy. This is partly because Diet members of the opposition parties do not have ready access to bureaucrats, but do have ready access to reporters who can tell them what is going on in the bureaucracy, the mood among government officials in this or that institute, and even opinions held by the bureaucrats toward the leaders and leadership style of the opposition parties. LDP Diet members see reporters as more cooperative than their colleagues from other party factions.

---

5. For example, the private secretary of former Prime Minister Ikeda Hayato was previously a reporter from the economic desk of the *Nishi Nippon;* Sato Eisaku had a former desk member from the *Sankei* as a secretary; Tanaka Kakuei had two former reporters from the *Tôkyô Times* and the *Kyôdô News Service* as secretaries; Miki Takeo had a secretary who was a former reporter from the *Sankei;* Fukuda Takeo, as secretary-general of the LDP, had a reporter from the *Kyôdô* as a secretary; and Nakasone Yasuhiro had a secretary who was a reporter from the *Yomiuri.* During the late 1980s, the staff of one of the up-and-coming new leaders of the LDP, Abe Shintaro, included the former head of the political desk of the *Mainichi,* who resigned from the newspaper to help Abe achieve the premiership.

And, like Diet members of the opposition parties, they find reporters more cooperative than bureaucrats when questions of access to information or practical advice are raised. Several LDP Diet members opined that it is obvious that reporters are more focused on assisting them than are government officials. One said:

> Mainly for this reason, in most cases reporters transmit information concerning the bureaucracy, but they will not tell the bureaucrats everything concerning the activities or plans of our party, unless, of course, we ask them to leak something to bureaucrats.

Another member of the same party said:

> At times, reporters obviously know that some of the information from the LDP's most reliable information sources is intentionally leaked to manipulate the bureaucracy; nevertheless, they write stories and help us to achieve our goals and to successfully lead Japan.

From the Diet members' point of view, the bureaucrats do not always have the ability to obtain input from reporters as to what kind of information is true and which has been intentionally leaked for some specific reason.

Asked to comment on the notion that reporters cooperate with Diet members on various occasions, a leading Diet member noted that such cooperation between the two groups is "quite natural." And then he added, "After all, Japanese Diet members and reporters are both wheels on the same car."

Part 5
Conclusions

CHAPTER 9

Politics and Political Information in Japan

Selecting the News

The news media assume a significant and crucial role in a present-day democratic, representative political system, in which the general public elects the legislators and leaders who will control the basic direction of government. It serves as a major channel of information about the leaders and government activities to most of the public. By utilizing experience, analysis, and the knowledge obtained from politicians, scholars, and other experts, it also serves as an important source of explanation and interpretation about the functioning or malfunctioning of the political system and political leaders. By channeling the attention of the public to, and facilitating the understanding of, certain political or social issues, activities, and processes taking place within the political environment, the news media often influence the behavior, knowledge, interest, or other attitudes of consumers and others, some of whom are not necessarily directly exposed to messages of the news media.

Given today's complex society and global state of affairs, the news media cannot always inform the public of every political, social, and economic event taking place in the world. On one hand, the news space and time that can be devoted to each event is limited. Thus, the news media must process and select what is to be reported from an infinite number of events that occur during a given period of time. It must decide, often based on its own criteria of news value or news interest, which events it can (or should) give more attention, which merit less attention, and which can be ignored. On the other hand, the news media may be limited and restricted in their attempt to obtain information about certain issues. Restrictions may also apply to the publications of certain kinds of information. Such restrictions may be imposed by law or informal regulations, either of which limits the capability of the press to fulfill its responsibilities vis-à-vis the general public. Whether the limitation is attributable to a lack of space or time, legal or other constraints that prevent reporting on a specific matter, the process of selecting the news that reaches the public is an integral part of press routines the world over. This, in itself, has several implications. Most notably, it results in a populace less informed about the socio-politico-economic environment. It is actually a kind of biased

193

reportage, often regarded as an attempt to manipulate a certain segment (or all) of society to the benefit of a particular social group.

Japan, from this point of view, is not exceptional. Processing information for publication in this country is unavoidable, not because of legal constraints (none exist), but because of the enormous amount of political, social, and economic information reaching the news media from across the nation. This information flows to reporters via the press clubs located in every important government agency, political party, and faction headquarters in the form of briefings, lectures, and news releases. Moreover, the constant direct contact reporters have with information sources (as well as other Diet members and officials) from morning to night, enables them to gather an endless stream of information by morning visits, *kondan* and "night attacks." In view of the huge amount of information and the limited space for political-related stories, reporters and editors must carefully screen what will be published. In Japan, perhaps as in other countries with a free press, news selection involves two processes: the extent to which political news is selected for publication and the way certain types of news is selected from all the activities occurring in the same time frame. Because of the large circulation of newspapers in Japan, and because the Japanese people get a high rating with regard to exposure to politics, political information, and political awareness via the news media (even though the level of active participation in politics is generally low, Kawakami and Feldman, 1988) news selection may have far more significant implications on behavior and attitudes than in other countries. Thus, the news media must be very careful in the way they process information.

Although this study discusses the two news selection processes in Japan, because of its relative importance, the latter process is given more attention. In the national dailies, the political editor or political desk members usually make the final decision concerning the value of a news item, whether to publish it, the length of the related story, the location in the newspaper, the headline, the subheadlines, etc. The initial selection is made by the reporters in the field, however. These reporters often consult (or are instructed by) their editors or members of the desk as to the importance of attending (or writing about) a certain event. On a routine basis, however, these reporters make the ultimate decision as to whether to write a story, how to write it, and what issues or processes to refer to. Because reporters spend most working hours everyday in the center of Japanese politics, either in the *Nagatachô* or *Kasumigaseki* districts, they have sufficient knowledge to judge the value of any event and item of information. Staying away from their news agencies' offices also contributes to the autonomy they experience.

Although reporters use their own judgment to decide which news item is suitable for a particular story, they often discuss with colleagues from another news media channel whether the activities or statements of certain Diet members are worth reporting. Because of the large number of newspapers, rival reporters (and editors) compete intensely to obtain information. Neither the reporter nor the newspaper wants readers to feel that a rival newspaper carries more information about a happening. Concern over the possibility of another news medium nabbing a scoop is typical. As a result there is a tendency among reporters to pack together and to monitor each other and to share the news with other media representatives. Notably, reporters belonging to a group such as a *ban*, (i.e., reporters representing different news media channels who work together in covering the activities of a certain Diet member), usually discuss among themselves which of the activities of the political (or bureaucratic) figure they are covering are most important, including which ideas should be emphasized in a story, and which aspects of that person's everyday activities merit special attention. Moreover, while Japan has a rather favorable legal structure for the press, the pack journalism syndrome causes the Japanese reader to get rather bland coverage, much of it done by recycling press handouts. Pack journalism thus affects the nature and the content of the political coverage and is perhaps contrary to a high-quality press and a correspondingly well informed reading public. When reporters are packed together, a special type of journalistic conservatism develops, producing a routine consensus about what is news, what is important, and how to handle that news.

Not less important is the fact that on a regular basis, and almost instinctively, every reporter assigned to cover activities in *Nagatachô* is capable of easily differentiating between information that can be used in a story and that which should be ignored. From the political reporter's point of view, information gathered in *Nagatachô* is broadly divided into two types. One remains in the cycle of *Nagatachô*, the "property" of the reporters themselves, a few Diet members, notably leaders of parties and factions and their close aides, and perhaps the secretaries of such Diet members, since they are knowledgeable of activities and schedules. In some cases, such information also reaches government bureaucrats and ranking officials in *Kasumigaseki* (significantly through reporters), but it rarely reaches the general public. When it does reach the public, it is always through the "back doors" of the Japanese news media, usually the weekly or monthly journals. (For this reason some claim they are the real mass media of Japan.) This type of information includes disagreement, differences of opinion, and other personal matters involving the struggles over cabinet seats or other important posts within one or another of the LDP factions and the party as a whole; general personal affairs within the LDP; ongoing contacts and negotiations between the LDP and opposition parties regarding a certain process in the Diet's regular work, or a committee's work; and contacts between government bureaucrats and leading Diet members of the LDP.

A detailed story on such activities, considered an *ura,* or the back side of Japanese politics, is rare. Interestingly, in most of these activities, reporters are not simply observers (who see the development of events or receive updates from Diet members), but often assume an active role by passing information between Diet members of the various LDP factions, between Diet members of various political parties, and between bureaucrats and Diet members. This kind of information, which reporters experience first hand and thus are extremely familiar with up to the last detail, rarely finds its way into published stories. Conversely, the other type of political information is used by reporters when writing their stories. This consists of the center and the majority of the so-called *Nagatachô gyôkaishi* (the Industry Pages of *Nagatachô*), i.e., all of the political related stories, especially the domestic ones appearing on the political pages of the national dailies. These stories are dominated by coverage of the regular sessions of the Diet and its most important committees (especially the Budget Committee) and the routine activities of the leading Diet members, including leaders of political parties, cabinet members and, particularly, the prime minister and leaders of the LDP factions. Questions about what these leading people do, who they meet with, and what their opinions are, are the heart of the political coverage. Indeed, politics in Japan is personalistic and therefore the news-gathering effort is focused on covering people, and most intensely on the few at the top that have all the inside information. The key reasons for high levels of contact between reporters and Diet members (most of them leaders of the ruling party) is thus mainly related to the nature of news reporting and the emphasis placed on being able to anticipate strategic factional political moves. These require a close monitoring of the ever-changing personalistic ins and out of politics, rather than a simple understanding of the facts and positions in a particular policy area that are less likely to change quickly.

The press club system (including news-gathering methods reporters employ) facilitates the interaction between these political leaders and reporters and enables the reporters privileged access to any place where the leading Diet members are, including briefings of the prime minister, ministers, vice ministers, and government officials. In these ways reporters are able to collect information on, and to report on, the personal aspects of the background of every political and parliamentary activity. The distinct group of reporters located in the press club, and the particular reporters who cover the activities of leading figures of the LDP, are the functional equivalent of the British Westminster Lobby correspondents (the "Lobby") and of the White House press corps in the United States, though they differ in the informal news-gathering methods and the various customs that characterize the activities in *Nagatachô* and *Kasumigaseki*. Their constant contact and access to leading Diet members through peculiar news-gathering methods place reporters in a unique position from which to observe and report upon every activity that takes place at the heart, as well as the periphery, of the Japanese political system. Thus, the press club refers not only to the association of political (or other) reporters, but also to the culture and organization of much of Japanese journalism. While working at the press club, reporters become specialists in political process, political parties and politicking, and parliamentary procedure. The press club (and likewise the British Lobby) thus serves as a hotbed that allows the reporter to become something of an expert on world affairs and, consequently, to play an important (sometimes even decisive) role in two ways. First, they function as vertical communicators because they produce stories that are in the front (or political) pages, to be read by the electorate, who depends to a considerable extent upon the information that is predominantly gathered by press club reporters. And second, reporters play a key role in horizontal communication in two respects: they produce stories that are in the newspapers and are read, though selectively, by other government bureaucrats, party officials, Diet members, and other politicians, including the prime minister; and, they transfer information directly between and among Diet members and government officials.

Because Japanese reporters have almost the same privileges as their British counterparts in the Lobby, who report on the political scene within Westminster, Tunstall's (1970, 88) description can apply to them as well: "coopted Members of Parliament, whose lack of voting and other rights is balanced by superior access to information and to outlets for publicizing their views." And like the unique role played by the Lobby in the British political system, Japanese press club reporters can be suspected of being what Seymore-Ure (1968, 198–240) and Tunstall (1970, 21) refer to, in the case of the Lobby, as "the messenger boys of (British) democracy."

The Soft Stomach of the Press

Although the political information published by the dailies is mainly intended to give the public a broad insight into the activities of political institutions and leaders, it has several weak points, notably the biased coverage of events and the vague nature of political stories.

Not intentionally biased by reporters, political coverage is more likely biased because it reflects the political situation and the fact that the LDP plays the major role in domestic politics and decision making. This leaves the press with no choice but to follow up and report the activities and statements of the leading LDP Diet members, more than those of any of the other political parties. Even though reporters meet Diet members from the opposition parties and obtain information from them, these meetings are less significant than those with LDP Diet members and so get less emphasis in political coverage.

(How could it be otherwise when the LDP has such an overwhelming number of supporters?) The LDP has the strongest ties to the bureaucracy with which it collaborates in initiating bills, constituting an almost perfect union (Odawara 1984). LDP Diet members, especially those veterans who have long experience in the Diet, are intimately familiar with all the political processes in the cabinet, in the LDP factions, and between the LDP and all other political participants. By their very nature, they are the main sources of information. And since LDP leaders hold the top positions in the nation (including prime minister and cabinet posts), what they say and do usually directly affects the life of every citizen. Moreover, reporters have better accessibility to LDP Diet members, who are generally willing to talk openly about any topic. The press is likely to continue to allocate the most coverage to the activities of the LDP and to depend on sources within the party to obtain political news and interpretations as long as the party maintains its leadership in Japanese politics.

Second, the political stories in the national daily newspapers tend to lack clarity in at least two respects. The information presented in them is often confusing in that one has to read between the lines to understand the real meaning, and, the source of the information is not always revealed. The content of the political stories is unclear and political process and events are often described in only general terms. Stories are often characterized by the choice of vague words and a sentence syntax which uses expressions such as *narisô* (it looks as if), *to iwareru* (it is said that) or *to mirareru* (it can be said to appear as if). When trying to give meaning to and interpret a certain political event, often-used expressions are "it is possible to say that," "it can be said that," and "it looks like it is going to be." And to describe a particular phenomenon, a reporter may resort to the following expressions: "looks like," "seemed like," "there is a strong possibility that," "the perspective is getting stronger," or, "the conditions are getting stronger toward a specific direction."

At least three plausible reasons can be advanced to explain the prevalence of such ambiguous expressions and lack of clarity. One is the ambiguous nature of the Japanese language. For one thing, clear logical argument has never been highly esteemed in Japanese culture, as it is in Western culture. Typically, to avoid offending someone, or in an effort to avoid "the loss of face" (which means the loss of self-respect and dignity for both the speaker and the listener as a result of public humiliation and embarrassment), Japanese refrain from expressing definite opinions, from taking clear-cut positions on issues, and from demanding, rejecting, asserting, or criticizing straightforwardly. Vagueness in the use of language is designed presumably to maintain harmonious human relations in Japanese groups and to avoid conflicts (Nakane 1972). Tsujimura (1968, 1977) noted that the tendency to use indirect expressions rather than direct ones in communication, is, along with the tendency toward taciturnity, the most important characteristic of the Japanese. These tendencies are based on three concepts. First, the spiritual aspect of *ishin-denshin* (or *haragei*, stomach act), i.e., communication of thoughts from one mind to another without using language. Second, racial and linguistic homogeneity, i.e., the idea that people can understand each other easily with few words as they are monolingual and monoracial. And, the experience of oppression in the long feudal era, during which Japanese subjected themselves to restraint and to the regulation of speech under a totalitarian system.

The second and more important reason for the ambiguous political coverage is that politics is still a very sensitive issue in Japan. Some groups on the left and the right fringes will resort to intimidation or even violence against reporters if they do not like their stories. Even if a reporter does not have to fear physical violence, a clear negative evaluation of a particular group is likely to meet with an emotional response directly against the reporter or his or her newspaper. Conspicuous in this regard are the rightist groups. During the 1980s, the Japanese right was composed of some 800 different groups with a total membership of about 120,000, one-fifth of whom are highly active, showing their presence in the streets with uniformed young men in speaker trucks, with flags and banners, booming out military music. The right-wing groups hold that the emperor constitutes the "holiest of holies" in Japanese culture, and is thus inviolate. They also publicly assert the propriety of terror in achieving their goals. During Emperor Showa's illness in 1989, Japan's right-wing extremists intimidated and attacked the daily newspapers on their coverage of the deterioration of the emperor's health conditions.

One group, *Dai Nippon Shuko-kai,* which tried to bomb a New Left mass meeting and has conducted military training in the Philippines, demanded, in an article published on November 15, 1989, in the group's organ, *Shuko,* the immediate resignation of the president of the *Mainichi* over the publication of an editorial in the English-language *Mainichi Daily News* on September 26. Another group, *Dai Nippon Seisantô,* which is linked with the former Black Dragon Society, an ultranationalist association founded during the Meiji Era, published in the group's official organ, *Chuô Jôhô Tsûshin,* an emotional attack on all the national newspapers, demanding that they apologize to the emperor. And, the *Asahi* became the target of criticism for other rightist groups, particularly the *Issui-kai,* which published emotional attacks on this daily in their organ, *Le Couquista.* In 1989, the *Asahi*'s offices were attacked with smoke bombs believed to have been thrown by a right-wing group, and in 1987 a reporter from the *Asahi* was murdered by a gunman thought to belong to an extreme rightist group. To avoid such attacks, reporters and desk members are often purposely vague, hoping that those who share their views will be able to read between the lines and grasp the real intent of their criticism.

Last, political stories are vague also because of the way political activities in Japan are managed and because of the general nature of the Japanese political process. Because of the constant need to know the desires and intentions of the other participants in order to prevent a clash of ideas over leadership positions or presenting a bill in the Diet, there are long and subtle negotiations between all political participants. To achieve a consensus on the promotion of a certain issue, lengthy negotiations go on behind closed doors between the leading Diet members of different political parties. Sometimes reporters pass information from one group of leaders to another, facilitating the interaction between leaders. Nevertheless, the negotiations are often complicated and involve concessions as well as less formal agreements. On one side of the coin, reporters may feel that articles elaborating on all the processes of achieving an objective, on the consequences of the concessions made, and on the agreements achieved by one political group or another, would make for very difficult reading. And so reporters and editors tend to pay limited attention to, and only briefly report on, such negotiations. On the other side of the coin, however, the long and subtle political process involves many political participants. Systematic inquiry to get all of the details and opinions of participants would take too long. To meet the deadline of the newspaper and perhaps also the competition of other news media channels, the reporters tend to generalize when writing their stories.

Even when a reporter gathers detailed information on an event, movement, or decision, he or she may prefer not to write a story that will disclose all the details. This is out of fear that the event will be short lived, several hours for example, caused by a sudden development that portrays a situation completely opposite to the details of the story. To avoid such a situation, reporters find that generalizing is a safe first step until the situation is clarified.

Another factor in the formula that makes political stories confusing and their content unclear is mainly related to the press club system. Through the press club, reporters are given easy and ready access to information sources, information, gossip, and leads; but these privileges are part of a complex trade off. Their access to the heart of the political system exists under the conditions of not attributing their stories to any specific source of information, either because they are asked not to disclose the person's name or because the reporter chooses not disclose it to avoid inconveniencing to the source. This is the case, particularly, when the information is given off the record; either gathered during *kishakon* (off-the-record *kondan*) or during a *memokon* meeting (in which reporters cannot use a tape recorder or video camera but can take notes); or because it was a leak or *hikoshiki hatsugen* (an informal statement from the source that is not supposed to be published). Because most of the political information gathered by reporters for use in their stories is acquired through at least one of the aforementioned methods, few political stories identify the source by name.

One immediate consequence of the nonattribution practice is that reporters use various phrases to disguise their information sources. The information is attributed to *seifu shunô* (a top government official), *gaimushô shunô* (a top official in the Ministry of Foreign Affairs), *tôshunô* (a leader of political party), *seifu suji* (a source within the government), *zaikai kankeisha* (a source related to economic circles) or *shushô shûhen* (a source close to the prime minister). Notably, the daily newspapers are fond of the term *suji mono* (according to the related people) as the source for nearly 90 percent of all political stories. The use of this term is especially prevalent because reporters often gather identical information from several sources. The Japanese press is severely criticized for not making known the source of information. The tendency not to do so makes many readers suspect that a certain news item was not really obtained from a top official, leaving them to wonder about the real intentions of the anonymous source.

To what extent does this nature of political stories in the national dailies affect the general behavior and attitudes of readers? Although no extensive research has been aimed at answering this question, at least two interrelated effects can be suggested. First, the lack of detailed coverage of political events and the difficulty in understanding stories tends to divert readers from political stories to the easier ones, such as social reportage. Fewer and fewer readers are then exposed to political stories, which results in people being less informed about the political environment. In turn, these people tend to show less interest in political activities and, perhaps, in supporting political institutions (Kawakami and Feldman 1988). Second, the overly generalized and vague stories may be directly connected to the general pessimistic view the Japanese have of politics. If events are not explained in detail and if interpretations are unclear, a reader may feel that political matters are too difficult to understand and that they have no ability to influence processes or institutions. This can directly affect their sense of involvement in politics and drive them toward political cynicism, which indeed characterizes the Japanese (Feldman 1992).

The Ruling Party and the Political Reporter

There are several ways of evaluating the findings reported in this book. One way is by referring to the two general questions posed in chapter 1: namely, how the huge influence that newspapers (or the news media in general) have on society affects Diet members; and how the dominant status of the ruling party affects overall political coverage.

Regarding the second question, there is an understandable tendency of the press to depend more on sources within the LDP for political information and to pay much attention to the LDP and the activities of its leaders. There is little doubt that the press enhances the LDP's domination, through its constant coverage of the LDP, resulting in obviously one-sided stories that reflect only the establishment view of the news. This, in turn, makes the party and its leaders even more newsworthy, stimulates reporters and editors to refer even more to events within or around the LDP, and to allocate more story and picture space to the party. Nearly every domestic and international activity is observed through the prism of the LDP. The press has no alternative; it must follow the LDP and its leaders, for they are not only the party leaders but the leaders of the nation as well. Of course, the close attention paid to the LDP has other related implications. One is that by focusing on the activities of the party, the press directly diminishes the activities of the opposition parties. Providing explanations and interpretations about the LDP contributes to public knowledge of the party's plans, the motives behind each step the party takes, and the objectives of the leaders. At the same time, this diminishes the opportunity to obtain knowledge and thus perhaps to understand and support the activities of the opposition parties. Perhaps because of the limited space in newspapers, most of which involves topics related to the LDP, the opposition parties are perceived as ineffective, weak, and timid. They are considered less capable of offering alternative policies or ideas compared with the many initiatives of the LDP and they are perceived as focusing mainly on political negativism.

By focusing on the LDP, the press directly emphasizes the gap between the LDP and the opposition parties, especially the gap between the LDP and the largest opposition party, the SDPJ. The two parties are contentious, not only in terms of basic policies such as diplomacy, defense, and energy (specifically nuclear-power generation), but in the tax system, fiscal and agriculture policies, and market-opening measures. Some readers may view this emphasis on the LDP as press support of the LDP's ideas and policies vis-à-vis any other party. The function of the press in this regard is especially crucial (and reflected more sharply) during important political events such as election campaigns. During elections, because the press devotes more attention and space to coverage of the activities and policy plans of the LDP while almost neglecting the opposition parties, especially the SDPJ, it may appear to the electorate as advocating the LDP. This directly or indirectly influences the behavior of a large number of voters.

Turning to the first question, concerning the extent to which the status of the press and its impact on society influences Diet members, several observations are instructive. It is obvious that in a country like Japan, in which the press and other communication channels are widely used, elected politicians and candidates seek every chance to exploit the influence of the news media to realize personal objectives. First, exposure via the news media (on the national and local level) helps a Diet member to mold his public image. This function of the news media, especially television, was confirmed by several studies and, in particular, has been the case of the so-called *tarento kôhosha*. These are television personalities such as newscasters, reporters, and television stars who run for election to the Diet. Through their frequent appearances on television, these candidates have been able to shape their public image to the extent that at election time, they have a decided advantage over the other candidates, often winning a Diet seat rather easily and moving smoothly from the media world to political life.

Also, exposure via the news media greatly helps a Diet member inform supporters and voters of the work they do, the people they meet, and which Diet members and leaders they associate with. Diet members operate on the principle that their first goal is to get elected, otherwise, they can accomplish nothing. And the Diet member who gets elected usually wants to be reelected. Diet members are thus sensitive to getting an idea of what people in their constituencies think and need, and of how to inform the electorate of their activities to meet those needs and demands. Each Diet member has several means of informing constituents about their activities. Among them are meetings with their support groups. As Diet members perceive the press as an "authority," exposure via the print media gives a Diet member a certain status among colleagues and voters. His or her name appearing in the press means that he or she is important. Few Diet members take this lightly. In fact, when a Diet member is written about in one of the newspapers, the secretary usually clips the story and photograph and runs off photocopies, which are then sent to supporters and leading public officials in the Diet member's constituency. This tendency is especially prevalent among junior Diet members, but the more senior ones act this way as well. No less important, when the name of a Diet member appears in the newspapers, it is a source of pride for the secretaries, aides, staff in the constituency, and voters.

How sensitive a Diet member is to news media coverage depends, generally speaking, on the frequency this Diet member has to run for reelection. In comparison to Upper House members, who run for election every six years, members of the Lower House serve two- or three-year terms and actually never stop campaigning—their election activity goes on 365 days a year. They are readily accessible to reporters, and in order to achieve exposure in the press, each of them, junior and veteran, is readily willing to meet (or initiate a meeting) with reporters at just about any time and place. They aim to provide the press with not only hard facts but opinions, in some cases flooding reporters with self-serving publicity, about their current and intended activities. For example, if he or she intends to pose questions at one of the Diet committees, the Diet member will often put the questions to the press beforehand to attract attention and hopefully spark a story.

Diet members are aware that they can get information, advice, and suggestions helpful to their work from reporters, and they know that reporters possess certain tools that can help them achieve their objective, but only if friendly relationships are developed. Diet members thus see the value in meeting with reporters frequently. The two main objectives for doing this are to establish a friendly liaison and maintain an overall good relationship. When they meet with reporters, Diet members chat informally, exchange gossip, and invite them to social events. Their relations exceed thus the framework of the "gray office at *Nagatachô*," to the extent that their relations are compatible, they often see things from a similar perspective, have the same values, and even the same orientation toward specific political activities; they even appear to have what Tunstall (1970, 88) observed in the case of British politicians and reporters, "very similar definitions of news values."

Generally, Diet members have more contact (and also prefer to meet) with newspaper reporters than with representatives of other news media. About one-third of the Diet members regularly meet with reporters of national newspapers. Another third regularly meet with reporters from local and bloc newspapers. Some 21 percent meet with television reporters, 14 percent meet with wire service representatives, and only 0.2 percent meet with radio representatives. The preference for newspaper reporters is partly attributable to the huge circulation of newspapers and their potential influence on society, though other reasons can be cited. One is the fact that newspaper reporters are in contact with Diet members throughout the day, whereas representatives of, say, the television networks, cover only specific events that they deem as valuable news. For this reason, and because reporters from the daily newspapers spend much more time with Diet members, they have, in contrast to other news media representatives, a great potential to broaden a Diet member's knowledge on a variety of matters and to give the Diet members advice and suggestions.

The fact that reporters obtain information from Diet members and the Diet members obtain political data from the reporters creates a situation in which members of these groups serve as primary information sources for each other. This is to the extent that Diet members, particularly those in leading positions in their parties and factions, do not need to rely on the newspapers (or any other news media channel) to gather information since they get it directly and faster from reporters. By obtaining information concerning other Diet members, political party or LDP faction activities or intentions, leading Diet members, especially those in the ruling party, see reporters as an important communication link between members of the Diet, and between themselves or their colleagues and the bureaucrats; veteran Diet members from the LDP see reporters as a bridge connecting the different parties and factions and as making a significant contribution to their work.

Indeed, this role of connecting/informing is the center of reporters' participation in politics. It is the nature of Japanese culture and political process that enables reporters to play more than just an observer and chronicler role. In particular, because consensus is a key concept in the Japanese decision-making process, decision makers depend on the formation of positive support from a majority of the parties involved in a certain matter, to advance their views, ideas, or course of action. To this end, decision makers need first to explore the opinions and desires of all the relevant sides and then try to achieve concessions that will lead to consensus of opinion, enabling them to achieve the final target. Because one needs to gather information from all the concerned parties and negotiate before adopting a specific position on which most agree, the Japanese mode of decision making is relatively slow in reaching an ultimate decision (but relatively solid in terms of commitment to a decision once it is reached). The role played by reporters, from this viewpoint, is crucial. By informing all parties involved, and serving as go-between for political leaders, reporters speed up and smooth the process of negotiations between the various parties (and between leaders who lead political parties and factions).

Reporters are those who, much more significantly than any group of Diet members, play the role of empathic communicators. They first listen and collect crucial information and understand what one side thinks about a certain problem. Then they transfer messages between the various leaders, informing the other of respective stances, ideas, and desires, trying to help them to achieve flexibility and concessions regarding the issue and its related activities, and finally mediate the time and place that leaders will meet each other face-to-face to bridge their differences directly. The role of reporters is not only needed to facilitate the flow of information, but reporters are the only people who can do it in Japanese politics. Their assistance is so decisive that Diet members in leading positions call them at crucial times and send them to their counterparts to establish channels through which information can be quickly transferred. The reporters' role thus benefits the Diet members who need this information; it benefits reporters who learn more about various aspects of the politics from "inside"; and, no less important, benefits the political system as a whole.

Because the press club reporters are at the center of political newsgathering and newsmaking (and transferring), the whole issue of the press club should perhaps be seen thus as not only an issue of propriety in journalism but, as Seymour-Ure (1977, 17) noted in the case of the British Lobby correspondents, "an issue in British politics itself." Reporters' activities should thus, with all their possible implications, be taken into consideration in any further inquiry into the shape of politics in Japan.

Appendix

Research on the relationships between Diet members and reporters in Japan was conducted at two different periods: from July to December 1983, and from June 1984 to August 1986. During these periods, extensive data was gathered from Diet members and reporters by a variety of methods: by a questionnaire sent to Diet members' offices, by interviews with Diet members and reporters, and by personal observation, and they were the initially intended and preferred method of obtaining information, and they were adequate for receiving data from reporters. Certain obstacles, mainly hectic schedules, prevented this from being the only way to obtain information from Diet members. Thus the need for a questionnaire arose.

Questionnaire to Diet Members

To study political communication in Japan, its components, and the relationship between Diet members and reporters, a questionnaire was sent to the offices of Diet members. The 24-question questionnaire was in two parts; the first part was devoted to determining the context of the relationships between Diet members and reporters of the news media, with emphasis on the reporters of national newspapers. The questionnaire was designed to obtain the Diet members' opinions of the press and of what newspapers print, particularly the articles and editorials concerning political life and activities. Several questions concerned political trends as reflected in some newspapers, and others concerned the connections that characterize the individual relationships between reporters and Diet members. The second part of the questionnaire, answered anonymously, was designed to obtain career details such as: which house of the Diet, political party, and party faction the Diet member belonged to; his or her position in the Diet; how many times the Diet member had been elected; and the constituency.

During the questionnaire's preparation, preliminary meetings with the private secretaries of several Diet members took place for evaluating the questionnaire. At these meetings, it was determined that if the questionnaire was sent to the Diet members, they would probably not have sufficient time to consider it seriously. The secretaries suggested that the questionnaires be sent directly to them, and they would respond on behalf of their employers. Two reasons were suggested for this. First, even if the Diet members received the questionaires, they would most likely assign the task of filling it out to their private secretaries. Second, the private secretary is closest to the Diet member. This person accompanies the Diet member through the workday and late-night meetings. The secretary prepares the schedule, selects visitors, screens reading material, and represents the Diet member at important public and supporter meetings and at party gatherings. In many cases, the secretary even lives at the Diet member's residence, and so this person has full knowledge of the Diet member's activities around the clock. Their knowledge of the attitudes, beliefs, and behaviors of the Diet member is extensive. Experts, consulted before the questionnaire was distributed, supported this method as the best way to achieve the desired objectives. The consensus was that sending the questionnaire to the private secretaries would ensure that the Diet members would be informed of it, and that they might be eager to respond personally. In later meetings with Diet members who I interviewed, it was found that almost all of them knew about the questionnaire and did, in fact, fill it out themselves. Some stated that as soon as they learned of the questionnaire, they instructed the secretary to show it to them upon completion. On more than half of the returned questionnaires, it was stated that the Diet member responded personally.

The first draft of the questionnaire, consisting of 30 questions, was shown to private secretaries of Diet members. On the basis of their feedback, it was reduced to 24 questions. One of the major problems in this study was how to deliver questionnaires to the secretaries. Since there is no direct access to the private offices of Diet members, a meeting was held with public relations officials of the LDP, the SDPJ, and the NLC. They agreed to deliver the questionnaires to the Diet members' offices and to attach a personal letter from the head of the public relations section of relevant political parties urging the Diet members to cooperate. Additionally, public relations officials agreed to collect the questionnaires within two weeks. Some Diet members and secretaries of the CGP and the DSP undertook this task themselves, volunteering not only to distribute questionnaires to the Diet members of their parties but to encourage these Diet members to answer it personally. The questionnaires were delivered directly to the Diet members of the *Sangiinnokai* group. Only the JCP refused to cooperate. Numerous phone calls were made and letters written, to no avail. Except for 43 JCP Diet members and 13 independent Diet members (there was no way to contact this small number of members), the questionnaires were sent to all Diet members in both Houses of the Diet. With nine Diet seats vacant at the time of the study, the questionnaire was distributed to 698 Diet members.

Recipients were: The LDP's five party factions (*habatsu*), namely the Tanaka faction (*Mokuyôkai*), the Suzuki faction (*Kôchikai*), the Fukuda faction (*Seiwakai*), the Nakasone faction (*Seisakukagaku Kenkyûjo*), and the Komoto faction; the former Nakagawa group (*Jiyûkakushindôyûkai*); independent Diet members who do not belong to any faction (*muhabatsu*), the SDPJ, CGP, DSP, and NLC—jointly with the USDP and the *Shinsei Kurabu*—and the *Sangiinnokai*. By November 1983, 402 questionnaires (57.6 percent) had been returned, a high number compared to other questionnaires that had been distributed to Diet members from academic sources. The information obtained was then compiled and cross-tabulated. Table A-1 lists the respondents and includes the LDP factions.

The fact that most political parties and the LDP factions returned 50 percent or more of the questionnaires helps to understand a general tendency in the Diet. Overall, 65 percent of the questionnaires returned were from the House of Representatives and 35 percent from the House of Councillors. Table A-2 lists the distribution of the Diet members who participated in the study according to the number of times they have been elected to the Diet.

The position that the Diet members participating in the study hold in the Diet and in their own political parties or party factions is noteworthy. Eleven of the 20 cabinet ministers and 20 of the 25 vice ministers participated in this study. Two LDP faction leaders, and 7 of 11 faction leaders (9 in the House of Representatives and 2 in the House of Councillors) within the SDPJ participated (formally, there are no factions in the SDPJ, or at least they are not as well-defined as those of the LDP). Also, 7 chairpeople of Diet committees, 4 political party secretaries-general (LDP, CGP, NLC, and DSP), 11 political party vice secretaries-general, 38 chairpeople of party commitees, spokespeople of parties and LDP factions, and party advisers participated.

Interviews

The interviews gave the participants great freedom in relating their experience and increased the scope of available information. To clarify some of the points that were later found to be problematic or unclear, some interviewees were visited three or more times. In particular, meetings with a number of reporters and Diet members were held regularly during the second term of the study, when their opinions on the development of the analysis and on the various findings were sought. With the exception of one female SDPJ Diet member, who did not want to be recorded, all of the interviews were recorded and transcribed soon after. Names are not attributed to the quotations in this book because participants were given a written promise of anonymity. The total interview time exceeded 270 hours, 80 hours with Diet members and 190 hours with reporters.

TABLE A-1. Number and Percentage of Questionnaires Returned from Diet Members, by Houses of Diet and Political Parties and LDP Factions

Party/Faction	House of Representatives			House of Councillors			Total
	Number of questionnaires returned	Actual number of Diet members	Percentage of returned questionnaires in comparison to total number of Diet members	Number of questionnaires returned	Actual number of Diet members	Percentage of returned questionnaires in comparison to total number of Diet members	Percentage of returned questionnaires in comparison to number of the Diet members in both Houses
Sangiinnokai	0	0	0	9	10	90.0	90.0
NLC	10	13	76.9	2	4	50.0	70.5
DSP	23	31	74.2	9	13	69.2	72.7
CGP	28	34	82.4	23	27	85.2	83.6
SDPJ	47	101	46.6	34	43	79.1	56.3
LDP							
Tanaka faction	41	65	63.1	15	53	28.3	47.5
Suzuki faction	31	62	50.0	15	26	57.7	52.3
Nakasone faction	30	47	63.8	3	6	50.0	62.3
Fukuda faction	23	46	50.0	14	24	58.3	52.9
Komoto faction	15	30	50.0	5	8	62.5	52.6
Nakagawa group	3	6	50.0	1	1	100.0	57.1
Independents	12	30	40.0	9	18	50.0	43.8
LDP Total	155	287	54.0	62	136	45.6	51.3
Total	263	465	56.6	139	233	59.7	57.6

TABLE A-2. Distribution of Diet Members Who Participated in the Study by Number of Times Elected

Party/Faction	Number of Times Elected									
	1	2	3	4	5	6	7	8	9	10
Sangiinnokai	6	2	1	0	0	0	0	0	0	0
NLC	3	4	1	0	0	3	0	1	0	0
DSP	3	10	12	1	2	0	3	0	0	1
CGP	8	5	12	8	4	14	0	0	0	0
SDPJ	11	24	12	12	4	6	4	2	2	4
LDP										
Tanaka faction	13	13	6	7	9	3	2	0	0	3
Suzuki faction	12	12	7	5	0	2	0	3	2	3
Nakasone faction	2	3	10	6	4	5	1	1	1	0
Fukuda faction	5	9	4	6	2	3	1	2	2	3
Komoto faction	2	3	0	1	2	3	1	3	2	3
Nakagawa group	1	1	0	1	1	0	0	0	0	0
Independents	4	8	2	0	1	1	2	0	0	3
LDP Total	39	49	29	26	19	17	7	9	7	15
Total	70	94	67	47	29	40	14	12	9	20
Actual number of Diet members	110	157	116	78	56	58	32	21	14	61
Percentage of returned questionnaires in comparison to total number of Diet members	63.6	59.9	57.8	60.3	51.8	69.0	43.8	57.1	64.2	32.8

The Diet Members

The interviews with Diet members had the following objectives: to verify the information obtained through the questionnaires and to obtain more details about the pattern of work of the Diet members such as their schedules and their attitudes toward their work, political parties, and colleagues, and contacts with reporters. A set of questions was posed to each Diet member. Most of the interviewees were also asked specific questions about their personal contact with reporters and their perception of the press and reporters based on personal experience. Seventy Diet members, from both Houses of the Diet and all the political parties (except the JCP and independent members) were interviewed. In conducting the interviews, special attention was given to the relative size of the political party (and LDP faction) and its strength in the Diet. Of those interviewed, 40 Diet members, representing all the factions within their political party, belonged to the LDP (35 from the House of Representatives and 5 from the House of Councillors), 14 to the SDPJ (8 and 6), 6 to the CGP (all from the House of Representatives), 7 to the DSP (5 and 2), 1 to the NLC (from the House of Representatives), and 2 members of the *Sangiinnokai* (both from the House of Councillors).

The positions of interviewees included a former prime minister, former cabinet ministers and vice ministers, current cabinet ministers and vice ministers, secretaries-general and their party deputies, chairpeople of Diet committees, party faction leaders, political party spokespeople, and other high-level decision makers. Among these, 10 had been elected to the Diet only once (6 of them belonged to the House of Councillors), 13 had been elected twice (7 from the House of Councillors), 7 elected three times (all from the House of Representatives), 6 elected four times (only 1 from the House of Councillors), 12 elected five times (all from the House of Representatives), 7 elected six times (1 from the House of Councillors), 6 elected seven times, 3 elected eight times, 2 elected nine times, and 4 elected ten times or more (all from the House of Representatives). Additionally, meetings were held with 10 political party officials, a number of Diet officials, and 20 secretaries of Diet members.

The Reporters

As in the case of interviews with the Diet members, the interviews with reporters also had certain objectives: (1) to study their views and opinions about the nature of their contacts with Diet members, their access to political news, and their methods of news gathering; and (2) to study their relationships with other reporters, i.e., those belonging to other newspapers, during the process of gathering information. In selecting the reporters to be interviewed, emphasis was placed on "working reporters," that is, those who report regularly on the activities of the government, political parties, and party factions—namely, political reporters, members of the political desk, political editors, and political commmentators. Meetings were also held with other section reporters. During the first period of the study, 45 reporters representing all branches and levels of the news media were interviewed. Special attention was paid to those from the national newspapers. Of these, 4 were from the *Yomiuri,* 5 from the *Asahi,* 6 from the *Mainichi,* 6 from the *Nihon Keizai,* and 4 from the *Sankei.* Reporters and members of the political desk of the wire services were also interviewed: 7 from the *Jiji Press (Jiji Tsûshinsha)* and 3 from *Kyôdô News Service (Kyôdô Tsûshinsha).* Of the remainder, 4 were from local newspapers, 3 from the Japan Broadcasting Corporation (NHK), and 3 from commercial television stations. Officials from the Japan National Press Club, critics, and others with connections to news media research were also interviewed.

Personal Observations

To ensure an in-depth study of the nature and scope of the relationships between Diet members and reporters, part of the field research was conducted through personal observations. Within this framework, I accompanied reporters from different news media at different times and observed them from morning until evening, gathering news, participating in press conferences, contacting reporters from other news media, and contacting Diet members. I frequently met reporters and Diet members in the members' offices or homes and discussed matters related to their mutual interaction, their views of each other's functions, and their attitudes toward Japanese politics in general. These observations led to a deeper understanding of the information obtained in the interviews and through the questionnaire.

References

Allison, G. T. 1971. *Essence of Decision: Exploring the Cuban Missile Crisis.* Boston: Little Brown.

Amamori, I., and Y. Koike. 1984. "Dai 5 kai zenkoku shimbun shinraido chôsa hôkoku" (Report on the Fifth National Survey on the Reliability of Newspaper). *Shimbun Kenkyû* 390:42–63

Arai, H., and N. Fujiwara. 1986. "Gendaijin no jôhô ishiki" (Japanese Views on Information). *NHK-Hôsô Bunka Chôsa Kenkyû* 31:227–78.

Arai, K. 1989. "Seron to masu media shiron" (Public Opinion and the Mass Media). *NHK-Hôsô Bunka Chôsa Kenkyû Nempô* 34:5–22.

Baluthis, A. 1977. "Congress, the Presidency, and the Press: The Expanding Presidential Image." *Presidential Studies Quarterly* 7:244–51.

Barker, A., and M. Rush. 1970. *The Member of Parliament and His Information.* London: Allen and Unwin.

Blumler, J. G., and M. Gurevitch. 1981. "Politicians and the Press: An Essay on Role Relationships." In *Handbook of Political Communication,* edited by D. D. Nimmo and K. R. Sanders, 467–93. Beverly Hills: Sage.

Brown, R. G., and J. B. Lee. 1977. "The Japanese Press and the 'People's Right to Know.'" *Journalism Quarterly* 54:477–81.

Carter, T. B., M. Franklin, and J. Wright. 1986. *The First Amendment and the Fifth Estate: Regulation of Electronic Mass Media.* Mineola, New York: Foundation Press.

Chittick, W. 1970. "American Foreign Policy Elites: Attitudes toward Secrecy and Publicity." *Journalism Quarterly* 47:689–96.

Cockerell, M., P. Hennessy, and D. Walker. 1984. Sources Close to the Prime Minister. London: Macmillan.

Cohen, C. B. 1963. *The Press and Foreign Policy.* Princeton, N.J.: Princeton University Press.

Cornwell, E. E., Jr. 1959. "Presidential News: The Expanding Public Image." *Journalism Quarterly* 36:275–83.

Craig, A. M. 1981. "Functional and Dysfunctional Aspects of Government Bureaucracy." In *Modern Japanese Organization and Decision-Making,* edited by E. F. Vogel, 3–32. Reprint. Tokyo: Charles E. Tuttle.

Crouse, T. 1974. *The Boys on the Bus.* New York: Random House.

Curtis, G. L. 1988. *The Japanese Way of Politics.* New York: Columbia University Press.

Davison, W. P. 1975. "Diplomatic Reporting: Rules of the Game." *Journal of Communication* 25:138–46

Deutsch, K. W. 1963. *The Nerves of Government*. New York: Free Press.

Doi, T. 1973. *The Anatomy of Dependence*. Tokyo: Kodansha.

Dunn, D. D. 1969. *Public Officials and the Press*. Reading, Mass.: Addison Wesley.

Dyer, C. S., and O. B. Nayman. 1977. "Under the Capitol Dome: Relationships between Legislators and Reporters." *Journalism Quarterly* 54:443–53.

Edelstein, A. S., Y. Ito, and H. M. Kepplinger. 1989. *Communication and Culture: A Comparative Approach*. New York: Longman.

Feldman, O. 1989. "Media-Politics in Japan," Paper presented at the 39th International Communication Association Conference, San Francisco.

———. 1992. *Imêji de yomu Nagatachô* (Perceiving Japanese Politics through Images). Tokyo: Miraisha.

Feldman, O., and A. Diskin. 1988. "Critical Periods of News Coverage during an Election Campaign: The Case of Japan." *Keio Communication Review* 9:85–99.

Feldman, O., and K. Kawakami. 1988. "Shimbun no seiji hôdô ni taisuru hyôka to imêji: chôsa kenkyû nôto" (Perceiving Political News Coverage: A Research Note on Newspapers Evaluation). *Shimbungaku Hyôron* 37:197–206.

———. 1989. "Leaders and Leadership in Japanese Politics: Images during a Campaign Period." *Comparative Political Studies* 22:265–90.

———. 1991. "Media Use as Predictors of Political Behavior: The Case of Japan." *Political Psychology* 12:65–80.

Fukui, H. 1978. "Japan: Factionalism in a Dominant-Party System." In *Political Parties and Factionalism in Comparative Perspective*, edited by F. P. Belloni and D. C. Beller, 43–72. Santa Barbara: ABC-Clio.

Gans, H. 1980. *Deciding What's News*. New York: Vintage Books.

Grossman, M. B., and M. J. Kumar. 1981. *Portraying the President*. Baltimore: Johns Hopkins University Press.

Hashiguchi, O., T. Takeshita, K. Sugiura, and T. Maruyama. 1977. "Taikenteki nemawashiron" (Empirical Study of *Nemawashi*). *Jichi-Kenshû* 203:2–17

Hayashi, C. 1973. "Shimbun kisha no taipu wo saguru: tajigenteki bunseki ni yoru" (Typology of Newspaper Reporters). *Shimbun Kenkyû* 267:56–68.

Hess, S. 1980. *The Washington Reporter*. Washington, D.C.: Brookings Institution.

Hirose, H. 1986. "Nihonteki jânarizumu to kurabu seido" (Japanese Style Journalism and the Club System). *Sôgô Jânarizumu Kenkyû* 116:6–14.

Hirose, M.. 1984. "Seitô to atsuryoku dantai" (Political Parties and Pressure Groups) *Jurisuto-Sôgô Tokushû* 35:52–56.

Ito, Y. 1990. "Mass Communication Theories from a Japanese Perspective." *Media, Culture and Society* 12:423–64.

Iwabuchi, Y. 1989. "Sôten hôdô to sôten sentaku: gidai settei kinô no kenshô" (Press Issues and Preference Issues: A Study of the Agenda-Setting Function). *Keiôgijuku Daigaku Shimbun Kenkyûjo Nempô* 33:75–94.

Janis, I. 1972. *Victims of Groupthink*. Boston: Houghton-Mifflin.

Kabashima, I. 1988. "Senkyo yosoku hôdô no anaunsumento kôka" (The Announcement Effect of the Election Prediction). *Shimbun Kenkyû* 439:47–55.

————. 1990. "Masu media to seiji" (Mass Media and Politics). *Rebayasan* 7:7–29.

Kase, H. 1978. *Nihon no ryôshiki wo dame ni shita* Asahi Shimbun (*Asahi Shimbun: The Newspaper who Spoils the Japanese Good Sense*). Tokyo: Yamate.

Kato, E. 1977. "Nemawashi to nihonteki fudo" (*Nemawashi* and the Japanese Climate). *Jichi-Kenshû* 203:18–26.

Kawakami, K., and O. Feldman. 1988. "Media Use, Political Attitudes, and Participation among Japanese University Students." Paper presented to the 14th World Congress of the International Political Science Association: Washington D.C.

Kennedy, R. 1968. *Thirteen Days*. New York: Norton.

Kim, Y. C. 1981. *Japanese Journalists and Their World*. Charlottesville: University Press of Virginia.

Kishimoto, K. 1981. "Diet Structure, Organization, and Procedures." In *The Japanese Diet and the US Congress*, edited by F. R. Valeo and C. E. Morrison, 39–59. Boulder, Colorado: Westview.

Kobayashi, Y. 1990. "Masu media to seiji ishiki" (Mass Media and Political Consciousness). *Rebayasan* 7:97–114.

Kokkai Binran 68. 1983. (The Handbook of Japanese Diet). Tokyo: Nihon Seikei Shimbunsha.

Konoe, S. 1987. "Chihôban no senkyo hôdô: 86-nen shû-san dojitsu senkyo no shimbun hôdô bunseki" (The Election Campaign Coverage of the Local Pages of Japanese Press: A Study of the 1986 Double Election for the House of Representatives and the House of Councillors). *Kagawa Hôgaku* 7:35–70.

Koyama, K. 1982. "Shimbun kisha no rinri wo tou" (Questioning the Ethics of Reporters). *Bungei Shunjû* (November): 94–114.

Krauss, E. S. 1989. "Politics and the Policymaking Process." In *Democracy in Japan*, edited by T. Ishida and E. S. Krauss, 39–64. Pittsburgh: University of Pittsburgh Press.

Kyogoku, J. 1987. *The Political Dynamics of Japan*. Translated by N. Ike. Tokyo: University of Tokyo Press.

Manabe, K. 1983. *Seron to masu komyuniksêhon* (Public Opinion and the Mass Media). Tokyo: Keio Tsushin.

Merril, J. C. 1988. "Inclination of Nations to Control Press and Attitudes on Professionalization." *Journalism Quarterly* 65:839–44.

Nakane, C. 1972. *Japanese Society.* Berkeley: University of California Press.

Nimmo, D. D. 1964. *Newsgathering in Washington: A Study in Political Communication.* New York. Atherton Press.

Nishiyama, T. 1988. "'Kisha kurabu' zakkan" (Impressions of the Press Club). *Shimbun Kenkyû* 442:52–56.

Odawara, A. 1984. "Seitô to kanryô no kankei ni tsuite" (On the Relationship between Political Parties and the Bureaucracy). *Jurisuto* 35:57–63.

————. 1987. "Mittchaku suredo yuchaku sezu; seiji no kyakkan hôdô shugi no genkai to kôyô" (Intimate but not United Relations: Utility and Limitation of Objective Political Reportage). *Shimbun Kenkyû* 427:46–50.

Pempel, T. J. 1984. "Organizing for Efficiency: The Higher Civil Service in Japan." In *Bureaucrats and Policy Making*, edited by E. N. Suleiman, 72–106. London: Holmes and Meier.

Reischauer, E. O. 1978. *The Japanese*. Cambridge and London. Harvard University Press, Belknap Press.

Seymour-Ure, C. 1968. *The Press, Politics and the Public*. London: Methuen.

————. 1977. "Government: The Lobby Correspondents." In *Studies on the Press*, edited by O. Boyd-Barrett, C. Seymour-Ure and J. Tunstall, 117–30. London: Her Majesty's Stationery Office.

Sigal, L. 1973. *Reporters and Officials: The Organization and Politics of Newsmaking*. Lexington, Mass.: D. C. Heath.

Sone, Y. 1986. "Nihon no seisaku kettei no henyô" (Changing Japanese Policies Formation). In *Nihongata seisaku kettei no henyô* (Changing Japanese Style of Policy Making), edited by M. Nakano, 301–19. Tokyo: Tôyô Shimbunsha.

Sugiyama, T. 1984. "Yomiuri Shimbun senmu Watanabe Tsuneo no Honseki wa 'Seiji' de aru" (Politics as the Home of the *Yomiuri Shimbun*'s Managing Director, Watanabe Tsuneo). *Bungei Shunjû* 62:284–303.

Takeshita, T. 1983. "Media gidai settei kasetsu no jisshôteki kentô" (An Empirical Examination of Media Agenda-Setting Hypothesis). *Tokyo Daigaku Shimbun Kenkyûjo Kiyô* 31: 101–43.

————. 1988. "Sôten hôdô to gidai settei kasetsu" (Issue Reporting and Agenda-Setting Hypothesis). In *Senkyo hôdô to tôhyô kôdô* (Election Coverage and Voting Behavior), edited by Tokyo Daigaku Shimbun Kenkyûjo, 157–96. Tokyo: Tokyo Daigaku Shuppankai.

Tsujimura, A. 1968. *Nihon bunka to komyunikêshon* (Japanese Culture and Communication). Tokyo: Nihon Hôsô Shuppan Kyôkai.

————. 1976a. *Shimbun yo ogoru nakare* (Warning to Newspapers). Tokyo: Takagi Shobo.

———— 1976b. "Seron to seijirikigaku: seifu, shimbun, seron no sankaku kankei" (Public Opinion and Political Dynamics: The Tripolar Relationship of Government, Press, and Public Opinion). In *Nihonjin Kenkyû*. Vol. 4:173–238. (Research on Japanese). Tokyo: Shinseido.

————. 1977. "Nihonteki komyunikêshon no tokushitsu to shimbun no arikata" (Characteristics of Japanese Communication and the Function of the Press). *Senmon Shimbun* 1:7–24.

————. 1981. *Sengo nihon no taishû shinri* (Mass Psychology in Postwar Japan). Tokyo: Tokyo Daigaku Shuppankai.

Tsuruki, M. 1982. "Frame-Imposing Function of the Mass Media as Seen in the Japanese Press." *Keio Communication Review* 3:27–37.

Tunstall, J. 1970. *The Westminster Lobby Correspondents: A Sociological Study of National Political Journalism*. London: Routledge.

Weiss, C. H. 1974. "What America's Leaders Read." *Public Opinion Quarterly* 38:1–22.

Williams, M. 1972. *Inside Number Ten*. London: Weidenfeld and Nicolson.

Yamaguchi, A. 1985. "Za Seijibu" (The Political Desk). *Chûô Kôron* 2:168–94.

Index